As Painting

As Painting: Division and Displacement

Philip Armstrong, Laura Lisbon, and Stephen Melville

Wexner Center for the Arts, The Ohio State University
Columbus, Ohio

The MIT Press
Cambridge, Massachusetts
London, England

This book was set in Sabon and Stone Sans by Graphic Composition, Inc. and was printed and bound in the United States of
America.

Published in association with the exhibition
As Painting: Division and Displacement
Organized by Philip Armstrong, Laura Lisbon, and Stephen Melville
May 12–August 12, 2001
Wexner Center for the Arts
The Ohio State University
Columbus, Ohio

Presented with major support from The Andy Warhol Foundation for
the Visual Arts.

Additional support provided by the Greater Columbus Arts Council,
Ann and Ron Pizzuti, Cultural Services of the French Embassy, the
National Endowment for the Arts, Etant donnés: The French-
American Fund for Contemporary Art, the Ohio Arts Council, Marsh
USA Inc., The Kettering Fund, and the Wexner Center Foundation.

Support for the works of Moira Dryer provided by The Judith
Rothschild Foundation.

Promotional support provided by WBNS 10TV.

Library of Congress Cataloging-in-Publication Data

As painting: division and displacement / [edited and organized by]
Philip Armstrong, Laura Lisbon, and Stephen Melville.
      p. cm.
   Exhibition held May 12–August 12, 2001 at Wexner Center for
the Arts, the Ohio State University, Columbus, Ohio
    Includes bibliographical references.
    ISBN 0-262-01183-2 (hc. : alk. paper)
      1. Painting, Modern—20th century—Exhibitions.
I. Armstrong, Philip. II. Lisbon, Laura, 1963– III. Melville,
Stephen W. IV. Wexner Center for the Visual Arts.

ND195 .A788 2001
759.13'09'04507477157—dc21
00-051960

In memory of Michel Parmentier, 1938–2000

We remain grateful for his intelligence, integrity,
and altogether too brief friendship.

Contents

An *As Painting* Anthology

Foreword

From the moment that three of our closest faculty colleagues at The Ohio State University first proposed *As Painting*, we were intrigued by their exhibition concept, as well as by the curatorial team itself. Their unusual mix of expertise—in painting, art history, and philosophy—held the promise of coaxing that rarest of curatorial alchemies between intellectual and visual intensity, matching rigorous argument with exquisite works of art.

After three years of dedicated effort, the result surpasses every expectation. Shaped by original thinking and driven by provocative debate, *As Painting* ultimately flourishes in the keenly honed selection and presentation of works whose seeming heterogeneity might at first perplex, even defy, those seeking cogent connections. But slowly, inexorably, the relational forces that move between and cut across these disparate objects emerge, catch our eye, and cue us to leave our preconceptions behind.

Stephen Melville, Professor of History of Art; Laura Lisbon, painter and Associate Professor of Art; and Philip Armstrong, Senior Lecturer in Comparative Studies, offer us a richly nuanced perspective on a few particular threads of painting's evolution since the sixties, elusive threads that ravel from the profound legacy of minimalism (but have heretofore been obscured by better-known skeins starting from the same point). In a gentle affront to critic Clement Greenberg's canon of painting's exclusive and irreducible attributes, the curators boldly posit that fluidity and an urge to morph may better describe painting's true character. In that sense, implicit in the heart of the exhibition is the assertion that paint itself, even in the hand of a minimalist, is a material fluid.

It is a great credit to the curatorial team that the complexity of their project and its sometimes abstruse philosophical excursions haven't sapped the enterprise of its pure experiential pleasures and discoveries. Instead, the precisely calibrated juxtapositions of thought and practice, message and medium, opticality and materiality, fixation and displacement, reverberate through the galleries and this publication with that distinctive pulse that marks every significant exhibition.

The curators deftly trace an intricate web of relationships among painting, sculpture, architecture, photography, and installation. Linking an unusual array of artists, they discover along the way some surprising convergences and parallel impulses across disciplines. That artists like James Bishop, Simon Hantaï, Jean Degottex, and Martin Barré are considered alongside Robert Ryman, Gerhard Richter, Agnes Martin, and Donald Judd suggests the degree of intellectual independence and courage with which the curators have culled their choices. And while it was never a matter of "resurrecting" careers nearly forgotten beyond French borders, *As Painting* undeniably casts fresh light on a number of French artists who, through the vagaries of cultural import and export, have largely slipped beneath international radar.

In keeping with the Wexner Center's commitment to encouraging artistic production, three artists have been commissioned to create new work for *As Painting*. Daniel Buren, Christian Bonnefoi, and Polly Apfelbaum will produce projects for the exhibition, and we're grateful for their unique contributions. Sherrie Levine and Mel Bochner will re-create previously realized pieces; their enthusiastic collaboration, along with that of so many other artists in the show, has been instrumental to its success.

As Stephen Melville notes elsewhere in this catalogue, *As Painting* constitutes something of an event. We are grateful to the many private collectors and public institutions that have collaborated with us to make such an extensive survey possible. Colleagues in the United States and Europe have been exceptionally gracious in responding to loan requests and helping the curators uncover relatively unfamiliar works, and I join the curators in thanking all of them. We are especially grateful to the department of Cultural Services at the French Embassy for encouragement and assistance throughout this process.

We are equally indebted to all those whose generosity has made the exhibition and this accompanying publication possible. Our thanks go to The Andy Warhol Foundation for the Visual Arts for major support of the project. We are also grateful to the Greater Columbus Arts Council, Ann and Ron Pizzuti, Cultural Services of the French Embassy, the National Endowment for the Arts, Etant donnés: The French-American Fund for Contemporary Art, the Ohio Arts Council, Marsh USA Inc., and The Kettering Fund, as well as to The Judith Rothschild Foundation for its specific support of works by Moira Dryer.

We're proud to have joined forces with our colleagues at the MIT Press to produce this in-depth publication to accompany *As Painting*. Special thanks go to Arts and Architecture Editor Roger Conover, who recognized the potential in this project from the outset and made an early commitment to copublish the catalogue, as well as to Paula Woolley and Matthew Abbate for their work on the manuscript. In addition to developing their own essays for this volume, the curators have assembled an intriguing and varied cast of contributors who offer thoughts on many of the artists and concepts that propel *As Painting*. We're especially pleased that many of these selections are appearing here in print (or in English) for the first time.

As always, the entire Wexner Center staff has also contributed immeasurably to the success of this venture, but I would be remiss not to single out a few key players from the exhibitions staff. Sarah J. Rogers, former Director of Exhibitions, first championed this project to the program team and persuaded everyone of its merits. Chief Curator of Exhibitions Carlos Basualdo embraced it enthusiastically on his arrival and generously shared his insights at later stages. Ellen Bethany

Napier, former Curatorial Associate, and Steve Hunt, Graduate Associate, successively filled the crucial role of project coordinator with grace and exactitude. Registrar Joan Hendricks brought her customary expertise and unflappability to negotiating loans from near and far, while Chief Exhibition Designer Jim Scott superbly guided the curators through a challenging installation. Exhibitions Manager Jill Davis presided over production schedules, budgets, and overall exhibition administration with great spirit and an unshakable grip on essential matters. A group of remarkable graduate student associates and undergraduate student assistants—among them, Cynthia Collins, Joby Pottmeyer, Amy Schmersal, Joanna Spitzner, and Aida Stanish—contributed to every stage of the endeavor.

A project of this scope and ambition is only conceivable when institutions enjoy the confidence, commitment, and unwavering support of a vital Board of Trustees. The Wexner Center is surely one such institution, and I am ever grateful to these uncommon patrons who believe so deeply in our unique mission.

In closing, I want to express once again my admiration and gratitude to our three guest curators for *As Painting*. Through their discerning lens, we are reawakened yet again to the fact that, just when we thought we had learned its lessons and mastered its mysteries, painting's unfathomed powers reveal so much more.

Sherri Geldin
Director, Wexner Center for the Arts

Acknowledgments

This exhibition started out as an idea hatched far too late at night in a small apartment just off Place Saint-Georges by three people who had very little idea what they were getting into. We had, in particular, very little notion of how much we would owe to so many people by the time we were through, nor how much pleasure there could be in accumulating so much debt.

Certainly foremost in any accounting must be our debts to all of the artists whose work appears in the show. And we are particularly grateful to the many artists whose generosity with their time and conversation contributed to the richness of both the show and our thinking about it. In France, we owe immense debts to Christian Bonnefoi, Daniel Buren, Daniel Dezeuze, Simon Hantaï, Michel Parmentier, François Rouan, Claude Viallat, and Jacques Villeglé; and in New York, to Polly Apfelbaum and Mel Bochner. We are likewise indebted, at somewhat greater distance, to Imi Knoebel, Sherrie Levine, Gerhard Richter, and James Welling. We also owe a special debt of appreciation to Michèle Barré-Gozland.

Work on the exhibition has brought us into repeated and deeply rewarding conversations with Mick Finch, Ann Hindry, Jan and Ben Maiden, Guy Massaux, Isabelle Monod-Fontaine, Alfred Pacquement, Paul Rodgers, and Tristan Trémeau. We are tremendously grateful to all of them, as we are also to Maurice Benhamou, Yve-Alain Bois, Lynne Cooke, Eric de Chassey, Hubert Damisch, Karen Dezeuze, Zsuza Hantaï, Bernard Joubert, Carmen Knoebel, Lucien Massaert, Catherine Millet, Marcelin Pleynet, Jean-Marc Poinsot, Robert Storr, Sylvie Turpin, Henriette Viallat, and Bénédicte Victor-Pujebet. Although, despite our many trips to France, we never quite managed to meet together, we obviously owe a great deal to Christian Prigent; we found no better title for our exhibition than the one he gave his fine study of Daniel Dezeuze: *Comme la Peinture.*

We deeply appreciate the generous cooperation of the collectors, museums, and galleries that have graciously provided works for this exhibition, as well as the many individuals who have assisted us throughout the loan process. In particular, this show would not have been possible without the advice, as well as the bottomless courtesy and tact, of Jean Fournier, whose Galerie Jean Fournier has played a pivotal role over the past thirty or more years for so many of the artists whose work we are showing; we cannot adequately thank M. Fournier and his very fine assistant Vincent Demeusoy.

For their advice and help in securing work and images, we are also grateful to Michel Durand-Dessert and Jean-Paul Robin at Liliane and Michel Durand-Dessert, Paris; Jacques Elbaz at Galerie Jacques Elbaz, Paris; Elyse Goldberg at James Cohan Gallery, New York; Gary Hulton at Zabriskie, Paris; Joseph Jacobs at The Newark Museum; Bernard Jordan at Galerie Bernard Jordan, Paris; Daniel

Templon and Élodie Rahard at Galerie Templon, Paris; Adam Sheffer at Danese, New York; Véronique Smagghe at Galerie Véronique Smagghe, Paris; Gabriel Salomon and Delphine Perru at Galerie Laage-Salomon, Paris; and Virginia Zabriskie at Zabriskie, New York. For their help with catalogue contributions and permissions, we would like to thank James Meyer, Georges Didi-Huberman, Eric Franz, and Jean Clay. Jacky Beillerot, Dominique Bollinger, Piet Coussens, Herman Daled, Agnès Foiret, Alberte Grynpas Nguyen, and Chloé Ziegler all provided crucial assistance and advice.

Additional assistance with loans, images, and myriad other details has come from: Sophie Streefkerk, assistant to Daniel Buren, Paris; Alessandra Carnielli at the Maria Gaetana Matisse Collection; Darlene Farris, formerly of John Weber Gallery, New York; Annette Ferrara, formerly of the Alan Koppel Gallery, Chicago; David Gray at Margarete Roeder Gallery, New York; Steve Henry at Paula Cooper Gallery, New York; Rodney Hill at Gorney, Bravin + Lee, New York; Jean-Marc Prévost at Musée départmental d'art contemporain de Rochechouart, France; Jacqueline and Caroline Rabouan-Moussion and Rémy Hoche at Galerie Jacqueline Rabouan-Moussion, Paris; Catherine Tieck and Georges Benero-Floride at Galerie de France, Paris; and Sean Ulmer at the Herbert F. Johnson Art Museum, Cornell University.

At The Ohio State University we owe particular thanks to Anthony Allen for his translations of much of the material in the catalogue; to Eileen Doyle and Candice Madey for their work on the extensive database; and to Ruth Melville and Lisa Florman, whose friendship, conversation, and interest have helped sustain this project from very nearly its inception. A Seed Grant from the College of the Arts assisted with some of the early work on the project.

Given our considerable unpreparedness for an endeavor of this kind, we are hugely grateful to all those with whom we have worked at the Wexner Center and at MIT. We echo Director Sherri Geldin's acknowledgments to the *As Painting* team and add personal thanks for each individual's contribution. In addition, Wexner Center Editor Ann Bremner and Assistant Editor Ryan Shafer brought valuable observations and careful attention to preparations for this publication. We also express gratitude to Sherri herself, for her willingness to support this project throughout its development; to former Curator at Large Donna De Salvo, for thoughtful conversations early on; and to Chief Curator of Exhibitions Carlos Basualdo for interest and support through later moments. Finally, *As Painting* would never have happened without the extraordinary support and guidance of Sarah J. Rogers, former Director of Exhibitions, Ellen Bethany Napier, former Curatorial Associate, and Steve Hunt, Graduate Associate, to whom we express our heartfelt gratitude.

Our broader intellectual debts are, we hope, made sufficiently clear within the body of the catalogue itself. What the normal apparatus of citation fails entirely to capture is the very real pleasure, and challenge, of feeling oneself engaged with a community that exists above all as a willingness to place things at stake and to repeatedly renew the work of articulation set in motion by that. We hope we have contributed to that work.

Philip Armstrong
Laura Lisbon
Stephen Melville

As Painting

Counting /As/ Painting
Stephen Melville

As Painting is intended as an exhibition of painting. At this level of description, the show has in principle no limits: what it claims to make visible is presumably as fully there to be seen in Giotto or Caravaggio or Poussin or Rembrandt or David as in any of the works that will in fact be found in the galleries. One can of course draw closer to what is in the exhibition, and the sense of disparity will perhaps seem less striking: these same things are also there to be seen in Manet and Picasso and Mondrian and Pollock and Stella. Inevitably many viewers will have their own lists of artists and works that appear so close to what we have chosen as to feel like bodies of work overlooked by or excluded from the exhibition, and at least some of the time they are bound to be right—there's no point in pretending that our particular choices are made in anything other than a relatively small clearing limited by ignorance and conditioned by interests.

In saying that we have attempted an exhibition of painting, we must mean that we hope we have created conditions under which other work can be compellingly seen, that what the show hopes to offer is a way to go on—with Stella or Manet or Poussin or Giotto. Its stakes are there, in painting.

It is of course true that the various lists I've offered are far from innocent; they answer well enough to a historical understanding that many visitors can be expected to bring into the galleries or to these pages. It's one that distinguishes between an activity seen as "traditional," another recognizably "modernist," and a third that is, these days, palpably uneasy, possibly "postmodernist," and notably uncertain how far it can recognize an interest in something called "painting." The array of objects, practices, and techniques represented in *As Painting* certainly suggests that the exhibition takes some special interest in this last moment, so the claim to show "painting" is evidently not without some relation to time or history. My opening sentence might then be revised to read, "*As Painting* is intended as an exhibition of what counts as painting," with the understanding that counting, regardless of the historical depth of the things being counted, always happens in the present. The exhibition means to articulate a certain node around which painting can be seen to crystallize. Some general features of this "node" are clear. It is committed in advance to an understanding of painting as having no essence outside of history, thus gathering, dispersing, and regathering itself at every moment; the exhibition and its supporting texts presumably have a specific interest in addressing this dynamic as part of their more general address to painting. It seems equally clear that if the general claim about painting as something that gathers and disperses itself at every moment is serious, this claim must nonetheless admit its partiality from the outset. This too is an element of what is shown, something the exhibition and the catalogue texts are obliged to address.

Texts and works do this, of course, in different ways, and the various texts in this catalogue offer significantly different angles into these matters. The purpose of the present essay is to explore in the most general terms possible the conceptual apparatus we take to be entailed by the work itself, so whatever sense it makes has finally to be measured against one's experience of that work. Whatever may be gained from my efforts to work, part by part, through the notion of something "counting as painting," the works themselves have to count that way—count as painting—or it all comes to nothing (theory offers no relief from judgment; at best it offers a useful gloss upon it).

There are some very straightforward things to be said about the work in *As Painting*. It is, for example, strongly tempting to describe the show as placing a particular body of French painting relatively little known in the U.S. into a particularly American context of minimalist and, especially, postminimalist work, much of which is not recognizably painting. This seems about right, although it is important that there are also a number of works in the show that cannot be directly assimilated to this description. Because the French work is less known and stands in greater need of introduction, there is inevitably some skewing of things, both in the galleries and in the catalogue, toward it. So it's important to say early that the French work hardly constitutes a "tradition," and that if it can be seen as reflecting something like a conversation, it is not always a polite conversation. Differences in it run deep—deep enough that the showing of this range of work together constitutes something of an event. If one of the wagers of the exhibition is that the French and American work can serve to bring each other into greater visibility, another is that such visibility also brings greater articulation, opening out differences as well as commonalities.

Another strong and legitimate temptation is to see the exhibition as about the situation of painting in the wake of minimalism or as attempting to construct such a situation. Under this description, a number of other features stand out, the most notable of which are perhaps, first, its refusal to conflate questions of painting and questions of abstraction and, second, its considered lack of interest in the varieties of overtly self-referential painting that have been particularly prominent in American art over the past decade or so.

The identification of painting with abstraction was crucial to the formalist understanding of abstract expressionism, and the continuing power of this identification is evident in any number of recent exhibitions that undertake to explore once more the interlocking of these terms. It seems to us that one of the clearest and most direct consequences of minimalism was the displacement of the opposition between abstraction and representation that supported this identification in favor of an opposition between abstraction and what came to be called "concreteness." The exhibition offers a view of what that might mean for painting.

One might fasten the interest in self-referentiality in painting to pop art, particularly as it developed in the U.S. as an interpretation (and parody) of the "self-criticism" invoked by the Greenbergian account of abstract expressionism. This particular reading of "self-criticism" undoubtedly partakes of a widespread tendency in the late fifties and, particularly, the sixties to pick up on questions of identity and the like as questions of knowledge (as opposed to, say, questions of action or being, both of which are also ways to construe criticism and, especially, self-criticism). If we see minimalism as defeating or otherwise transforming the terms in play in abstract expressionism, we equally see it, or strains within it, as offering an alternative to the path opened by pop. The refusal of any direct identification of painting with abstraction and the lack of interest in self-referentiality show something about the overall shape of the informing curatorial judgment—so also something about what work cannot find a place on these particular walls or floors, cannot show in the space *As Painting* claims.

The more direct way to put the same point would be to say that in the recent past it is minimalism above all that seems to have placed painting radically in question. If painting finds itself most fully only where it is most deeply in question, it is just here that one might expect to find whatever measuring or discovery of itself painting is yet capable of. It is this work of measuring or discovery that determines what counts as painting.

/Counting/

By the Numbers

As Painting contains some 110 works by 26 artists. But if one were to ask how many paintings there are in the show, things would immediately become much more difficult: there's a good bit of work here that does not seem to partake of any of the elements associated with painting, there's work that seems to do so but in highly ambiguous ways, and there's work that appears close enough to what we normally mean by painting but that behaves in ways we don't expect, so that its limits or possibilities appear peculiarly unclear.

Not so many years ago, this could not have been the case. Paintings came clearly as wholes and came one at a time. The only numbers needed to count them were real, whole, and integral, and the further reaches of arithmetic—complex numbers, imaginary numbers—seemed safely out of view. Painting appeared entirely capable of doing its own sums, of summing itself up, and indeed the tendency was strongly to see painterly achievement happening as the summing up within a single work of painting as a whole. One could imagine saying of, for example, a Jackson Pollock or, later, a Frank Stella something on the order of "This is what it is for something to be a painting" or "This is painting if anything is." Such sentences have everything to do with what Clement Greenberg meant in speaking about "purity" (a term both absolutely necessary and always uneasy in his writing) or its more particular gloss in terms of "opticality."

Painting that counted this way—integrally, summing itself up—happened in particular ways, most often as some kind of "breakthrough," and presented itself in equally particular ways: as if apart from or without any thinkable need for our words, as if silence were the natural concomitant of the visual presence that was its achievement, its way of counting and indeed the very act of its counting. The strongest critical writing about such work was, at its best, neither description nor interpretation but something closer to evocation. And when—the beginning here is perhaps Stella—its presence began to be supplemented by words doing more or other than that, painting was already starting to count differently.

While these remarks take undeniable advantage of the idiom "counting as," it's important to see that they actually touch fairly closely on aspects of abstract expressionist practice—on, for example, the tendency to replace titles with numbers or, closer to the point, Pollock's desire to retitle *Number 31, 1950* as *One,* removing it from a sequence so that it might stand as a unity that would also be an origin. We catch a glimpse here of a central and defining scene: it consists of a single painting through which all of painting can come into view—a moment of reduction in its strong, theoretical sense as a determination of the means by which the terms of a practice are rendered transparent and wholly mutually translatable. At this moment, in this painting, painting is secured in itself and above all *is*.

If this scene is a fantasy, it is a powerful one that ought not be easily set aside: it captures much of what we must want if we take painting to be more or other than a peculiar form of interior design, and it seems extraordinarily adequate to the objects it's built around. It nonetheless also bears the betraying marks of fantasy—after all, the critic is there with his or her words; the numbers do not stop, the one painting giving itself always back over to a seriality whose logic escapes it; and behind the pure counting of *One,* there is the "literary" supplement of, for example, *Full Fathom Five,* dragging in tow an entire unconscious filled with oceanic depth, Oedipal violence, and blindness. It is hardly surprising that subsequent art will make itself to a high degree out of just these slips or symptoms, as if obliged to acknowledge—to work through and transform—both the power of this scene and the limitations on which it depends. Such art discovers new ways of making itself count, so that, in the work and wake of such key figures as Jasper Johns and Donald Judd, language, seriality, and something partly like theory and partly like blindness are increasingly put forward as dimensions of the work itself and not simply conditions adjacent to it. In Stella's early painting, something like the direction of our counting, from outside in or inside out, suddenly seems to matter—the instant of our seeing it in its wholeness and instantaneity subtly fractured from within.

The costs of seeing these changes, as many have wanted to, as amounting to a radical break, as a passage from the old order of painting to a new order of objects or objecthood, are exceedingly high. It's perhaps better to stay close to the model arithmetic itself offers—it doesn't take much playing around with whole numbers to discover that division is one of their processes and that it quickly produces new kinds of numbers that are not resolvable into the initial terms, which now turn out to be special cases within a more complex system.

After minimalism it's not clear that painting counts at all, let alone that it counts in the way it had seemed to. Certainly such counting as may still belong to it has been transformed in a way that makes things like division central to it, and if some of the numbers now put into play are best called complex or imaginary, then we may have to admit work that can never fully count or can be counted only insofar as it is in some special way contiguous to or continuous with work that does count.

One might expect to find in a field expanded in this way an absence of breakthroughs, a sliding off of integral achievements, and an end to the imagination of a certain visual silence. One might expect that painting and related forms—because surely they are now in some sense a part of the equation—might find themselves taking time to take their own measure, as if trying to either find or displace some abruptly obscure relation between number and identity.[1]

As Painting cannot disavow its relation to the scene of the one integral painting; it shares at some level the wager that painting in exhibition either counts or doesn't. But it takes the conditions of such showing to be newly complex in ways that make the earlier scene unimaginable. It seems fair to say that the little "as" that accompanies "counting" is an index of this increased complexity, so it is worth noting that this "as" seems to do several kinds of work. Certainly it opens up a gap between number and identity and underlines the difficulty of nonintegral counting. But it also marks the need to go beyond this initial literal address to counting, points to what in "counting" already moves beyond this. (And, in all these ways, it points to excess in play.)

Mattering

In saying that something counts as something, we most often mean more than that it can be sorted into this pile rather than that. We are usually saying something also about how it matters. Like "counting," the word "matters" opens easily enough in several directions—its usual meaning, as a verb, is something like "makes a difference," as a noun, it's the plural of "matter," and with a little tweaking it can serve as verb for what matter might be thought or said to do. When we say that something counts as painting, we probably also mean that it matters that way, and in exploring that thought I want to take as full advantage as I can of the possible inflections of the word. Just as I claimed earlier that the twists and turns of "counting" were not simply imposed upon a recent history of art in the U.S., so also I will claim that the happy accidents of this English word find real resonance in pertinent strands of recent French intellectual life.

There is a particular strand of materialism that emerges in France in the fifties and sixties. This phrasing suggests Marxist foundations, but in its broadest, and I'd suggest deepest, form the thought at issue is not peculiarly Marxist. In terms of French intellectual history, it's probably most accurately thought of as carried along in the general assimilation of Hegel and as capable of supporting a Heideggerian as well as a Marxist inflection. At its core is the proposition that "matter thinks"; the thought that painting might also think would be a corollary of this.

A version of this thought informs Claude Lévi-Strauss's *The Savage Mind*, with its claim to engage what it calls a "science of the concrete," and becomes fully explicit with the "Overture" to *The Raw and the Cooked,* where he writes:

> The aim of this book is to show how empirical categories . . . can nonetheless be used as conceptual tools with which to elaborate abstract ideas and combine them in the form of propositions. . . .
>
> I intend to carry out an experiment which, should it prove successful, will be of universal significance, since I expect it to prove that there is a kind of logic in tangible qualities, and to demonstrate the operation of that logic and reveal its laws. . . .
>
> I [have] tried to transcend the contrast between the tangible and the intelligible by operating from the outset at the sign level. . . . We can thus hope to reach a plane where logical properties, as attributes of things, will be manifested as directly as flavors of perfumes. . . . Our task then is to use the concept of the sign in such a way as to introduce these secondary qualities into the operations of truth.[2]

Much of the detail here is particular to Lévi-Strauss's anthropology, but its main lines—the emphasis on a thought carried in and as the concrete, the determination of the sign as the place where this becomes graspable—are much more widely shared. And though these propositions are at the heart of what we recognize as structuralism, something close to them is already at work in the late work of Maurice Merleau-Ponty, to whose memory *The Savage Mind* was dedicated. It's particularly to the point to notice how much the ambition articulated here by Lévi-Strauss shares, despite the shifted means, with that articulated by Merleau-Ponty in, for example, *Sense and Nonsense.*[3]

The late and unfinished *The Visible and the Invisible* extends Merleau-Ponty's version of this ambition in a particularly influential way that is clearly informed strongly by his dealings with visual art, most notably that of Cézanne, as it presses toward a formulation of vision as a gap the world opens within itself as a modification of its continuous contact with itself—a kind of crossing, fold, or, as Merleau-Ponty calls it, "chiasmus."[4] This opening, a version of Heidegger's "clearing," is the world's giving itself over to articulation, the making, then, of its differences; it is the thought within which we find ourselves and which makes possible what we call our thinking, the form of which it must also ultimately determine.

Merleau-Ponty's account of the articulate lucidity of the world is strongly echoed in Jean-Luc Nancy's recent rewriting of philosophy's founding parable of the cave:

> Let us imagine the unimaginable, the gesture of the first imager. He proceeds neither at random nor according to a project. His hand advances into a void, hollowed out at that very instant, which separates him from himself instead of prolonging his being in his act. But this separation is the act of his being. Here he is outside of himself even before having been his own self, before having been a self. In truth, this hand that advances opens itself this void, which it does not fill. It opens the gaping hole of a presence that has just absented itself by advancing its hand.[5]

Here, as with Lévi-Strauss and Merleau-Ponty, the opening of the world, the birth of the work, is at once the founding and foundering of a subject that finds itself only as a certain folding of the world on itself. This is the core of the "antihumanism" associated with this body of thought, as also of its theses on "the death of the author." In this form, it is bound to a notion of work that presumably will have consequences at the level of such things as composition—the terms through which a work holds itself together and makes itself visible. Turning specifically to painting, this often appears in France as the question of what constitutes the *tableau,* although it can also serve as the ground or justification for practices that cast themselves against what would then be the factitious unity of the *tableau.*

I've noted that the proposition that matter—and therefore painting—thinks can be given a distinctively Marxist inflection, and this shows up perhaps most explicitly in and around the journal *Tel Quel.*[6] It likewise shows up in the early writings of Hubert Damisch, where it is partly supported by reference to Harold Rosenberg's writings in ways that make it count as part of a French reception of the American painting of the fifties—a reception in which Pollock and Kenneth Noland, Greenberg and Rosenberg find themselves, from an American perspective, oddly mixed.[7] What American formalists tend to read as a triumph of opticality is received in France more nearly in terms of an engagement with materiality: Pollock's skeins of paint count in their thickness and Morris Louis's *Veils* in their display of the material facts of canvas and pigment. If in Greenberg's writing Jean Dubuffet appears in the late forties as an ultimately defeated rival to Pollock, in France Dubuffet's "materiological" practice continues to set conditions for Pollock's reception.

These references will have to serve as the rough outline of a distinctively French field in which certain painting practices can discover themselves in the sixties and after. Any fuller account would turn into a history of the interplay between phenomenology and structuralism that eventually produces the various intellectual positions we now recognize as poststructuralist. Such an account would have to be responsive both to the range of fields across which the underlying intuition gets articulated and transformed and to the complex moments of convergence and divergence proper to its full elaboration. One would expect no more homogeneity among artistic practices in this field than in its discursive forms. One can nonetheless draw out some general statements that appear to belong to the field as a whole:

1. Matter thinks. "Thinks" here evidently means "makes a difference," so the proposition is that matter gives itself over to difference or to a process of difference.

2. This process must be grounded in matter opening itself to sense though some interruption of its apparent absolute continuity with itself; the ground of thought is something like a cut or a fold, a moment of delay or excess, in which substance refigures itself as relation.

3. Because thought taken this way is above all articulation, matter is not conceivable apart from language and the structures of difference to which it gives particularly compelling expression. There is no perception and so no visibility that is not also a work of articulation, and so also no visibility not structurally worked by invisibility, blindness, reserve.

This is the history that produces what in the U.S. comes to be called "theory," so it is especially worth noting that, as I've tried to sketch its foundations, such theory is not something that needs to be brought to objects. It is something at work within them, a constitutive part of what or how they are. This is the foundation of claims for a "theoretical practice" or a "theoretical object," terms that can be thought of as translations or revisions of Lévi-Strauss's commitment to "concrete thought."

Some Accounting

These first two sections have tried to offer brief and partial summaries of bits of historical background important to *As Painting*. They no doubt divide too neatly along too many lines—too simply American versus French, much too simply minimalism against pop—but they also too simply, if more implicitly, play Kantian concerns with the autonomy of art against a rather different view of art's work rooted in Hegel. If one can hope to work the apparent opposition between French and American traditions into a different place and do something to open the way toward a different imagination of the relations between work and intellectual contexts, it is unlikely that one can claim to undo the more intractable differences between Kantian and Hegelian views of art. Indeed, that opposition is importantly continued in the ensuing sections of this essay. Perhaps the best we can say here is that our sense of what art, and most especially painting, might be remains deeply divided in just this way, and that this dividedness and difficulty is our best access to it.

There's a way to put this less burdened with the heavy weight of philosophy: Modernism has seemingly wanted always to be a revolution, to do some final work of delivering us either to or from our selves or our situations. Sometimes we have imagined this as art's achievement and sometimes we have imagined it as art's overcoming or defeat. More recently we have seemed to want a postmodernism that would deliver us somehow from modernism, either by accomplishing its unfulfilled promises or by definitively vacating them. The hard thing, evidently, is to take modernism, in all its irresolution, as our fact, as the place where such differences as can be made continue to be made and can continue to do the obscure and difficult, unfinished and uncompletable, work of making sense.

/As/

The little word "as" has already been called upon to do a certain amount of work in this essay, carrying the first meditation on counting beyond simple arithmetic and modulating the notion of "mattering" so as to render audible in it a sort of confluence of the brute and the significant or sensible. Clearly its role in the title *As Painting* is in some way to carry the viewer and reader across the obvious differences between things on the wall and things on the floor, things made with a camera and things made with pigment and canvas: all of these the exhibition apparently asks one to see *as* painting.

But of course there are questions one has every reason to ask here. Why should one see this or that as painting? And what would that mean anyway? Can I see the view out my window as painting if I just look at it the right way? That's just what a landscape painter might be said to do—but then the proof of seeing it as a painting just is the painting, which is what there is to see. The view out the window remains merely that, and although I may recall the painting as I look out, no amount of squinting is going to make the view be that painting. By the same token, when I see a painting, that's what I see. What you see is what you see.[8] "As" just ain't in it.

In an important and well-known footnote to "Art and Objecthood" Michael Fried makes repeated use of "as" in ways worth attending to. He writes, in part:

> Moreover, seeing something as a painting in the sense that one sees the tacked-up canvas as a painting, and being convinced that a particular work can stand comparison with the painting of the past whose quality is not in doubt, are altogether different experiences: it is, I want to say, as though unless something compels conviction as to its quality it is no more than trivially

or nominally a painting. This suggests that flatness and the delimitation of flatness ought not to be thought of as the "irreducible essence of pictorial art," but rather as something like the minimal conditions for something being seen as a painting; and that the crucial question is not what those minimal and, so to speak, timeless conditions are, but rather what, at a given moment, is capable of compelling conviction, of succeeding as painting. This is not to say that painting has no essence; it is to claim that the essence—i.e. that which compels conviction—is largely determined by, and therefore changes continually in response to, the vital work of the recent past. The essence of painting is not something irreducible. Rather, the task of the modernist painter is to discover those conventions that, at a given moment, alone are capable of establishing his work as painting.[9]

Trying to focus particularly on the work "as" is doing in this passage, it's useful to bracket it with two other passages that also make central use of this word:

That which is explicitly understood . . . has the structure of something as something. . . . That which is designated is understood as that as which we are to take the thing in question. That which is disclosed in understanding—that which is understood—is already accessible in such a way that its 'as which' can be made to stand out explicitly. The 'as' makes up the structure of the explicitness of something that is understood. It constitutes the interpretation.[10]

Instead, we must be able to view the ocean as poets do, merely in terms of what manifests itself to the eye—e.g. if we observe it while it is calm, as a clear mirror of water bounded only by the sky; or, if it is turbulent, as being like an abyss threatening to engulf everything—and yet find it sublime.[11]

The first of these is from Martin Heidegger's *Being and Time*, and it asserts a general and radical interpretability of the world—the thought that nothing is except by being *as* the thing it is. This is a thesis that has become central to much contemporary thought in the humanities and human sciences and that clearly can figure powerfully in attempts to work out the kinds of positions sketched in the previous section. The second is from Immanuel Kant's *Critique of Judgment* and belongs to his account of a particular form of aesthetic judgment, the judgment of the sublime. The Heidegger passage is an explicit reflection on the place "as" occupies in our experience of the world, whereas Kant uses the word in ways that suggest it is necessary for capturing a particular, possibly defining, feature of an experience or region of experience distinct from other such regions.

Fried's statement can be taken as negotiating a certain path between these two, as if arguing that, while it is indeed a general possibility of our experience that anything flat and delimited is a candidate for interpretation as a painting, this interpretation can only be secured by another painting, which is to say it can only be secured through a specifically aesthetic judgment. To insist on the adequacy of the first possibility by itself is, at some level, to refuse or deny the experience that gives that possibility whatever sense it actually has. Granting experience its weight in the sense interpretation makes or fails to make seems, by contrast, to shift the center of interpretation away from us and toward the relation one work establishes, or fails to establish, with another, so that the work itself now appears as interpreting—as, let's say, making itself responsible for being a work and not simply an object we might classify one way or another. The "as" that we might have imagined ourselves to bring to the encounter has now slipped inside the work, become part of its structure, part of what shows in the painting or part of what makes it a painting.

But if this is the case, then it's not at all clear that the idea of some minimal condition that establishes something as a candidate makes any sense here at all: it will be enough that a work shows itself as painting—that it be able to, as Fried puts it, "stand comparison with the painting of the past whose quality is not in doubt," or, as I would put it, that it offer an experience that we recognize as continuous with what we know to be the experience of painting—for it to be a painting.

Working through Fried's passage in this way, we have done two things. First, we've crossed over the line between the general interpretability of experience and the more specific structure Kant attributes to aesthetic experience, or at least one major form of it. But we've also crossed over a line between two interpretations of interpretation—one that sees interpretation as something we accomplish by meeting conditions and securing an outcome within them, and another that sees interpretation as a dimension of things and thus a part of our experience not insofar as it is ours but insofar as it is *of them* (this is presumably part of what Heidegger means in speaking of understanding as disclosing an "as" that is already there). While there is more to be said about each of these crossings, what is perhaps most important is their interlacing: the way the particular region of experience Kant calls "aesthetic"—and so the particular kinds of things we call "works"—appears to force a redistribution or rearticulation in our larger understanding of how objects and experience and interpretation stand with regard to one another. Works of art have something to do with the shapes of inhabitation we find or fail to find the world offering: this is certainly close to the heart of Kant's interest in the aesthetic, and it is a proposition that only gets deepened and extended by such later thinkers as Heidegger and, closest to us, Jean-Luc Nancy. That's certainly one way painting could count.

On the more confined matter of interpretations of interpretation, a few things are worth saying briefly. The first is simply to note how close this thought of competing interpretations of interpretation appears to be to Fried's central claim that there are in modernist art two sensibilities at stake. As he famously or notoriously puts it, "Literalist sensibility is, therefore, a response to the same developments that have largely compelled modernist art to undo its objecthood, more precisely, the same developments seen differently, that is, in theatrical terms, by a sensibility already theatrical, already (to say the worst) corrupted or perverted by theater."[12] It presumably takes a work of translation or interpretation that I will not attempt here to bring Fried's assertion fully into line with Jacques Derrida's equally famous or notorious assertion, made at Johns Hopkins just a few months before the appearance of "Art and Objecthood" in the June 1967 *Artforum:*

> There are thus two interpretations of interpretation, of structure, of sign, of freeplay. The one seeks to decipher, dreams of deciphering, a truth or an origin which is free from freeplay and from the order of the sign, and lives like an exile the necessity of interpretation. The other, which is no longer turned toward the origin, affirms freeplay and tries to pass beyond man and humanism. . . .
>
> There are more than enough indications today to suggest we might perceive that these two interpretations of interpretation—which are absolutely irreconcilable even if we live them simultaneously and reconcile them in an obscure economy—together share the field which we call, in such a problematic fashion, the human sciences.[13]

Part of what is difficult in translating these two positions fully into one another, however close they may be, is that just where Fried wants to fully divide the two sensibilities from one another, Derrida writes:

> For my part, although these two interpretations must acknowledge and accentuate their difference and define their irreducibility, I do not believe that today there is any question of choosing—in the first place because here we are in a region (let's say, provisionally, a region of historicity) where the category of choice seems particularly trivial; and in the second, because we must first try to conceive of the common ground, and the différence of this irreducible difference.[14]

Derrida's position implies, as his writings make abundantly clear, the necessity of embracing the monsters that arise under such circumstances. And isn't this what modernism has always asked of us?

A second thing one might say, still more briefly, is that interpretation itself remains exposed to interpretation, thus underlining not only the irreducibility of the "as" that belongs to the structure of our experience but also how it works to uproot what we so repeatedly try to pin down with "is." This is a way of taking on the weight of Derrida's critique of Heidegger, of pushing what he takes from Heidegger toward a work of explication that does not return to interpretation.

The Kant passage in which I've partially framed Fried's remarks is lifted from his discussion of the experience of the sublime. This is a category that has been in and out of favor, mostly out, since its moment of romantic privilege. Barnett Newman famously appealed to it in the fifties; more recently it has appeared, somewhat uneasily, as a relay within accounts of or claims to "postmodernism," most notably that of Jean-François Lyotard. The little word "as" I've been so assiduously tracking appears in Kant's sentence three times, although it is easy to overlook its first, rather workmanlike, appearance. The experience Kant is giving instances of is one he has earlier analyzed: it is the experience, under suitable conditions, of something overwhelming, that we lack in an important sense any equipment for handling (it's too big or too powerful) but by which we are nonetheless finally not overwhelmed and that we are in some sense able to handle—an experience that begins in something like pain and ends in something equally like pleasure. The pleasure lies importantly in the discovery of a capacity within ourselves (Kant calls it Reason) that we did not know ourselves to have (or perhaps did not know ourselves to have to that degree or in such circumstances; it does not seem to be a discovery made but once). This new capacity does not succeed in doing what our existing capacities could not: we could not take in the power of that storm and we still cannot, Reason awakened as it may be; it continues to escape us, remains "outside."

And yet. What strikes the eye—and, finding no entry, evidently bounces off, remains outside—we also make something of, and "as" is the operator of this transition: the ocean's vastness escapes us and yet we see it before us as . . . a clear mirror bounded by the sky. The infinity of the starry sky escapes us, and yet it remains spread there as . . . a vast vault encompassing everything.

It looks very much like what's being discovered in these examples—and what Kant glosses primarily in terms of our capacity for freedom and thus our moral agency—is most concretely a capacity for metaphor.[15] Certainly, a part of what makes Kant's sentence difficult and interesting is the way it moves from an "as" that evidently aims at the most brutely literal—merely in terms of what manifests itself to the eye—to what is clearly a metaphor, also introduced by an "as," although now differently weighted or inflected. The distance between these two is somewhat muted by the invocation of the poet, but the passage is saying that the poet is the one in whom the brutely literal and overwhelming finds its necessarily bounded and displaced—this is all "adequate" can mean in this circumstance—expression.

The experience or judgment of the sublime arises from an encounter with something that escapes human measure (these things are necessarily "natural" even if what that means inevitably depends in some measure on one's culture), so it's interesting that just this dynamic seems to be at work in Kant's account of how fine art is possible—an account of what he calls "genius." Imagine a classroom of sorts where most of the students—copyists, we have to imagine—are doing perfectly good work, but one (the one that interests Kant) is doing something more or other than that. Kant writes, "The artist's ideas"—and by this he means the work being copied—"arouse similar ideas in his apprentice if nature has provided the latter with a similar proportion in his mental powers." The formulation here is directly that of the sublime, so Kant is giving us a moment in which the work taken as beautiful by most of the students is, exceptionally, experienced by this one as sublime: awakening a power or capacity for what Kant calls "originality" and "original sense" that will find its ultimate expression in a work of beautiful art that will itself become exemplary, indicating a theretofore unavailable way to go on and so capable also of renewing this cycle of experience.

This suggests a curious view of art written into the interstices of Kant's accounts of the beautiful and the sublime: if natural beauty consists in something like a thing's appearing wholly contained within itself, cutting itself out and apart from all the terms and interests that otherwise lace it into a world, and if the sublime in nature consists of what overruns all bounds, art seems to make itself out of both these things at once. It appears as a play of self-enclosure and excess—a continual passage and displacement back and forth through an "as" that is the mark of the work's difficult and divided showing of itself "as the work it is."

There's one last bit of Kant that needs attention, a sentence that can turn us back toward the more familiar terms of recent art and criticism. Every translation of the third *Critique* phrases it a bit differently; the German reads:

> Die Natur war schön, wenn sie zugleich als Kunst aussah; und die Kunst kann nur schön gennannt werden, wenn wir uns bewußt sind, sie sei Kunst, und sie uns doch als Natur aussieht.[16]

The path that's brought us to it suggests a rendering along the following lines:

> Nature is beautiful when it also seems as art; and art can only be called beautiful when we are conscious that it is art and it nonetheless seems to us as nature.

This lacing of "being" and "being called," of what is and what seems, of art and of nature, in and out of an "as" that is already implicated in each of these pairs and whose force and mobility becomes extraordinarily apparent in the spread of existing translations—all this feels like the exactly phrased center of what Kant has to say about art.

Elements of it have figured strongly in the strain of American criticism that has been repeatedly associated—by its practitioners and others—with "Kantian formalism." It's not hard to pick out the impulse in Greenberg's writings on Pollock to say that a part of the achievement of his art is its seeming as nature. And it is surely not wrong to see certain broader tendencies in the reception of Pollock—

to make out something of nature and landscape in or behind his painting, or to see these things as happening someplace where the beautiful and the sublime find themselves resolved into one another—as outgrowths of this more specific claim.

It's clear enough now what this costs us in Pollock (at the least, it costs us his thumbtacks and cigarette butts and handprints; at the most, it costs us his painting). But we also pay a considerable philosophical cost in forgetting that beautiful nature has never been available as an independent criterion against which to measure art's achievement but instead attains its visibility only in a world in which seeming as art is already a possibility.

Fried can appear to be at uneasy grips with these costs in "Art and Object-hood," on the verge of reopening the actual interlacings and seams through which Kant arrives at a notably difficult imagination of art. Once nature is put out of play as a condition for, and aspiration of, art and instead becomes one of its shifting concomitants, any number of other things shift as well. For example, "conven-tion" will no longer seem opposed to "nature" but deeply entwined with it (this is how Fried can write of artists "discovering" rather than, say, "inventing" the con-ventions capable of establishing work). One can begin to spin further thoughts out of this as well: for example, that abstraction and representation might be less op-posed than one had thought, that they are simply varied modulations of the "as" through which work renders itself visible; or again, that "self-criticism" in the arts is less a matter of a work's having a stance toward itself (that is, the name for an option it might or might not take up) than a particular tuning in it of the way it turns through and finds its limits, something like a name for what in other kinds of work one would call its "composition" (and in still other kinds of work might take the name of "noncomposition").

Fried's remarks emerge at a moment of crisis; one of their effects is to bring to explicitness an "as" that is internal to what we mean in speaking of a work but that is thus internal only by virtue of belonging to the movement by which the work at once establishes and overruns its limits, making itself out of that play. In its moment—one that *As Painting* takes as still somehow ours—this crisis is pecu-liarly a crisis of painting, and it is that term or practice or medium that remains to be considered.

/Painting/

It's important that the passage from Fried that I've tried to use to reopen a negoti-ation with Kant's view of fine art is responding to, in effect, two versions of the same enemy. A significant part of its work—for all that Fried's writing is normally linked to Clement Greenberg's—is to show the complicity between minimalist "lit-eralism" and Greenberg's appeals to what he often calls "positivism." What's at stake for Fried appears to be the notion of "medium" itself as it is threatened on the one side by reduction to sheer convention and on the other by elevation to something like a natural fact.

Greenberg famously makes the case for the centrality of medium at the beginning of his career as an art critic in "Towards a Newer Laocoon," and it's still worth looking at the sleights of hand through which that essay yields up the irreducible object "painting" and thus sets the terms in which he will later advance his claims for Pollock and the strong painters that follow him.[17]

The essay is intended as a defense of abstraction as the necessary form of an art aiming to claim its exclusive and proper ground, which means that the bulk of it is an account of how painting found itself in the position of making such a claim. Greenberg thus offers an expansive account of painting's history and position among the other arts of a kind he never really provides again. This involves an opening admission that "confusion of the arts" is genuinely possible and that there is at least enough of a relation among the arts that at one time or another one medium may be so "dominant" that the other arts are led to take their criteria, function, and so on from its model. In the relevant recent past of painting, literature has, in Greenberg's view, exercised just such an influence on painting, bending whatever interest painting itself might have in realism toward the exigencies of subject matter and the effects and meanings it could bear. Greenberg sees two strong currents that contribute to painting's assault on subject matter. The first is direct: he writes of "Manet . . . attacking subject matter on its own terrain by including it in his pictures and exterminating it then and there" (a statement, like so much of Greenberg's best writing, that is still stunning in its economy and exactness). The second is indirect: painting finds elsewhere in the arts, specifically in music, a relay that relieves it of the weight of literature. Greenberg devotes most of his attention to this second path because it is the one that delivers up "purity" as an artistic goal and defines it in terms of the internal means and proper effects of a given medium. (On Greenberg's description, Manet's path alone does not produce "purity" as a criterion—indeed it seems more nearly to embrace a certain impurity as the condition within and against which painting is to achieve whatever is its to achieve.)

This is a curious argument. Beginning from a field characterized by a range of relations among the arts, it offers an account of how the resources in play within that field lead to its reconstruction as so many separate and noncommunicating activities, each in search of its "purest" form—as if (although Greenberg does not put it this nakedly) a system of the arts dominated by literature is one open to various forms of merger or confusion while one dominated by music no longer apprehends itself as a system. From the point of view of this essay, the scare quotes Greenberg never ceases to place around "purity" are permanent markers of purity's being, in the end, not painting's word but music's, an ambition painting imagines its own but which is actually inscribed upon it from elsewhere.

By and large, and increasingly over time, Greenberg fastens his own writing more and more closely to painting's forgetting of what is constitutively impure in its aspiration to "purity"—this is his frequently avowed positivism. But traces of this uneasy "purity" continue to work his best writing, perhaps most clearly in his attempts to come to grips with sculpture and his various moments of willingness and unwillingness to recognize how sculpture's contemporary possibilities are themselves formed by a certain dominance of (and so also internal relation to) painting rather than arising at some simpler distance from it. The thought one might begin to have is that the internal possibilities of a medium are not fully or adequately thinkable apart from some reflection on the other mediums with which it is in relation. One might further think that painting's inability to give rise to such a thought would itself be a product of its particular place within a system of such relations at a particular time.

This general idea—that a medium must be thought of in terms that actively link its internal possibilities to a larger system to which it belongs—is crucial to *As Painting.* It is also an idea that has received one notably strong development in G. W. F. Hegel's *Lectures on Fine Art,* which both offers suggestive ways to think about the inner constraints of an art or a medium in relation to a larger system of the arts and brings them to a particularly interesting focus around painting.

Unlike Kant, Hegel has no time for natural beauty and does not derive his account of art from such considerations. "Art" is for him a sustained, but finally limited, element within the history of human thought, which is itself always an action of sorts—say, a making of differences. And this means that he is not tempted by any imagination of pure form: content is integral to art, which just is a content's finding adequate sensuous form. Hegel further takes it that "adequate form" cannot be sorted out apart from some reasonably full account of that content, because only that content can say what would count for it as adequate form—so that sometimes overt disjunction between a form and its content will be a more adequate expression of that content than some more harmonious and unified binding of the one to the other. Hegel's account of art necessarily unfolds along two axes—one historical and driven by considerations of what is available to material or concrete thought at any given moment, and one systematic, bearing on the ways in which one or another thing can be thought to what effect. These are independent but also interlocking: what is available for or in need of thinking at any given moment will determine one or another form as more nearly adequate to it.

This yields a historical narrative in which art is closely entangled with religion, working its historical way from East to West, from "natural" polytheism to Christianity (which is finally modern secularity), through phases Hegel distinguishes as Symbolic (characterized by the inarticulateness of its content and so the arbitrariness of its most adequate form), Classical (characterized by the thoroughness of its articulation and so the absoluteness of its external expression as form), and Romantic (characterized by a renewed recognition of the essential inwardness of thought and so also by forms that take reservation or limitation as one of their dimensions). As a global history or narrative, this clearly will not do, but it remains interesting insofar as it offers a way of thinking about how art might have a history and how a certain temporality linked to its content might be an internal feature of it. One might imagine that although "the history of art" as such either does not exist or does not exist in this way, art itself is always working through temporal rhythms that are built along these lines.

On the systematic side, we have a general theory of forms or mediums that will gain most of its real value through the more fully fleshed-out accounts it enables, but that in its broadest formulation distinguishes three major regions of form: the architectural (form understood most directly and simply as what contains a content and has little other articulated relation to that content), the sculptural (form understood as the full expression of content), and the painterly (form understood as the acknowledgment of a necessary withdrawal or reservation of content). This last moment is actually more complex—poetry and music are also among its privileged forms, and indeed a part of what it privileges is just this plurality of forms, a key point to which we will return.

Putting the two together, one gets a grand scheme in which the historically Symbolic is linked to the primacy of architecture, and so on, and in which these two dialectics—historical and formal—are also active within one another, so that the Symbolic includes its own Classical and Romantic moments, just as the privilege of architecture does not go apart from practices of sculpture or painting that both answer to it and in some measure contest it. However interesting this may be as a scheme, its real worth presumably lies in and is tested by the accounts of work it can actually sustain, which is why Hegel's lectures occupy some 1,400 pages and include, again in marked contrast to Kant, explicit treatments of a substantial number of works of art, general tendencies, and so on.

What is it that art is thinking across all this? At one level, it's thinking whatever is evidently there to be thought—things like who we are, how we are together, what it is for us to face or turn away from one another, what it is for the gods or nature to have or not have a shape, and so on. And at another level it is always thinking (working through, finding new articulations for) what it is to think at all: how it is that this activity takes place in the world and is clothed in its stuff, in sounds and marks and gestures and so on, and so also what kinds of barriers or limits this worldliness imposes on the work of thinking. Over its longest haul, the sustained episode of art takes us from the apparent arbitrariness of language to a recognition of its transparency as pure thought now able to discount or abstract itself from its material envelopment. This entails the notable Hegelian thought that art comes to an end, indeed has come to an end, and does so—has done so—as philosophy.

Art's "autonomy" is, on this account, only a passing moment within a history in which it does not, finally, find any ground of its own. Classical sculpture, the fullest assertion of that autonomy (and the moment in Hegel that most nearly answers to Kant's beauty), is given the lie by everything that precedes it and by everything that follows from it.

To persist with art, the making of it or the caring about it, in the wake of Hegel is to take it that there is no end to the dealing with the materiality of our thought and so equally to take it that there is no place thought comes simply to rest within this materiality. We are willing to take this as a description of the fundamental conditions for *As Painting*. Such a situation is marked by a certain impossibility of the Classical, which would also be a certain impossibility of sculpture, and a distinct interest in painting at the edge of discursivity and at radical grips with a reserve inseparable from its showing. *As Painting* thus explores the terms of visual practice in a field for which language is an ineradicable given; in doing so, it aims at a visuality not so much supplanted by language as possessed of an articulation or thinking internal to it. This would be what it means to speak in terms of a "theoretical practice" or a "theoretical object." "Theory" here would be less something a critic or historian brings to the work (perhaps to decode it, perhaps to justify it) than something to be traced in it, and writing would belong to such work as a part of its unfolding, a continuation of the conditions of its appearing.

If we go on to say that the contemporary impossibility of sculpture and painting's coupling of reserve and showing are one another's inner lining, we move into a space where the internal capacities of one medium cannot be thought apart from its relation to other mediums, and we enter it not as the space of a general proposition but as one specific to painting. This is to say that it seems to be a feature of Hegel's account that the various mediums have each a certain ability (and certain inability) to think the plurality of the arts. Architecture thinks it as the general fact of a variety of activities that can, as it were, take place under the same roof, whereas sculpture tends to think that same plurality as something that can be summed up by and as a single achievement (so the temple sculpture takes its architectural surround not as its container but as its further expression). Painting, as the art that takes reserve and limitation as its fundamental condition, can imagine neither art's simple self-containment nor its central summing up within one of its forms but is instead obliged to acknowledge a system of interdependent limitations and possibilities. The moments of painting's dominance are thus moments also of a certain dispersion, figured in Hegel by painting's sharing its moment of historical privilege with poetry and music. This emergence of an ordered dispersion of the arts itself figures or prefigures the shape Hegel's own philosophy—the work of thought freed of the limitation of art—will take as what Hegel famously calls "the System." The terms of painting's composition—what holds it together—are not available apart from the larger system of material implications and articulations within which it finds itself. This "system" is oriented to finitude and to the permanence of matter; it is finally unabstractable from the occasions of its articulation and is continuously produced, reproduced, and transformed in those occasions. "Radical self-criticism" can serve—has served—as a powerful name for this, and it is one that is particularly powerful insofar as it makes clear how painting's thinking through itself is always also a thinking through of the historical moment Hegel called Romantic and we are more likely to call Modernist. (But this power will remain partially concealed or baffled if we too quickly construe self-criticism as unproblematically oriented to something imagined as "purity.")

One might then say that minimalism occupies a special place in relation to the work in *As Painting* just because it opens up and insists on the lateral field of the arts in their mutual relation and interference as the field in which the thought of painting can be continued. This would be absolutely distinct from the widespread current tendency to imagine thought as belonging to painting by virtue of some special reflexivity or self-reference (a tendency that seems to gain strong, if different, forms of expression in pop and conceptualism).

There are several formulations that look particularly interesting here.

One might, for example, try out the thought that minimalism by and large works to mark the impossibility of sculpture as such—putting a kind of end to what had been under way in the work of David Smith and Anthony Caro—and so forces a concrete redescription or revision of both architecture and painting as practices that are predicated upon this now explicit impossibility. That architecture should appear this way suggests something about a path mostly not taken in *As Painting*, although thinkable in relation to it.

"Impossibility" does not, of course, mean that sculpture cannot in fact be made or has somehow dropped out of our imagination of art. Indeed, the aspiration to expressive integrity and totality carried by sculpture remains both defining for art and foreclosed to it—as if it were possible neither to surrender Kantian criteria nor to meet them. Painting's counting—of itself—would thus continue to be crucially relayed through this impossibility and would find in that relay a crucial element of its self-relation.

Sculpture does continue to be made, and the assertion of its integral impossibility underlines how the most powerful instances of contemporary sculpture will be made out of what it cannot be. This might be a way of beginning to think again about the work of David Smith—about the ways in which it appears as sculpture only under conditions set by painting; about the ways in which, under those conditions, it realizes a certain pure exteriority, an unfolding wholly into its aspects, in ways that nonetheless display an absent center that Classical sculpture had, on Hegel's account, no need to conceal; and about the ways Smith's sculpture ever more urgently moves to re-create the conditions of group sculpture—for

Hegel, the beginning of sculpture's fall away from itself—within the guise of the individual human form. Or one might attempt to think about Richard Serra, working on the far side of the break minimalism makes, trying once again to make a sculpture that would have something like the force of Kantian nature, and finding his own way to a late resolution or revision of that aspiration in a renewed practice of group sculpture now fully broken away from Smith's Classicism.

Remarks of this sort begin to sketch a field intimately related to the field of *As Painting* but also quite distinct from it.[18] That a certain range of work might indeed be shared among such fields points to a particular undecidability or interdisciplinarity variously at work within and between them, at once dividing and multiplying the effects of such names as "painting" and "sculpture" without being able to simply let them go. And this suggests that our histories here must be both plural and deeply bound to one another, making their differences inside each other, weaving and reweaving the nonintegral texture of our art and its forms.

Sculpture shows itself in its impossibility only under Romantic conditions. Hegel's Romantic era, and the partial dominance of painting that is one of its leading features, is the transition toward the full emergence of a content no longer bound to material form—which is to say, toward the philosophic writing that in a sense both rivals and supplants the Classical achievement of sculpture. Our insistence on Modernism marks the failure of this transition and the permanence of philosophy's entanglement with the material conditions out of which art makes itself. Where Hegel sees painting withdrawing into finitude because engaged with a content that goes beyond it, *As Painting* insists on painting's finitude—or its finish, a pun richly exploited by Jean-Luc Nancy[19]—as a recognition of a division internal to it, a condition of its appearing that does not lead beyond it. Where Hegel takes the surface of the painting to divide us from its content, we take division to be the essential fact of that surface as a surface.[20]

This is what it means to say that painting happens and counts always as painting. This essay has worked—no doubt the labor is all too palpable—to separate these two terms in order to fully demonstrate, make fully explicit, the terms of what is, in the end, so deep a solidarity between them as to make them but two routes to a single thought; but that thought is itself deeply a thought of difference and the effects of displacement. The phrase "as painting" is as fully a proper as an improper name for painting. Better: it is not a name at all—it is an attempt to mark within a practice the limit that belongs to its objectivity and not simply its nominal definition; it marks painting as, let's say, all edges, everywhere hinged, both to itself and to what it adjoins, making itself out of such relation.

What Counts as Painting?

To begin with, painting counts as painting. It has always done so. This essay has tried to sketch out something of what this means, and it has done so with one eye cocked toward the terms set in play across a certain range of postwar art and criticism. But it has also assiduously avoided any direct reference to the particular works and artists visible in *As Painting,* and so it has willingly maintained a gap between its own theoretical terms and the more directly material terms of the works themselves. What to say, then, by way of turning or returning to them in their concreteness?

Two closely related remarks by the philosopher Stanley Cavell open a path here. The first asks a question that goes to the heart of any claim to show painting—that is, to the heart of any claim for something to be painting. Cavell asks,

> What does it mean to say that a painter discovers, by painting, something true of all paintings, something that everybody has always known is true of painting generally? Is it a case of something hidden in unconsciousness becoming conscious? It is like something hidden in consciousness declaring itself. . . . Any painting might teach you what is true of all painting. A modernist painting teaches you this by acknowledgment—which means that responding to it must have the form of accepting it as a painting, or rejecting it.

The second remark fills in a bit more about what kinds of things might come to be acknowledged by painting in the way Cavell means.

> There may be any number of ways of acknowledging the condition of painting as total thereness—which is perhaps to say that there are any number of ways in which that condition can present itself, many different significances it may develop. For example, a painting may acknowledge its frontedness, or its finitude, or its specific therenesss—that is, its presentness; and your accepting it will accordingly mean acknowledging your frontedness, or directionality, or verticality towards its world, or any world—or your presentness, in its aspect of absolute hereness and nowness. Or a painting may declare that a painting, like nature, is of more than one color, and that its colors occur simultaneously.[21]

"Total thereness" is Cavell's placeholder for whatever it is that painting inevitably expresses or acknowledges in some more particular form. He glosses it in terms of the way painting is "wholly open to you, absolutely there in front of your senses." These are facts we are probably happier registering slightly differently—in terms of painting as something above all exposed and to which one is exposed, something that essentially shows—and we are inclined this way because acknowledgment only makes sense, only becomes necessary and only carries any weight, where something is somehow less than totally there, which is why painting's acknowledgment of the conditions of its presence is always an acknowledgment of some finitude apart from which painting would not be at all.

Let's imagine that what *As Painting* takes as in most general and sustained need of acknowledgment is painting's superficiality. We'll follow Cavell as well in imagining that any adequate registration of this will also be an acknowledgment of our superficiality. This is close to what Hegel thought of painting, although it would perhaps be more accurate to say that for him painting acknowledged, precisely by withdrawing from sculptural fullness to the limitation of its two-dimensional surface, a depth that necessarily escaped it (and so it was capable of bringing us to an acknowledgment of the depth of our inwardness). For Hegel the painting's surface was above all there as a limit fixed between us and art's deepest truths even as it also provided the only concrete access such truths could have. To say that for us the works in *As Painting* show themselves above all in or as an acknowledgment of painting's superficiality is to say that they take whatever depth painting may have, whatever reserve it marks the visible limit of, as itself a feature and dimension of that surface and not as something that lies beyond or outside it—so the technical and material means of the works are those proper to the surfacing of things. These include, in ways we discuss in detail in our comments on individual artists, such things as cutting and folding; the emergence and persistence of edges; the inevitability of adjacency; what is given in reversibility or transparency; what shows itself not as representation but as displacement on or into a surface; what supports an inscription or becomes visible only through its inscription; what belongs to a surface as the limit—the outside or the compression—of a volume; what is discovered in color's passage into its own articulation; the persistence of ground across or as its own remarking. . . .

As one works through this list it rapidly becomes apparent that this is not simply a matter of surface as the marker of a limit but of surface as itself having the structure of a limit, of being that place in which visibility and invisibility discover themselves as one another's inner lining, thus surface as itself a kind of event, a tension sustained and held open by an outside it touches everywhere but that has no thinkable existence apart from that touch. Hegel's painting, pointing always beyond itself, here finds itself only ever folded back through itself, its materiality the unsurpassable condition for what, in it, passes beyond it. There is no depth to this painting apart from its laterality—its extension, across the canvas, across the relation of one canvas to another, across the discontinuities that bind it to its adjacencies. This is what we hoped to capture in the phrase "division and displacement"—terms intended to make visible how painting's ability to hold itself together, to show itself as painting, includes and structurally depends upon an internal detachment that makes its departure from itself a dimension of its achievement.

I began this essay by raising questions about how this exhibition finds its limits, about the conditions under which one thing or another might show or fail to show in its context, and I've tried to work this question into the fabric of painting itself insofar as it exists as or happens on its own limit. It is this deep orientation to a logic of limits that justifies the opening suggestion that counting the works included in *As Painting* calls for something more like a calculus than a straightforward arithmetic. How, then, might one begin to think about what is not in the show? What will it mean to imagine some particular work or body of work to have been overlooked or excluded?

Recognizing that there is an inevitable fringe of work we wanted but could not for one reason or another obtain, granting sheer ignorance its due weight, and admitting the limitations that come with the show's particular focus will take care of some of this. But the question about the structure of the exhibition, about how it stands toward or finds its own limits, will remain intact.

One might begin by saying that "absence" is already at play within the logic of limits around which the exhibition is formed and so has to be taken up in some active relation to questions of acknowledgment that emerge there. At least three things can be said.

The first is that "acknowledgment" is not an easy or gentle term. One need think only of the simple human dramas that can turn around it. The term clearly opens onto such other terms as "criticism" and "self-criticism," so that it does not function apart from some notion or practice of "judgment." Not all displays of, stagings of, what I've called "superficiality" count as—function as—acknowledgments of it or as acknowledgments of it in painting; this boundary is then a particularly active or urgent one for *As Painting*. But if "acknowledgment" has in this way its harder edge, it remains always an exposed term, one that cannot be guaranteed in advance or held apart from the world in which it is called for. If we can wear the absence that arises from the various forms of ignorance relatively lightly—in the way one can wear one's simpler failures of recognition—failures of acknowledgment, curatorial or painterly, are more difficult matters: they are places where things are at stake and for which one remains responsible, to which one is (obscurely, polemically, problematically) obliged.

The second begins from the thought that acknowledgment, unlike recognition, does not have any simple stopping place, cannot be accomplished once and for all but always offers ways to go on—some of which may well ultimately open onto a ground that feels very different from that initially claimed. Acknowledgment remains open to the possibility of something's coming to be transformed beyond recognition, thus needing to find new words for its accomplishment. This would be an open limit on *As Painting,* a matter not of what it excludes but of what can only be gone on to.

The third is that it is part of acknowledgment's grammar that it can never be perfect. *As Painting* offers particular terms for thinking this. These are terms that remain importantly finite or occasional, but there is nothing that can stand in for them that will not be equally concrete, finite, and occasional. *As Painting* imagines its absences in part as what is folded into it, figuring within it as a certain reserve that is not an active withholding but a structural feature of the showing of painting as such. This limit would be neither open nor excluding and would not take the form of some boundary around it; rather, it would traverse the whole surface of the exhibition in the form of an invagination through which its intention is repeatedly unfolded as its extension. Just as *As Painting* cannot imagine the one painting that would be painting, so also it cannot imagine the showing of painting as a simple and simply enclosed totality.

All three of these thoughts are ways of trying to mark out the specificity of the appeal to something one might call "theory" in and around *As Painting*. "Theory" doesn't set the boundaries of the exhibition, but is importantly staked by the work within it. This stake is variously taken up both by the artists themselves and by us in bringing this work together in the way we have. But such "theory" is, finally, a part of *As Painting*—something that gains its visibility there. It is the exhibition that sets a certain limit to theory: what happens in its internal folds and at its apparent boundaries is perhaps a stilling of the voice of theory, perhaps its transformation toward another voice or another idiom. This would be a way of saying what it means to go on with painting, as well as a way of saying how theory counts, how painting does and does not count (on) it. In the end, it will be painting that counts *As Painting*.

1. See also Lucy Lippard, "As Painting Is to Sculpture: A Changing Ratio," in Maurice Tuchman, ed., *American Sculpture of the Sixties* (Los Angeles: Los Angeles County Museum of Art, 1967), pp. 31–34.

2. Claude Lévi-Strauss, *Introduction to a Science of Mythology I: The Raw and the Cooked,* trans. John and Doreen Weightman (New York: Harper and Row, 1969), pp. 1, 14.

3. Maurice Merleau-Ponty, *Sense and Nonsense,* trans. Hubert and Patricia Dreyfus (Evanston: Northwestern University Press, 1964).

4. Maurice Merleau-Ponty, *The Visible and the Invisible,* ed. Claude Lefort, trans. Alphonso Lingis (Evanston: Northwestern University Press, 1968).

5. Jean-Luc Nancy, *The Muses,* trans. Peggy Kamuf (Stanford: Stanford University Press, 1996), pp. 74–75.

6. For a useful overview in English of this moment, see Paul Rodgers, "Toward a Theory/Practice of Painting in France," parts 1 and 2, *Artforum* 17, no. 8 (April 1979): 54–61, and *Artforum* 18, no. 7 (March 1980): 53–61.

7. See Hubert Damisch, *Fenêtre jaune cadmium, ou les dessous de la peinture* (Paris: Editions du Seuil, 1984).

8. The phrase is, of course, Frank Stella's. See Bruce Glaser, "Questions to Stella and Judd," in Gregory Battcock, ed., *Minimal Art: A Critical Anthology* (New York: E. P. Dutton, 1968).

9. Michael Fried, "Art and Objecthood," in *Art and Objecthood: Essays and Reviews* (Chicago: University of Chicago Press, 1998), p. 169.

10. Martin Heidegger, *Being and Time,* trans. Joan Stambaugh (Albany: State University of New York Press, 1996), p. 139 (§149).

11. Immanuel Kant, *Critique of Judgment,* trans. Werner Pluhar (Indianapolis: Hackett, 1987), p. 130 (§270).

12. Fried, "Art and Objecthood," pp. 160–61.

13. Jacques Derrida, "Structure, Sign, and Play in the Discourse of the Human Sciences," in *Writing and Difference,* trans. Alan Bass (Chicago: University of Chicago Press, 1978), pp. 292–93.

14. Ibid., p. 293.

15. See Timothy Gould, "The Audience of Originality: Kant and Wordsworth on the Reception of Genius," in Ted Cohen and Paul Guyer, eds., *Essays in Kant's Aesthetics* (Chicago: University of Chicago Press, 1982), and Ted Cohen, "Figurative Speech and Figurative Acts," *Journal of Philosophy* 72, no. 19 (November 6, 1975): 669–84.

16. Immanuel Kant, *Kritik der Urteilskraft* (Wiesbaden: Suhrkamp Verlag, 1957), §45. Pluhar's translation reads: "Nature, we say, is beautiful if it also looks like art; and art can be called fine art only if we are conscious that it is art while yet it looks to us like nature."

17. Clement Greenberg, "Towards a Newer Laocoon," in *Perceptions and Judgments, 1939–1944,* vol. 1 of *Collected Essays and Criticism,* ed. John O'Brian (Chicago: University of Chicago Press, 1986).

18. For a related argument, see Rosalind Krauss, "Sculpture in the Expanded Field," *October* 8 (Spring 1979): 30–44, reprinted in Krauss, *The Originality of the Avant-Garde and Other Modernist Myths* (Cambridge: MIT Press, 1985). Krauss's essay has had a significant influence on the conception of *As Painting,* and readers are invited to imagine how far the exhibition can be thought of as exploring painting in an expanded field structured by "photography" and "sculpture."

19. See Nancy, *The Muses,* especially "The Vestige of Art."

20. See also Rosalind Krauss, *The Optical Unconscious* (Cambridge: MIT Press, 1993). A number of Krauss's formulations in this book have also played a formative role for *As Painting.* Considerations of space have precluded a fuller discussion of Krauss's work here; a version of the relevant arguments is forthcoming in *Art History.*

21. Stanley Cavell, *The World Viewed: Reflections on the Ontology of Film* (New York: Viking Press, 1971), p. 110.

As Painting: Problematics

Philip Armstrong and Laura Lisbon

Problematics

Still

> . . . the dialectical circle of the question asked of an object as to its nature,
> on the basis of a theoretical problematic which in putting its object to the
> test puts itself to the test of its object.
>
> —Louis Althusser

At first glance, the various objects displayed in *As Painting* appear without relation or attachment to anything other than themselves. In the catalogue, of course,
things appear a little differently, for here the work takes its place in a situation that
continues the convention of listing the artists in alphabetical order, with the presentational information one usually expects from such contexts. But in the attempt
to situate the various pieces so that they convey something compelling about *painting*, nothing seems to justify their belonging together in the actual exhibition space
other than the creation of a "conversation" that remains closed and somewhat in-
sular. In spite of the desire to prolong a conversation about painting (against what
odds? with what risk?), in spite of the desire to establish a conversation that takes
the form of what Maurice Blanchot terms an "entretien infini," this is a conversa-
tional space that appears closed off and even hermetic. The exhibition has a self-
enclosed coherence that is already prescribed by the "formal" terms the work has
established for itself in advance of its showing.

In more specific ways, the presentation of the paintings does not insist on any
opposition between the figurative and the abstract, so there is no represented theme
that leads to a discursive analysis at this level. Not that the exhibition is oblivious
to a number of conceptual issues, some of which are historically circumscribed
within the context of the work's reception, some of which relate more obliquely to
concepts employed in the history of art, and some of which, more tendentiously,
the work even attempts to "create." (Enough of the artists are cited in the margins
of Gilles Deleuze and Félix Guattari's *What Is Philosophy?* to justify this last
claim.) But neither the galleries nor the catalogue are labeled according to established themes, concepts, or historical markers, and there is no point of orientation

that would lead toward the definition or comprehension of the work in terms that are purely thematic, conceptual, or historical. Nor has any attempt been made to "represent" a given artist's career. Nor again has the gender of the artist played any determining or significant role in the choice of works exhibited.

It would no doubt be appropriate to acknowledge that the phrase "theoretical practice" plays a prominent role in the initial production and reception of much of the work, at least as Louis Althusser gives us this phrase to think *with*.[1] But the work in the exhibition is not an illustration of "theory" either. Perhaps it offers a resistance to theory, to theoretical speculation about painting, a resistance echoed in the work's insistence on a material dimension that is a decisive aspect of its exposure as painting. But this is not a presentation of painting in theoretical terms that it does not already assume for itself as a theoretically inscribed object or "praxis." In short, there is nothing in the presentation of the work in *As Painting* that identifies it in terms other than a questioning of its own identity, nothing here that is not an incessant pursuit of the *limits* of what painting *is,* and thus nothing that does not attempt to show painting's own exteriority—its divisions and displacements—in and *as* painting.

If the work is presented without relation or attachment to anything other than itself—a "formalism" that doesn't preclude a certain pedagogy or even didacticism—then it is also presented in terms that are always other than—irreducibly different from—that attachment. *As Painting* is not an exhibition about self-referential or self-reflexive painting, not a gratuitous mirroring of painting back onto its own conditions of possibility, if only because there is no prior "self" to find itself reflected in. Here, any "self" that painting is said to possess is always missing from its place, detached from any essential form on which to support such a self in the first place.[2] If the exhibition insists on a questioning of painting's identity and limits, it does so as an acknowledgment and affirmation of painting, but there is nothing assured in advance of that acknowledgment and affirmation, nothing a priori—no tradition—by which we might know what "difference" painting makes. Even the negatives in all these various formulations (this suite of "nothings" and "nots") are difficult to pin down with any determinate sense. But an initial approximation might be that this is and is (again) not a "fundamental painting" exhibition, at least insofar as what is fundamental to painting is also what is most resistant to painting as such. What grounds painting and what holds painting most intimately to itself is also what is most distant—detached—opening the same work to a torn intimacy (a permanent crisis) that inaugurates painting's (in)finite dispersion and the origins of its own displacement.[3]

It would be tempting to say that *As Painting* presents also a "space" for painting. The gallery space is not simply a container in which we find a number of paintings but becomes the space *of* painting, a painting space, in the sense that Blanchot will write of "l'espace littéraire"—the title of a book that had a decisive influence on many of the artists included here. Space and painting are not distinct but folded together in an exhibition space—Peter Eisenman's Wexner Center—which itself participates in questions of structure and architecture that much of the work already explores as a dimension of what it is doing (or undoing) as painting. In this sense, the exhibition has no single theme, and it offers us nothing in particular that draws us toward an identifiable center other than the space of an exhibition in which painting poses—and poses again, repeats, and so displaces—the question of its own identity. With Blanchot, we could say that the center of the exhibition is a question of the "space" of painting, and that if it has a "fixed" center, it is not one that can be discerned thematically, conceptually, or historically but one that (at least if it is "genuine") *displaces itself.* Curating *As Painting* would then be approached "out of desire for this center and out of ignorance," and the feeling of having touched this center might very well be "only the illusion of having reached it."[4] As an exploration of painting's own limits, this experiment then plays at the limit of what can be presented or what—and this is more difficult to discern—comes *into* presence here (indeed, *The Presence of Painting* was one of our working titles at an earlier stage of this project).[5] *As Painting* thus remains open to the fundamentally paradoxical question of how (and when, and where, and for whom) some "thing"—called painting, or that calls itself painting—can be *exposed* in a way that shows, reveals, and so discloses its limits. How painting becomes, in other words, something that we can still turn back to. And that *still—* once (and) again—turns away.

Theoretical Problematics and Painting

In presenting our contribution to *As Painting* in terms of "problematics," we can repose the question of painting and the exposure of its limits somewhat differently.

Our first concern is the use of the word "problematic" itself, which we owe to Louis Althusser. The word thus participates within a larger philosophical project of understanding Marxism as "a theory of epistemological history" and as a measure of the potentially transformative consequences of this thinking as a "theoretical practice." In this sense, a problematic takes its place within Althusser's attempt to locate the "irreducible specificity" of Marxist theory, a theoretical commitment that is termed "scientific" and thus distinguishable from a tradition of speculative idealism with which it seeks to break. Such a rupture with this idealist tradition equally distinguishes Marxism's specificity from any reliance on conceptual categories inspired by, or serving to reproduce, both humanist discourse and the historicist narratives that sustain it.

As a pivotal concept in Althusser's texts *For Marx* and *Reading Capital,* both from 1965,[6] a problematic constitutes "the internal essence" of an ideological thought, at least insofar as the essence of this thought does not possess an ontological identity but "a determinate unitary structure." More particularly, a problematic designates "the particular unity of a theoretical formation," one whose structure is both discernible and historically circumscribed: "understanding an ideological argument implies, at the level of the ideology itself, simultaneous, conjoint knowledge of the *ideological field* in which a thought emerges and grows; and the exposure of the internal unity of this thought: its *problematic*" (*FM*, 70). In light of this definition, our interest in Althusser's reference to a "problematic" in the context of *As Painting* prompts some preliminary observations.

First, emphasis on a problematic suggests a way to introduce the painting in the exhibition, to give the painting visibility from a determinate (or overdetermined) position. The use of the term simultaneously situates that approach within the context of an ideological argument. In other words, any reference to a problematic would necessarily offer a way of situating the ideological implications of an exhibition devoted to painting today. This is not in fact the way the exhibition has been conceived or developed, but reference to an ideological context would now become—belatedly—the first consequence of any appeal to Althusser's concept of a problematic.

Of course, the "ideological field" in which painting has emerged has been explored at length by others. Art history is littered with commentaries on the ideological implications of painting, and our modernity would perhaps not be (already) our (post)modernity without the repetition (itself ideological) of this claim. But this particular "ideological field" is not our primary concern here. For what remains especially difficult to circumscribe is the specificity of painting's relation to "the internal unity" of this thinking, to the "systematically interrelated set of concepts" that structure painting's emergence into an ideological field. Indeed, how does painting relate to "the particular unity of a theoretical formation"? And what would be gained or lost in posing these questions to—or, more pertinently, *in*—painting in the first place?

Second, our evocation of Althusser is less an arbitrary choice to give a theoretical introduction to *As Painting* than an attempt to recall the language of a historical moment (a "conjuncture") that is past (perhaps too distant for some, certainly not distant enough for others) and in which much of the exhibited French work was produced. And even if some of the work was not directly associated with the cultural context inspired by Althusser, reference to a problematic provides the terminological context in which much of it was critically received. So the reference to Althusser has, at this level, its own historical justification.

Considerably less known in the American context of *As Painting* (at least outside specialist circles) are the visual practices current in France in the years following the publication of Althusser's seminal texts. Indeed, while French "theory" has been imported and has become, for many, common currency, there has been a virtual effacement of (or a refusal to face) many of the visual practices that existed in France from the late sixties on and that found their first voice within this intellectual context and political moment. One of the initial motivations behind *As Painting* was to understand how a number of artists working in France—some individually, many collectively—oriented their work according to these same theoretical and political questions posed (in one form) by Althusser, in a critical language that was, for artists and critics alike, deeply informed by Althusser's texts or at least the shared intellectual commitments they generated. Our insistence on the concept of a problematic is, we hope, a fitting emblem of this initial motivation.

Perhaps even stranger for the American reception of the work included here is the realization that the visual practices that accompanied the writings of Althusser were *painting*. And it is work that has no hesitation in calling itself painting, even when it looks nothing like painting in any usual sense of the term, and even when (for certain artists) what it wanted to demonstrate was a "deconstruction" of painting (another word in vogue at the time, at least since Jacques Derrida's first publications). It would be no exaggeration to say that this work has been effaced from, at best simply ignored in, Anglo-American art historical narratives since the late sixties, even by those (once?) fully sympathetic to the political ambitions of this historical moment that we have come to call "'68."[7]

A number of causes of this neglect could be raised, starting with the assumption that New York had already "stolen" the idea of modern art, with the result that there has been little attempt in the U.S. to see any of the French work that might have followed in the wake of this theft.[8] If Clement Greenberg also plays a pivotal role in the earlier receptions and misreceptions of French art, both his most faithful followers and his most vehement critics have often shared a refusal to acknowledge French painting from the late sixties on.[9] The rhetoric of postwar art analyzed by Serge Guilbaut would then find its natural extension in someone like Donald Judd, whose chauvinism and New York provincialism concerning the relative values of European (and other) art are only too well known. One might also point to the ways in which the painting that did accompany the American reception of French "theory" was either of "historical" interest or already illustrative of the claims in which philosophers in particular seem to have found so much solace. Even those social historians well versed in the intellectual and political commitments Althusser represents have tended to avoid the contemporary visual practices associated with his work in France, turning to the nineteenth century or earlier, to postwar American art, or away from painting altogether. If we look back over the last thirty years at the reception of "theory" in relation to the visual arts in Anglo-American contexts, it is clear that the theoretical and political interests we have been exploring in reference to Althusser have been received and transformed in the most extraordinarily dense and conflicting ways, but never in any significant sense in relation to painting, finding their home above all in studies of film, literature, photography, and popular culture.[10] One could also point to the ways in which French painting of the period was ignored here because its often militant politics were considered unacceptable or naive—or note that the predominantly collective practices it inspired (from the demonstrations of Daniel Buren, Olivier Mosset, Michel Parmentier, and Niele Toroni in the late sixties to the Supports/Surfaces or JaNaPa exhibitions in the early seventies) found no easy commercial reception. We could say that the work was already provincial enough to have become nothing more than a domestic conflict within French borders, a belated (the last?) form of avant-garde militancy. Then again, a failure to acknowledge this work may suggest nothing more than that it was seen but was judged to be uninteresting, a claim no doubt supported by any number of willing critics and artists already working in France as well.

These narratives have all had their play in the last few decades. But perhaps the easiest thing to say here is that the French work included in *As Painting* has come to seem of mere historical interest, even if some of the artists are still exhibiting widely today. Indeed, on both sides of the Atlantic—and this we increasingly found in our conversations as we prepared for the exhibition—there is an overwhelming sense of historical closure. So that if this work is becoming increasingly available in the United States, there is a sense that it represents a moment that is not only past but of only historical value. (Cadere's *batons* are the most fitting emblem of this sense of closure, or at least of the "politics" that has disappeared from the work's initial reception.) And of course, on both sides of the Atlantic, not a few academic dissertations are beginning to appear.

As Painting refuses to subscribe to this sense of historical closure. It does, however, intend to recall what remains an undoubtedly strange confluence of texts and events, in which Althusser's appeal to a problematic finds itself explored in relation to something that insists on calling itself painting. By the same token, it hopes—at least through this brief introduction—to evoke a situation where Blanchot's writings on the "space" of literature (or Roland Barthes's *Writing Degree Zero* or Julia Kristeva's early writings) could find an echo in a journal like *Peinture: Cahiers théoriques,* sympathetic in certain essays to a discourse of both Maoism *and* painting, in whose pages Greenberg's writings on modernism or an essay on Poussin could find themselves next to a manifesto appealing to painting's epistemological "rupture" with bourgeois values; a situation where experimental practices of "writing" and what Philippe Sollers once termed "the experience of limits" could inform the interior and exterior spaces in which an artist chose to exhibit; where painters like Parmentier or Buren might proclaim militantly that "we are not painters," and so inaugurate a new limit-experience for painting, refuse all forms of conceptualism, and still appeal to Cézanne or to Beckett's dialogue on Bram van Velde for justification; where the exhibition *Art of the Real* (first shown in New York in 1968 and then seen in Paris) could find its very title read through Jacques Lacan and Althusser, thereby transforming the terms in which one might call a work of art "minimalist"; where the history of art itself could be replaced by "a theory of epistemological history" or where painting could assume responsibility for producing an "epistemological object";[11] and where *all* of these references—however disparate and antagonistic—could not only play a determining role in the contemporary alignments between art and political events but simultaneously offer a way of acknowledging how the formal and technical procedures of Pontormo or Poussin or Cézanne or Matisse or Picasso or Pollock or Newman might still *count* (to use Stephen Melville's felicitous phrase), might still matter as a way of thinking, as a way of producing something that makes a difference to the ways things are.

We have no desire to efface the fundamentally contradictory nature of the thinking evoked in this schematic overview, nor to reduce the complexity of the potential analyses to which these various references may give rise by explaining them away. Even less is it a question of restoring these references and the events they recall to their contemporary relevance, even as they begin to collide in ways that appear strangely disturbing for those in an Anglo-American context convinced that questions of formalism or traditions of painting (even through a rereading of Greenberg's "Eliotic Trotskyism") are not the place in which we are to find our most resonant political ambitions or theoretically informed interventions. There is no place for nostalgia in *As Painting,* and no desire to revise the past, through Althusser or whomever else might come to figure in his place. If we insist on situating the work included in *As Painting* in rapport with Althusser's concept of a *problematic,* it is not only to preserve the full complexity of the references and events raised here but to refuse the historical closure to which much of this work—and painting itself—has been consigned.

"An Informed Gaze"

In what ways does situating painting in relation to a problematic demand a simultaneous interest in, and displacement of, notions of "medium-specificity," with the essentialist categories and historicist patterns the term implies?

Our insisting on a problematic intends to reopen painting to a reading informed by a question of its structure rather than its essential properties—of its structural articulation, the play of its limits, more than its purported meaning (or lack of meaning). Attention to the problematic of painting further intends to advance the work's *autonomy* as itself a structural articulation through which the definitions of the work's interiority and exteriority are radically redistributed in ways irreducible to any opposition between its form and its historical context. In situating the work in *As Painting* in terms of a problematic, we are seeking a certain amount of lucidity—today—about the questions that are posed to (or articulated with) its objects. But any claim to lucidity is also structured by an opacity. And this too is a fundamental aspect of what Althusser suggests of a problematic.

Althusser's appeal to a problematic aims to remove all appeals to "subjectivist" concepts informing an idealist interpretation by foregrounding the "system" of questions that are posed of its objects. A problematic is what brings together all the theoretical presuppositions that enable a given thought to find coherence. It seeks what gives the objects contained within its field their visibility: "To think the unity of a determinate ideological unity . . . by means of the concept of its *problematic* is to allow the *typical systematic structure* unifying all the elements of the thought to be brought to light" (*FM*, 67).

Althusser's appeal to a problematic here testifies to his well-known debts to a discourse of psychoanalysis, specifically to a "symptomatic" reading, so that the aim is to identify the theoretical structure informing those objects within a given field. Attention is paid as much to what is excluded from that field as to what is present, as much to what is invisible as to what comes into visibility. But if the reading Althusser offers overcomes ideological mystification, then attention is not simply given to the invisibility that structures the visible; nor does it give us better knowledge of a given object. If the "science" Althusser aspires to is to sustain itself as a measure of the transformative or revolutionary consequences of a "theoretical practice," then this science and the "reading" it insists on must inaugurate the *production* of a new theoretical problematic or "a theory of epistemological history." In short, the reading aspires to the production of what Althusser terms "an informed gaze."[12]

In light of this claim, it is worth quoting Althusser at length here, if only because the very language in which he articulates a reading of a problematic informs much of the exhibited work, as well as any number of writings in France from the late sixties on by artists and critics alike. Writing of the possibility of advancing this "science," he argues:

> This opens the way to an understanding of the determination of the *visible* as visible, and conjointly, of the invisible as invisible, and of the organic link binding the invisible to the visible. Any object or problem situated on the terrain and within the horizon, i.e., in the definite structured field of the theoretical problematic of a given theoretical discipline, is visible. We must take these words literally. The sighting is thus no longer the act of an individual subject, endowed with the faculty of "vision" which he exercises either attentively or distractedly; the sighting is the act of its structural conditions, it is the relation of immanent reflection between the field of the problematic and *its* objects and *its* problems. (*RC*, 25)

Insisting on the problematic of painting refuses the unmediated vision of an object as that which grants us knowledge of that object; as Althusser writes, "we must abandon the mirror myths of immediate vision and reading, and conceive knowledge as production" (*RC*, 24). If knowledge is conceived as production, the object of this knowledge must be contained *immanently* within the very problematic in which it is articulated, so that what comes into visibility "is the relation of immanent reflection between the field of the problematic and *its* objects and *its* problems." It is "the act of its structural conditions."

Of course, everything turns on what Althusser implies by this sense of immanence, notably its rapport with a "sighting" that is phrased in terms of its "structure." The difficulty can be rephrased by insisting on the ways in which this immanence does not secure a closed and essentialized condition, a mirror reflection between a problematic and the objects contained within its field of vision. Nor is Althusser suggesting that we are now caught within a vicious circle. For in his insistence on the notion of "immanent reflection," he is reopening this vicious or hermeneutic circle into a "dialectical circle." This transformation is captured in our opening epigraph, where Althusser refers to "the dialectical circle of the question asked of an object as to its nature, on the basis of a theoretical problematic which in putting its object to the test puts itself to the test of its object" (*FM*, 38).

A number of consequences follow from this change in emphasis.[13] A theoretical problematic is not constituted as a preconceived "theory" that is applied to the work. It does not offer a theorized relation to the work. It is not a question of "turning around" in this circle either, as if such reflection was simply a self-reflection, the "recognition" of the object (and of the "self" that secures this recognition as a form of representation or a logic of mimesis). This is avoided, Althusser insists, because this dialectical circle is not "the closed circle of ideology, but the circle perpetually opened by its closures themselves" (*RC*, 69), the dialectical circle that opens the possibility of a "theoretical practice" and the production of a new theoretical problematic. For a problematic of painting opens a way of measuring what is beyond (or prior to) measure: "The problematic of a thought is not limited to the domain of the objects considered by its author, because it is not an abstraction for the thought as a totality, but the concrete determinate structure of a thought and of all the thoughts possible within this thought" (*FM*, 68). Transforming a hermeneutic circle into a dialectical circle is the initiating moment of a radical transformation of any theoretical practice (including the *writing with* with which it is articulated).[14]

Althusser insists on pursuing such a mode of reading not only in terms of the structured "limits" of a problematic but also in terms of what he calls the "gaze." It is precisely this term that becomes the conceptual pivot around which he distinguishes between a hermeneutic circle and a dialectical circle, further recalling the language of visibility and invisibility we have been tracking here:

> To see this invisible, to see these "oversights" [in a given text], to identify the lacunae in the fullness of this discourse, the blanks in the crowded text, we need something quite different from an acute or attentive gaze; we need an

informed gaze, a new gaze, itself produced by a reflection of the "change of terrain" on the exercise of vision. (*RC*, 27)

This reference to a "change of terrain" can be elaborated by citing several other texts that date from this same time. As we have noted, *For Marx* and *Reading Capital* were first published in 1965. In light of the language in which a problematic is presented, it is useful to recall that Maurice Merleau-Ponty's *Le visible et l'invisible* was first published (posthumously) in 1964, and that Lacan's seminar on "The Four Fundamental Concepts of Psycho-Analysis" (with its attention given to Merleau-Ponty and the "gaze") was also first presented in the same year. If we recall these dates and texts, it is because they inform some of the most sustained theoretical writing on the visual arts over the last thirty years. If we go on to notice that Michel Foucault's *The Order of Things* (with its reading of *Las Meninas* as its preface) was published a year later in 1966, we might obtain a further measure of Althusser's reworking of the language of the "gaze"—of the visible and invisible—informing his concept of the problematic.[15] But above all else, these citations bring us back to the painting from the late sixties and early seventies that attempted to draw a number of conclusions from this very cluster of texts, pursuing their consequences for the "theoretical practice" of painting and its claims for the production of new knowledge. This reading not only informs the repeated calls for a "change of terrain"; it recalls the numerous texts by critics, art historians, and above all the artists themselves that explore the various thoughts of painting as a form of epistemological model or theoretical practice—of painting in which what comes into visibility "is the act of its structural conditions."[16]

Of course, investigating the work in *As Painting* in light of a problematic of painting will raise the question of our own blindness or lack of lucidity (which the French at least take care to term the curator's *parti-pris*). But we are willing to declare an insistence on limits for two reasons. The first is because attention to the work's structural limits has no sense outside an exposure to the work and its "space." Attention to the work's structural limits can only ever find its play around the "absent center" that organizes the ways in which the work included in *As Painting* hangs or folds together.

Our emphasis on the problematic of painting is also offered in order to refuse the appeals to pluralism that characterize most recent discussions of painting, appeals that have done little more in their recent celebration of painting's continued viability than maintain the ideological interests that any appeal to pluralist practices always serves to reproduce. Against the opportunities offered by many of the most dominant practices and discourses of recent painting, we have decided to explore the structural limits of work that engages us within a dialectical circle that is "perpetually opened by its closures themselves," and with all the contradictions and overdeterminations this necessarily implies. For the knowledge it opens, there remains, as Althusser reminds us, only reading. And writing (or writing *with*). And (with a little luck) a "metamorphosis in the gaze," the creation of an "informed gaze," as we walk through the galleries. These days, this knowledge already demands a great deal, as well as the incessant work (and unworking) of articulation.

Problematics of Painting

To explore more closely the work actually gathered in *As Painting,* we now turn to four areas of inquiry that engage many of the artists presented. These areas—structure and "reduction," color as language, technique, and serial thinking—extend the initial motivation to situate painting in terms of Althusser's concept of a problematic and thus further measure painting's originary divisions and displacements.

Structure and Reduction

As Painting opens two asymmetrical impulses in contemporary art—one toward the structural, the other toward reduction—into their fullest possibilities. Both impulses reveal a vested interest in anticompositional strategies that reinvent the relationship of parts to wholes; in literal, factual, or "simple" aspects of the object; and in a shared refusal of gestural expression. Even though the discourse of reduction in relation to minimalism is tied to a streamlining of elements, culminating in various endpoints, including the monochrome, geometry, and the proclamation of the "end of painting," the paradox proper to both impulses is that in burrowing toward the structural elements of a work a surplus is unearthed, a displacement or pulverization of the volume is produced, or an excess, reserve, or "spacing" is made "visible."[17] Our concern is what this paradox suggests for the work included in *As Painting.*

On the one hand, structure and reduction in painting are associated with the pure, nearly blank aesthetics and industrially manufactured objects we associate with American minimalism.[18] On the other hand, and as a counter to this minimalist impulse, an inquiry informed by certain aspects of structuralist thinking opens the "ground" of painting's possibilities to a more dialectical thinking that ties presence to absence, the visible to the invisible, surface to "thickness," color to its dimension as language, visual to "written" space, form to formlessness. To think of *As Painting* as only extending out from minimalist practices, or only as an exploration of painting after minimalism, is thus to miscontextualize many of the artists in the exhibition. For minimalism and a discourse of reduction are simply not relevant as a way of thinking for many of the artists, even for some of those most frequently associated with these terms. Instead, we emphasize their close association with a theoretical tradition inspired by a discourse of structuralism, phenomenology, and psychoanalysis that figures in many of the artists' own writings. If the reception of this thinking plays an important role in certain strains of Anglo-American critical writing over the last thirty years, then the introduction of much of the French or European work in *As Painting* might suggest a way of engaging and dislodging some common assumptions concerning reductive work—and so further exploring the question of continuing painting "after" the minimalist and conceptual practices that announced its end.

The distance in perceptions between a discourse of reduction and an attention to structure is clearly demonstrated by Yve-Alain Bois in his 1991 essay on Donald Judd. Reflecting on the evolution of his own reception of the artist, Bois acknowledges:

> It may well be that, once again, I simply remain too European, or even "Continental," to use the American expression: from a common stock (Hume's empiricism, for example) Continental philosophy produced the phenomenology of perception, while the Anglo-Saxon tradition produced pragmatism and logical positivism. I see Judd's *oeuvre* through the eyes of Merleau-Ponty, so to speak (I'm certainly not the first to do so, but perhaps I'll be the last), whereas most of the time he himself speaks the language of Rudolf Carnap, Charles Morris, John Dewey and other philosophers he studied during his stay at Columbia University. Every time Judd invokes "clarity"—which he does even more now than he used to—I can't help interpreting it dialectically: a thing has to be simple in order to demonstrate that it will always remain unattainable, that nothing can ever be known of its "essence."[19]

Judd's own writings against compositional practices, against any kind of hierarchical or conventional relationship of the part to the whole, do not strike Bois as proposing anything particularly new.[20] Indeed, as Bois admits, it wasn't until after viewing Judd's *Untitled* (1977) in 1980—a piece consisting of six plywood boxes set up in a row—that he experienced the particular way in which Judd sculpts voids and planes to provoke the phenomenological reading of his work first suggested by Rosalind Krauss.[21] But this phenomenological reading did not obscure the ways in which Judd's rethinking of anticompositional practices remained, at least in his writings, relatively oblivious to a long tradition of similar ambitions.

Situated in relation to these essays by Bois and Krauss, Judd's own comments about the "specific object" reveal (what may have been there all along) that "specific" objects are also *perceptual* objects. As much as Judd attempts to make the structure of his forms fully accessible, an inescapable excess is nevertheless produced through this effort to present the object's specific "thereness" or facticity. The "specific objects" he proposes reveal the emergence of a complex dynamic of transparencies, shifting viewpoints, bisected wholes, and obliqueness. Paradoxically, concentration on a specific wholeness of the object ends up producing not a reduction but an introduction of the "unattainable" (the fact "that nothing can ever be known of its 'essence'"). This unattainability informs the work of many of the artists in *As Painting*. Indeed, it is now a condition of painting, a measure of its *simplicity*, opening it to a "reserve" or "excess" (a limit-experience) that *is* painting.[22]

What happens when the effort to rethink the part-to-whole relationship meets a practice of painting? For Judd, the response in his celebrated essay "Specific Objects" is unambiguous. He moves into three-dimensional space: "Three dimensions are real space. That gets rid of the problem of illusionism and of literal space, space in and around marks and colors—which is riddance of one of the salient and most objectionable relics of European art. The several limits of painting are no longer present."[23] Judd appears unable to recognize the range of "limits" that are present in the examples of European anticompositional practices, because he refuses to acknowledge that there are several limits to negotiate within painting. And yet Judd clearly recognizes the challenges posed by the painting of Pollock. If we take seriously his comments on Pollock's way of composing, we might ask why it is that painting cannot sustain the very part-to-whole specificity that Judd espouses. Writing of Pollock in 1967, he argues:

> Pollock used paint and canvas in a new way. Everyone else, except Stella for the most part, used them in ways that were developments upon traditional European or Western ways of handling paint and canvas. This use is one of the most important aspects of Pollock's work, as important as scale and wholeness. The nature of this is difficult to make intelligible. It's one of the things which needs considerable verbal building. It's a different idea of generality, of how a painting is unified. It's a different idea of the disparity between parts or aspects and it's a different idea of sensation. . . . The elements and aspects of Pollock's paintings are polarized rather than amalgamated. The work doesn't have the moderated a priori generality usual in painting.[24]

Judd suggests that what Pollock keeps alive is the specificity of the whole we call painting at the same time as the specificity of its parts. Or rather, it is through a strategy of "polarization" of parts as opposed to their amalgamation that a "different idea of the disparity between parts" achieves a different kind of "unity" or "autonomy" in painting. Pollock's construction of a new kind of autonomy thus provokes painting with questions less of its reduction than of its structure. This would also suggest a rearticulation of painting not only in terms of its parts and wholes but of its "limits," the very limits that Judd himself once deemed "no longer present" or operative.

For many of the artists included in *As Painting*, any suggestion of moving away from the exhausted limits of painting into another space is a denial of painting's capacity to reconsider its own structure. Unlike Judd, who feels it necessary to move into three-dimensional space to make "specific objects," many of the artists here continue to rethink painting in terms of a space in which painting, in its assumed two-dimensional form, already poses questions of its three-dimensionality, temporality, or "spacing."[25] In much of the work in *As Painting,* it is above all through the concept of "thickness" (as folding, *tressage,* play of recto/verso, collage, etc.), and in an insistence on the divisions of supports and surfaces, that the three-dimensional is asserted as a "dimension" of the two-dimensional. At the same time, *As Painting* includes many three-dimensional works that engage both the conceptual and theoretical terms explored by painting. These terms are thus not exclusive to painting—and this is perhaps what Judd so provocatively proposes by moving a problematic of painting into a different dimension. We could even argue that Judd continues to make "paintings"; as he acknowledges in 1977, "my thought comes from painting even if I don't paint."[26]

What is it about structural thinking that is useful for continuing painting, termed as such, in the climate of its own reductive questioning? Perhaps a structural tradition reveals a play of the already jointed—divided, impure, or frayed—nature of any structure (including the conjoining of two and three dimensions). Just as Judd recognizes that Pollock achieves a "different idea of the disparity between parts" and thus a different kind of "unity," our hope remains that—through attention to both structural thinking and reduction—*As Painting* will be a provocation for painting to understand itself differently.

Color as Language

> . . . the name of a color is never anything but the result of a segmenting made by other colors, and so on. In this process in which words segment words, the name of a color risks losing its designated referent, even though it vouches for that to which it corresponds. To red corresponds crimson, vermilion and many others. The name of a color is the name of a name, along the lines of the nominalist paradox of infinite regression illustrated in [Duchamp's] *Tu m'* by the perspectival arrangement of the color samples.
>
> —Thierry de Duve

Color is not only one of the "parts" of the whole that interested Judd throughout his career; it presents one of the insurmountable challenges to painting's ability to continue in a strong anticompositional mode within two-dimensional space. The urgency of this challenge echoes in Judd's late essay "Some Aspects of Color in General and Red and Black in Particular": "In retrospect, and only so, the expansion of color is logical until the 1960s, concluding with the painting of Pollock, Newman, Still and Rothko. The need for color, the meaning of that need more than anything, destroyed the earlier representational painting, whether in Europe or Asia."[27] Given the obstacle that the "the need for color" presents for painting, Judd and other artists move into sculpture, for color in sculpture is freed from representation, even as it is now implicated in sculpture's development as a specific medium.[28] Within sculpture itself, two opposite impulses are notable in the work associated with minimalism—a use of primary colors and a commitment to the inherent color of the materials themselves. We might understand these different impulses as coterminous with a search for essential colors. But this is a misunderstanding if the use of primary colors is taken as an endpoint for the work or its reductive core.

If instead we understand the use of primary colors more nearly in terms of Duchamp's interest in the "prime word"—the word divisible only by itself, leading to a concept of nominalism as a dispersal of color from its referential function—then we might locate the use of primaries as structural and differential, closer to a dispersion of words and names without a demand for what de Duve in *Pictorial Nominalism* terms their "designated referent." If so many of the colors in minimalist works are primary or namable, they remain less attached to a logic of reduction than to a link between color and its name, a restructuring of color as *language*.[29]

A compelling reading of color in these terms is explored in Bois's essay on Ellsworth Kelly. As in his essay on Judd, Bois clarifies the different receptions of painting in France and the United States, particularly in relation to Kelly's *Colors for a Large Wall* (1951), a painting Kelly donated to the Museum of Modern Art in New York in 1969 in order, as Bois suggests, to set the record straight regarding his commitment to anticompositional practices. Read through a minimalist or reductive context, the painting of multiple solid monochrome panels (arranged in an 8 × 8 unit grid) would only appear to confirm the "additive elementarization" and "all-over grid" of the minimalists' anticompositional strategies. But this reading ignores two other anticompositional practices developed by Kelly during his early years in Paris, which Bois terms the "aleatory" and the "already made." (A renaming of Duchamp's readymade, the already made is related to a given or preexisting motif—a trace of shadows or the spaces between things—through which Kelly insists on an anonymity of reference.) The combination of his commitment to restructuring the notion of the whole in conjunction with his understanding of color as a particular already made distances his *Colors for a Large Wall* from a minimalist or reductive reading it might otherwise have been given.[30]

In the context of this argument, Bois refers to de Duve's reading of nominalism and Rosalind Krauss's notion of the "index," both in relation to Duchamp's *Tu m'*, to support his claim:

> Kelly deploys a similar, but more radical nominalism [than Duchamp] (after all, the color chart in Tu m' is still a representation, still an image, or, in

semiological terms, an icon, albeit the icon of an index). The monochrome panel as a color sample is an index of color as such, designating its own color without any transformations.[31]

It is the reference to color "as such" that interests us in the context of *As Painting,* notably as it relates back to the question of the work's structure. If we take the force of de Duve's and Krauss's claims fully, we can now extend the notion of a "color sample" ("an index of color as such") to the ways in which any color sample is an index of color *and* its name. But in order to focus this shift in emphasis and its implications, we need to return to the respective readings of Duchamp's *Tu m'*.

Although both de Duve and Krauss refer to *Tu m'* to underscore their interests in nominalism and the index, they discuss very different parts of the painting. Krauss focuses on its indexical signs—notably the painted shadows cast by Duchamp's readymades and the pointing index finger in the center—while de Duve attends to the squares of color: the receding chart of colored squares that stretch across the left half of the painting, as well as the segmented color diagrams that descend from the *stoppages-étalon* in the right half. If the index finger in the center is pointing to anything (for Krauss it is the indexical sign for the shifter "this," a term she derives from Roman Jakobson), it is pointing to an oblique, white square, one of the "grammatical" samples from the left of the painting that produces the ribboned color "sentences" on the right. The paradox is that the "sentences" of color cannot be decoded by the perspectival stack of colored squares that precede them on the left. They are meaningless in their literalness, a circulation of "names" according to a "nominalist paradox."

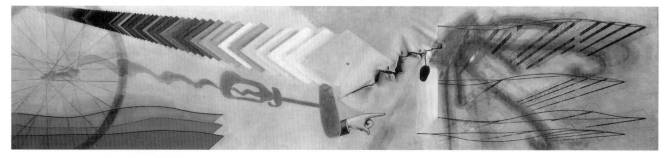

Marcel Duchamp
Tu m', 1918
Oil on canvas
27 1/2 × 122 3/4 in. (70 cm × 312 cm)
Collection Yale University Art Gallery; Gift from the Estate of Katherine S. Dreier
Photo: Joseph Szaszfai
Art © 2000 Artists Rights Society (ARS), New York/ADAGP, Paris

Throughout *Pictorial Nominalism,* de Duve develops a reading of Duchamp's move from painting to the readymade that centers on Duchamp's revelation that color is its name, the name of the tube of paint. In contrast to Kandinsky, who developed a metaphoric language of color, Duchamp realized that color is no more than a language. Of course, the nominalism that interested Duchamp in relation to his work and language opened art to do other things—to be literal, to pun, to be read, to reflect or challenge its institutional context, to be undone. But it found its original motivation in a thought of painting, as *Tu m'* clearly demonstrates. For *As Painting,* it is this recognition of the central problem of language and color that continues to offer painting a place to operate, opening spaces in which to work beyond the conventional, metaphoric, expressive, or pictorial registers of color.

If we return to Bois's reading of Kelly one last time, we can remark how the radically nominal nature of color is acknowledged by Kelly himself in a brief anecdote: "In 1952 I had a studio with a balcony overlooking a busy street. When I finished the first painting I had done in five horizontally grouped panels, I hung it on the balcony and went out to hear comments. A few people who noticed the painting were puzzled and said so. A child, pointing with his finger said: 'black-rose-orange-white-blue-blue-white-orange-rose-black.'"[32] One senses that *Tu m'* could be read in a similar way, where the index finger points to the successive names of color, a reading that produces radical possibilities for the structuring and destructuring capacity of painting, here mobilized as language. If Kelly's monochrome polyptychs are indexes of color, traces of color *as such* (rather than an image or icon of an index of color), then Kelly's anecdote equally suggests that the index is of color *and* its name. Indeed, if Kelly is read back through and out of Duchamp, his work will come to occupy a central place in any further debate concerning the question of color and painting, notably in the ways in which it already responds to Judd's challenge to painting with which we started.

An incisive confirmation of this displacement from color "as such" to a radical nominalism can be found in the work of Gerhard Richter. For it is possible to read Richter's abstract paintings (and not just the color charts and monochromes) as works that consider color as a name and thereby challenge our experience of painting as such. That color resists performing any one function in his work—it is not expressive, metaphoric, or compositional—seems to return Richter's color to Duchamp's palette, as a closed tube, but only insofar as his work explores the possibility of continuing or repeating painting after the "art in general" inspired by Duchamp. Richter's use of color happens in light of color's fall from its aspirations to purification or chromatic/symbolic expression. He begins the "abstracts" with buckets of paint that are easily namable—blue, red, yellow, green, etc. The surfaces of the paintings are open to the layers of color used, unable to gather into anything we are comfortable calling composition. The gray monochromes return color to its value on a gray scale. The films of color in the early work are sprayed over black-and-white paintings as a kind of colorizing activity. The photo paintings are meant to be in color, but that is not the same thing as using color, and the color charts resist collapsing the relationship of color to meaning in painting. By Richter's own admission, the color charts "all came down to the desperation of not knowing how I could ever arrange colours meaningfully—and I tried to fabricate that, as beautifully and as unequivocally as possible."[33] Richter acknowledges that to fabricate the color charts is to arrange the names of the colors. This is nowhere considered a meaningless or ironic act; it is an act of *unequivocation,* not only of color as such but of color as named.

The name of color is what differentiates one color from another and works to articulate painting as itself a process of differentiation. Beyond Richter (and Kelly), such nominalism finds a number of pertinent explorations in *As Painting,* including the mathematically derived color combinations of Cadere, the play with primaries in many of the works of Knoebel, the dating by color in the early work of Parmentier (blue in 1966, gray in 1967, red in 1968), the systematic production and structuring through color in Apfelbaum, the shifts in color in Simon Hantaï (as in his *Tabula* from 1980), the stripes of Buren, and the "specific" colors of Judd.[34]

Through an operation of color as its name, painting frees itself from the logic of composition, of form identifying with color. But this material interest in color as index need not represent a return to "beauty," "sensuality," or a reactionary playfulness. Nor does it suggest that pop art offers the only source for painting's future exploration of color, thereby reinscribing the very tradition of expressivity and metaphor that Duchamp had already challenged. Setting color and its name within the linguistic terrain enfolded within the visual field is a provocation to painting, mobilized by the concepts of the index and nominalism. This also returns us to Judd's "need for color," but only insofar as it reopens the closure he ascribes to painting in the sixties to another "logic," another sense of "expansion," another name.

Technique

If we return to the issue of composition and paintings' part-to-whole relationship (in light of Judd's discussion of "unity" in Pollock's painting), then a reading of Pollock informed by attention to structure reveals a distinctly different implication for another of painting's "parts": technique.

In an essay on Pollock from 1959, Hubert Damisch refers to the "invention" of Pollock's technique by suggesting: "The invention takes place, at the decisive moment when the painter raised this process, dripping—which after all had been only a means of 'padding' (*remplissage*)—to the dignity of an original principle for the organization of surfaces."[35] Commenting on the implications of this claim for painting, Bois suggests that Damisch's reading of Pollock explores a "threshold" where technique is to be understood as both "thought and invention": "For there is technique and technique, or rather there is the epistemological moment of technique, where thought and invention take place, and then there is all the rest, all the procedures that borrow from tradition or contest it without reaching that threshold that it is a question of designating."[36] "The epistemological moment of technique" takes us back to the discussion of Althusser with which we started, to the notion of a theoretical practice and an "epistemological break" echoed in Bois's reference to a "threshold." It can be argued that Damisch has not only drawn out the full consequences of Althusser's insistence on visualizing a problematic in terms of the language of the visible and the invisible but simultaneously transformed it again into a new register or model.

In much of the work in *As Painting,* we can remark not only a suite of different compositional and anticompositional strategies but the invention of numerous techniques. Indeed, it could be argued that specific, even original, techniques in much of the work are indissociable from the creation of "an original principle" for the organization of the works' surfaces and from the creation of concepts themselves.[37] More specifically, we can remark the conjunction of technique, "principle," and concept in the *tressage* of Rouan, the *décollage* of Villeglé and Dufrêne, the folding of Parmentier and Hantaï, the knotting of Viallat and Valensi, the cutting of Dezeuze and the *laissées* of Hantaï, the banding of Buren and Parmentier, the mathematical derivations of Cadere's *batons,* and the collage of Bonnefoi.

We might argue that the industrial methods associated with Judd and minimalism are also inventions of technique. But in comparison with the above practices, they represent a counterimpulse toward the generalizing of technique, toward its nonspecificity in industrially manufactured objects, as if the very indifference to technique was also raised to a "principle." This counterimpulse coincides with a displacement away from the privilege of painting as a medium into an array of other spaces and mediums, including photography and sculpture. The movement away from painting itself coincides with an apparent inability to secure painting's continuation as a theoretical object capable of rethinking itself, a refusal to acknowledge the ways in which painting as a discipline remains capable of sustaining technique as a measure of its "epistemological moment." The actual hanging of the exhibition sets out to explore some of the many implications of this issue.

Painting's displacement into other mediums and its attention to specific techniques share a similar fracturing of the (concept of the) whole and a similar reaction to the sense of excessive gesturality within an expressionist tradition. Paradoxically, in the context of *As Painting* this raises technique to an organizational principle or theoretical model: the originality of the techniques with which an artist's work can be identified share exactly the same refusal of gesture—the same refusal of subjective expression—as the reductive, industrially produced work of minimalism in which emphasis on technique has been radically effaced.

New concepts of the whole reverberate with a host of anticompositional impulses, many predicated on the claim that structuring wholeness is simultaneously a destructuring that demonstrates disassembly and reassembly of frayed parts into another concept of the whole. For many of the artists, articulation—dividing, jointing—becomes a key strategy that opens reserves and spacing to ways of rethinking any part-to-whole relation. The results are objects turned over or inside out, exposed simultaneously recto and verso, marked by continuities and discontinuities, attachments and detachments; surfaces pierced with holes, layered with pockets and folds, formed by *tressage* and knotting—paintings. But articulated ones, divided and displaced, outside in and inside out.

Series

> To the latest *flâneurs*, shouldn't it be signaled that a "*tableau*" (and without doubt in all senses of the term) is formally a "series of series" (*série de séries*)?
>
> —Michel Foucault

Serial practices elaborate decisive ways of thinking through the work's exposure—the object that it *is* and the inseparability of the objects *with, through,* or *to* which "the work" is articulated *as* a series, or as *essentially seriate.* Much of the work in *As Painting* turns on a critical rethinking of serial practices and their implications for painting. A schematic list could include Barré's series of structurally autonomous fragments, simultaneously articulated within (and from) a larger, architectural schema, or Bonnefoi's diagramming of the different series in his own work and writings. One might also consider the many ways the artists recycle materials from series to series: Degottex's residue, Rouan's *tressage*, Hantaï's *laissée* that is both a remnant and an excess. Other artists have explored serial extension through the rapport between parts and whole (Judd), questions of photographic reproducibility in relation to pictorial genres (Richter, Welling), issues of "appropriation" (Dufrêne, Villeglé, Levine), and variations in the display of the work or its architectural context (Apfelbaum, Smithson, Buren, Barré, Knoebel, the artists formerly associated with Supports/Surfaces). Also notable are the use of structural grids (Martin, Dezeuze, Barré, Bishop), perspectives (Smithson, Welling, Bochner), and mathematically based permutations (Bochner, Cadere, Judd). One might also consider practices in which color is the basis on which a series unfolds (Apfelbaum, Richter, Knoebel, Cadere, Judd, Parmentier, Welling), or in which identifiable forms or "signatures" are repeated, whether established through absolute detachment (Barré, Buren, Parmentier) or by a principle of incessant variation (Viallat). Many of these references are taken up further in the individual entries on the artists.

If serial thinking opens another thought of historical chronology than a historicist sequence of unique objects, a definition leveled at the dominant role of individual paintings within a presumed canon of modernism, then serial practices also play a fundamental role in any definition of modernism itself. In his discussion of "automatism" in *The World Viewed,* Stanley Cavell suggests that in modernist arts, "the task is no longer to produce another instance of an art but a new medium within it," a task, he argues, that shows us "the relevance of series."[38] Modernism creates the conditions, Cavell suggests, in which each and every "instance" of the work "calls" for other instances, "as if to attest that what has been discovered is indeed more than a single work could convey." In this sense, "a new medium establishes and is established by a series. Each instance of the medium is an absolute realization of it; each totally eclipses the others." The curious displacement between "instances" and "series"—the prior condition for thinking how a new medium is produced—is then captured in the seemingly paradoxical suggestion that, "in its absolute difference and absolute connection with others, each instance of a series maintains the haecceity (the sheer that-ness) of a material object, without the need of its substance."

What interests us in Cavell's reading of modernist painting is his suggestion that "the haecceity (the sheer that-ness) of a material object" is something minimal art also wants to convey. Drawing from Michael Fried's well-known discussions of minimalism in terms of "theatricality," Cavell argues that there nevertheless remains an irreducible difference between the ways in which material objects are displayed in series by the minimalists (he speaks of an environment that is "landscaped") and the ways in which modernist (i.e., post-Pollock) "instances" of painting are exposed to serial extension in order to acknowledge "an absolute realization" of painting's specificity as a medium. Modernist painting must acknowledge that each "instance" marks not only an "absolute difference" from other instances—this is the mark of its "closure" or "autonomy"—but also "an absolute connection," a radical "openness" (and an openness that is achieved in the work's serial possibilities).

We cite this well-known argument about the theatricality of minimalism in order to suggest the ways serial practices constitute the shared conceptual hinge around which modernist painting and minimalism are nevertheless distinguished. Cavell's argument opens the question of seriality in order to repose once again this distinction between painting and minimalism, and in such a way that the question remains how seriality is inscribed in the very "specificity," as it were, of "medium specificity," and thus inscribed so that it also becomes possible to claim that this specificity has the force to "eclipse" another medium.

This opens a host of other questions: If both the minimalist object and painting share the same quality of "sheer that-ness," is painting's acknowledgment of its specificity capable of making the distinction to which Cavell aspires? Is the shared emphasis on serial extension such that, for painting as a medium, "our acceptance of an instance determines whether its series is worth realizing"? Or does serial extension annul this implied *sequence* and its motivation in "worth"—the movement *from* instances *to* series—and fully inscribe seriality *in* and *as* the work painting does (or undoes)? In short, Cavell's text suggests how it is possible to re-mark serial extension inscribed in and as an "instance" of the work (and in this regard, his use of "instance" unfolds through not a few twists and turns of argument). Serial practices show that anything we term a work has an identity that is not only the condition for its acknowledgment but is also already displaced to—and by—the "instance" of the work's exteriority in and as its essentially seriate dispersion, a dispersion that places its "medium" in question. One could say that an "instance" of painting—the sense of its presence—is its simultaneous *ex-istence*, its standing outside of itself or its seriate ex-posure. And this existence cannot fully efface the sheer that-ness that painting shares with minimalism, a materiality that makes possible the essential exteriority of painting's presence, its *passage* to existence or its birth to presence.[39]

For both minimalism and modernist painting alike, "media are not given *a priori*," and, to Cavell, "the failure to establish a medium is a new depth, an absoluteness, of artistic failure." Serial practices for painting would be a way not only to insist on an "instance" of a work as the originary measure of its serial extension (the force of its potential extensity) but to acknowledge painting's "failure" in and as its own dispersion. It is through this "failure" that painting is capable of generating its self-divisions and (in)finite displacements, an emphasis that is irreducible to a concern with what falls either "between" mediums or in some position beyond mediums. It is this "failure" whose history also remains to be written, and it is in and through painting's essentially seriate dispersion that such a failure is most fully explored as the permanent measure of thinking painting's future.[40]

In light of this reading of serial practices, it becomes possible to isolate three consequences for the work included in *As Painting* that might invite further discussion and illuminate issues pertinent to the exhibition as a whole.

First, if serial practices are usually conceived in terms of the *extension* of a given work in relation to a series (which precedes it or in which the work finds its relative and thus exemplary place), then the possibility is now raised of a serial practice that is *intensive* to a given "instance." Thus we see series not as extensive (metaphoric) sequences of works held together (as parts to whole) but as the metonymic transformations of the work into something itself *essentially* seriate and thus dispersed. This would mark a shift in emphasis from the work's syntagmatic, lateral extension into paradigmatic intensivity (as "thickness").[41]

This displacement further foregrounds the inclusion of photography in *As Painting*, at least insofar as the mechanical reproducibility of the photographic medium now finds itself inscribed in an elaboration of painting's own temporally inscribed displacements and seriate dispersions. It's worth noting that photography has played a pivotal role in the elaboration of the work of many featured artists in addition to those represented by photographic images in the exhibition.

The second implication is the way serial practices open further questions of the relation of the work to its structure, and thus ways of inquiring how, in light of its structural articulations, a work can be *essentially* seriate and thus dispersed and not "reduced." For what initiates the heterogeneity of series in which the work endlessly divides itself into multiple and infinitely new configurations? And thus what constitutes the initial terms for describing a series if heterogeneity is *essential* to the work's existence?

In light of these questions, the essentially seriate nature of painting recalls the argument first presented by Gilles Deleuze that "the serial form is necessarily realized in the simultaneity of at least two series," that the serial form is essentially "multi-serial," a distribution set in play by what he terms a "paradoxical element" that allows for the possibility of movement between series but remains irreducible to them. What interests us in Deleuze's argument is his claim that the essential heterogeneity of two series—in which "the terms of each series are in perpetual relative displacement"—is the minimal condition of any "*structure*."[42] If we insist on situating the work in *As Painting* in terms of its structural articulation, it is because this is a necessary precondition for any understanding of painting's potentially seriate ex-istence.

The third consequence to examine turns on questions of fragmentation. Attention to the work's essentially seriate exposure is also a way of rethinking the work as a structurally articulated fragment. It is above all in the writings of Jean-Luc Nancy that this question has been most forcefully explored, notably through his distinction in *The Sense of the World* between two specific forms of fragmentation.

The first, which corresponds to "the genre and art of the fragment," returns us to what Nancy terms "romantic" fragmentation, which he describes as

> a certain recognized, accepted, desired state of detachment and isolation of the fragments. Its *end* is situated where the fragment collects itself into itself, folds or retracts its frayed and fragile borders back onto its own consciousness of being a fragment, and onto a new type of autonomy. Disruption transforms itself here into the gathering of itself into itself of the broken piece. The latter converts its finitude—its interruption, noncompletion, and

in-finitude—into finish. In this finish, dispersion and fracturing absolutize their erratic contingency: they *absolve themselves* of their fractal character.[43]

Nancy's second form of fragmentation is an attention to this "fractal character" itself. For if romantic fragmentation is an exploration of the "essence" or "identity" of the work of art, then the question Nancy asks is whether this "essence" has not itself been "delivered, thrown, projected, and offered like what one would have to call . . . a 'fractal essence'" (a term he transforms from the writings of Benoit Mandelbrot). He emphasizes, however, that the difference between these two kinds of fragmentation should not be over simplified and that they should not be considered to follow one another in a historical sequence.

> One must be careful not to oversimplify this opposition but, rather, to bear in mind that, although the second fragmentation—the one I have rather heavily called "fractal essence"—is indeed *happening,* it is happening at a distance from us and happens to be coming toward us across the entire history of art, a history that this fragmentation has always worked on and on which it has always bestowed a *fractal sense,* as the diffraction and spacing of linear and cumulative histories.

As Painting makes no claim to show work that has a "fractal essence,"[44] and it certainly does not assume that any appeal to the question of fragmentation is itself a symptom of some loss in our given notion of a cohesive, social totality, for which the work is the cultural expression. Nevertheless, a few brief implications of Nancy's discussion can be outlined for the work included here.

Nancy's appeal to a "history" of fragmentation radically recasts what we might mean by the "autonomy" of the work of art. The consequences of this displacement transform the customary accusations concerning the autonomy of the work within modernist discourse, at least insofar as the widespread denegation of painting's autonomy is assumed to coincide with a simultaneous denegation of formal inquiry. When Nancy refers to romantic fragmentation in terms of the way a fragment "collects itself into itself, folds or retracts its frayed and fragile borders back onto its own consciousness of being a fragment," and thus folds itself "onto a new type of autonomy," he leaves us to ask: What *self* (*soi*) is being posited in this form (or fold) of the work's own "self-consciousness"?[45] And does this "gathering of itself into itself" of the fragment already open such "gathering" into a simultaneous "dispersion" or an "erratic contingency" that is now made "absolute"? The term "absolute" in this context must in itself then be made out of what it folds into its own being other than itself. What "collects itself into itself"—its *col-legere*—now opens up as a ligaturing, and so a play of and on the limits of the autonomy of the "absolute," rather than a positing of its substance and self-propriety. It is thus not a question of the fragment collecting "itself into itself," "the gathering of itself into itself," as the English translation repeatedly suggests. For the autonomy of the fragment is less something that is essentially definable and locatable than the *passage* of this movement itself, the ligaturing of what folds "*onto* itself" (*sur soi*) and not "*into* itself," and so the opening of this "self" to the play of (non)reflexivity, to the simultaneous attachment and detachment of something whose interiority is made out of its own essential exteriority.

Perhaps this autonomy of the fragment is precisely the way in which what we call "theory" finds its most intimate mode of presentation, the way in which painting is capable of producing itself as it produces its own theory of this "self" (or loss of self), and thus another measure by which we can speak of a "theoretical practice," the work's "production," or painting as a "theoretical object," at least as Althusser gives us these phrases to think with. If the question of painting and autonomy is reopened through a rethinking of fragmentation, it also reopens in ways that are not unrelated—but clearly irreducible—to a confrontation between what Greenberg and Theodor Adorno are said to share or not share, however fertile such a confrontation has been in recent years.

Nancy's writings in this context indissociably reticulate across the further question of what begins to constitute the work's identity, specifically as any positing of a medium's identity implicates questions of what it means for a work to be finished or unfinished, what it means for a work to come to completion or incompletion, perfection or imperfection, achievement or "inachievement."[46] Nancy's attention to such terms might allow for further exploration not only of painting's rapport with serial thinking but of what is implied in any claim for painting's "end," "death," or critical "exhaustion." If questions of finish, (in)finitude, (in)achievement, and (im)perfection come to play a significant role in any attempt to write the history of painting, it is perhaps more than significant that all these terms found their most extensive critical elaboration in discourses about painting in the nineteenth century. The question that thus might be raised here is whether such critical elaboration of painting at the end of the nineteenth century is itself the simultaneous continuation and transformation of a problematic concerning the work of art's identity that precedes it historically and radically recasts our accustomed notions of painting's privilege within any discourse of our more recent modernity.

The terms in which Nancy advances this interrogation into fragmentation thus demand a permanent reference to a romantic and postromantic tradition in which to think the arts. Any further appeal to painting as a "model" will also find its renewed force in light of this tradition.[47] The consequences for painting considered in terms of fragments and fragmentation is a "history" that remains to be written. But whatever its outcome, and in whatever language it comes to be articulated, it cannot be considered in detachment from the various references and traditions to which we have briefly referred. Nor can it be considered in detachment from the serial practices that have come to haunt these references and traditions over the last forty years, practices that will also have their place in reopening these traditions and histories, and on which painting—formally, a "series of series"— might still insist in its refusal to accommodate itself to the tastes and opinions of the latest *flâneurs*.[48]

1. On thinking and writing *with* the work, we want to acknowledge our debt to Hubert Damisch, whose writings have continually demonstrated this practice and the "theoretical objects" that sustain it.

2. In this light, the concept of form is exposed to—internally riven by—its own aporetic condition (and this since Plato). Our second debt, here, is to Yve-Alain Bois and Rosalind Krauss's 1996 exhibition at the Centre Pompidou, *L'informe: Mode d'emploi.*

3. Which may be a more tortuous way of glossing Beckett's phrase "pour finir encore" (or Derrida's insistence on "pas"). See Michel Parmentier's essay in this catalogue for a further rethinking of Beckett's phrase.

4. The quotations are from Blanchot's opening statement in *The Space of Literature,* trans. Ann Smock (Lincoln: University of Nebraska Press, 1982).

5. This phrase is the title of an essay by Jean-Luc Nancy, to whose work we are broadly indebted.

6. Louis Althusser, *For Marx,* trans. Ben Brewster (London and New York: Verso, 1977), and Louis Althusser and Etienne Balibar, *Reading Capital,* trans. Ben Brewster (London and New York: Verso, 1997). Further references are cited in the text as *FM* and *RC* respectively.

7. This is evidently not the case in France, where the debates engendered by the same work are still a decisive feature of contemporary cultural life, state, institutional, and educational politics, and any number of generational divisions and animosities. The French contributors to this catalogue, both artists and critics alike, remain active participants in these debates.

8. See Serge Guilbaut, *How New York Stole the Idea of Modern Art: Abstract Expressionism, Freedom, and the Cold War* (Chicago: University of Chicago Press, 1983).

9. It is significant that Greenberg was first translated into French by the painter Marc Devade in the pages of *Peinture: Cahiers théoriques.* Edited by artists in close rapport with *Tel Quel,* the journal was the most influential in bringing Althusserian terms to a discussion of painting, as its name testifies.

10. The same could be said of the early writings of Pierre Macherey or Julia Kristeva.

11. This is undoubtedly an unusual way of characterizing work included in the former journal *Macula.* But it finds its justification in the extensive space *Macula* gave to two artists included in *As Painting,* Martin Barré and Christian Bonnefoi, whose work is clearly conceived there as the production of an epistemological object or model. The reference here is also to Marcelin Pleynet's widely read *L'enseignement de la peinture* (Paris: Editions du Seuil, 1971), in which Althusser figures prominently.

12. Althusser's concept of science has nothing to do with scientific discourse seen as empirical or positivist. As he notes, "When I say that Marx organized a theoretical system of scientific con-

cepts in the domain previously monopolized by philosophies of history, I am spinning out a metaphor which is no more than a metaphor" (*Lenin and Philosophy and Other Essays,* trans. Ben Brewster [New York and London: Monthly Review Press, 1971], p. 38). Some of the consequences of this reading have been raised by John Tagg in *Grounds of Dispute: Art History, Cultural Politics, and the Discursive Field* (Minneapolis: University of Minnesota Press, 1992).

13. Another start might be to take Althusser's rewriting of the hermeneutic circle in *Reading Capital*—in reference to Descartes, Husserl, and Heidegger—and read it in relation to Jean-Luc Nancy's *La partage des voix* (Paris: Editions Galilée, 1982). A further question here might explore the dialogue between the production of an epistemological object and Stanley Cavell's insistence on "acknowledgment," explored in Stephen Melville's essay in this catalogue.

14. As Althusser notes, "Allow me to recall that it is the peculiarity of scientific discourse to be *written;* and that it therefore poses us the question of the form of its writing" (*RC,* 69).

15. Foucault, of course, was one of Althusser's students. As Althusser notes in his review of the glossary of terms provided for English readers of his work (included in the translations of *For Marx* and *Reading Capital*), Foucault was the person who most clearly extended and transformed the concept of the problematic in his own writings. One might argue that Foucault's preface to *The Order of Things* is his most sustained "reading" of Althusser's notion of a problematic.

16. Althusser's phrasing suggests why artists could present their work less in terms of an "installation" than as an exploration of painting and its structural limits.

17. In *Modern Art 1890–1918* (London: Octopus Books, 1978), Jean Clay suggests a number of additional terms derived from attention to the work's structure.

18. As Daniel Buren remarks, any appeal to the terminology of "reduction" and "minimalism" is already a specifically American way of phrasing an interest in the work's limits. See his essay on Ryman in this catalogue.

19. See Yve-Alain Bois, "The Inflection," in *Donald Judd: New Sculpture* (New York: Pace Gallery; Paris: Galerie Lelong, 1991), n.p.

20. Bois cites various examples of European anticompositional practices unacknowledged by Judd, including "Russian Constructivism, the *art programmé* of Van Doesburg, Bill and Lhose, Strzeminski's Unism, the monochromes not just of Klein but of Manzoni and of the whole Zero Group, Kelly's Paris period random grids, the early Soto, the early Morellet . . . Rodchenko's modular sculptures." It is important to recognize that for many of the European artists included in *As Painting,* these are standard references for their own practice.

21. The reference is to Rosalind Krauss, "Allusion and Illusion in Donald Judd," *Artforum* 4, no. 9 (May 1966): 24–26.

22. In conversation, Michel Parmentier has evoked a similar appeal to simplicity by referring to a practice of painting that is "*bête,*" a term we have tended to translate more equivocally as "dumb."

23. Donald Judd, "Specific Objects," reprinted in *Complete Writings: 1959–1975* (Halifax: Press of the Nova Scotia College of Art and Design; New York: New York University Press, 1975), p. 184.

24. Donald Judd, "Jackson Pollock," reprinted in Pepe Karmel, ed., *Jackson Pollock: Interviews, Articles, and Reviews* (New York: Museum of Modern Art and Harry N. Abrams, 1999), p. 116.

25. The practice of "spacing" as a condition of structure is explored in numerous readings of Mallarmé, notably by Blanchot and Derrida. Since the late sixties, this cluster of texts has been a prominent reference for both painters and critics.

26. Quoted in the newsletter of The Chinati Foundation, vol. 4 (September 1999): 1.

27. Donald Judd, "Some Aspects of Color in General and Red and Black in Particular," *Artforum* 32, no. 10 (summer 1994): 77.

28. In 1967, Lucy Lippard suggests that "whereas color in painting can be judged within a relatively understood system of theory or experience, such a system, fortunately, is not yet established for sculpture." See her essay "As Painting Is to Sculpture: A Changing Ratio," in Maurice Tuchman, ed., *American Sculpture of the Sixties* (Los Angeles: Los Angeles County Museum of Art, 1967), p. 33.

29. See Thierry de Duve, *Pictorial Nominalism: On Marcel Duchamp's Passage from Painting to the Readymade,* trans. Dana Polan (Minneapolis: University of Minnesota Press, 1991); the epigraph for this section is from p. 135.

30. See Yve-Alain Bois, "Ellsworth Kelly in France: Anti-Composition in Its Many Guises," in *Ellsworth Kelly: The Years in France, 1948–1954* (Washington, D.C.: National Gallery of Art, 1992). We especially regret the absence of Ellsworth Kelly from *As Painting.* His inclusion might have avoided the more predictable readings of his work in terms of abstraction and minimalism, as well as acknowledging his historical importance for many of the issues explored in the exhibition.

31. Yve-Alain Bois, "Ellsworth Kelly in France: Anti-Composition in Its Many Guises," p. 28. See also Rosalind Krauss, "Notes on the Index," parts 1 and 2, reprinted in *The Originality of the Avant-Garde and Other Modernist Myths* (Cambridge: MIT Press, 1986), pp. 196–219.

32. Cited by Yve-Alain Bois in "Ellsworth Kelly in France: Anti-Composition in Its Many Guises," p. 28.

33. Gerhard Richter, *The Daily Practice of Painting: Writings and Interviews 1962–1993,* trans. David Britt (Cambridge: MIT Press, in association with Anthony d'Offay Gallery, London, 1995), p. 143.

34. We would also like to stress our disappointment at not being able to include any work by Blinky Palermo in *As Painting.*

35. Hubert Damisch, "La figure et l'entrelacs," in *Fenêtre jaune cadmium, ou les dessous de la peinture* (Paris: Editions du Seuil, 1984), p. 76.

36. Yve-Alain Bois, *Painting as Model* (Cambridge: MIT Press, 1990), p. 250.

37. Deleuze and Guattari's affirmation of the "creation of concepts" draws extensively from Damisch's writings. See Gilles Deleuze and Félix Guattari, *What Is Philosophy?,* trans. Graham Burchell and Hugh Tomlinson (London and New York: Verso, 1994).

Color Plates

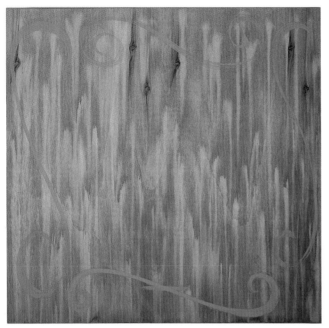

Moira Dryer
Headline, 1989
Collection Barbara Schwartz, New York
Photo © Zindman/Fremont, New York

Anne Truitt
Elixir, 1997
Courtesy Danese, New York
Photo: Zindman/Fremont, New York

Daniel Buren
Peinture aux formes variables, 1966
Courtesy of Daniel Buren
Art © 2000 Artists Rights Society (ARS),
New York/ADAGP, Paris

Sherrie Levine
Romulus and Remus, 1998
Graphite on walnut
2 panels, 12 1/4 × 7 1/2 × 7/8 in. (31 × 19 × 2 cm) each
Private collection
Photo: Adam Reich
Photo courtesy Paula Cooper Gallery

Christian Bonnefoi
Machine 78, 1978
Courtesy Galerie de France, Paris
Photo: Patrick Müller

Robert Ryman
State, 1978
Collection Albright-Knox Art Gallery, Buffalo, New York;
George B. and Jenny R. Mathews Fund, 1979

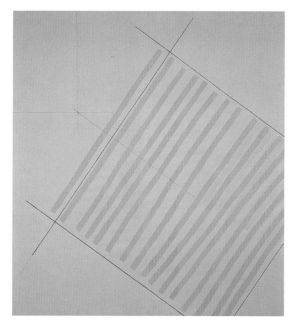

Martin Barré
75–76-B-174 × 164, 1975–76
Courtesy Galerie Laage-Salomon, Paris
Photo © André Morain
Art © 2000 Artists Rights Society (ARS), New York/ADAGP, Paris

Simon Hantaï
M.c.8, 1962
Collection of the artist, Paris
Photo: Sabine Ahlbrand-Dornseif

Robert Smithson
Slantpiece, 1969 (original)/1976 (reconstruction)
© Allen Memorial Art Museum, Oberlin College; Gift of
the Buckeye Trust in memory of Ruth C. Roush, 1980
Art © Estate of Robert Smithson/VAGA, New York

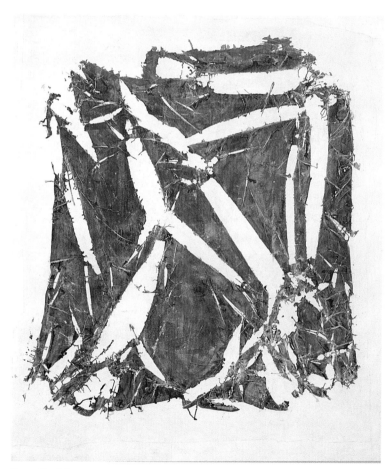

Simon Hantaï
Laissée, 1981–89
Collection of the artist, Paris
Photo: J. C. Mazur
© Centre Georges Pompidou

Daniel Buren
Peinture aux formes indéfinies, 1966
Courtesy Galerie Jean Fournier, Paris
Photo: J. Hyde
Art © 2000 Artists Rights Society (ARS), New York/ADAGP, Paris

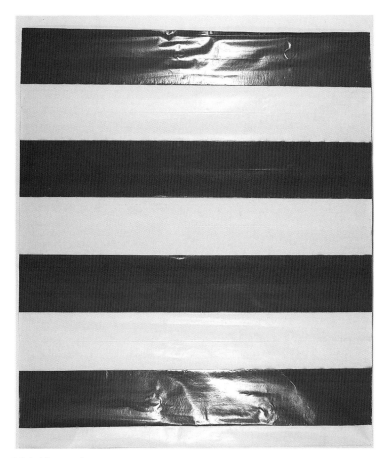

Michel Parmentier
5 octobre 1966, 1966
Collection Bénédicte Victor-Pujebet, Paris
Photo: Philippe Simon

Polly Apfelbaum
Still Life: Green/Orange/Blue, 1997
Courtesy the artist and D'Amelio Terras, New York
Photo: Adam Reich

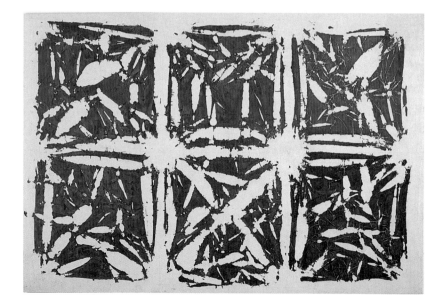

Simon Hantaï
Tabula, 1980
Collection of the artist, Paris
Photo: J. C. Mazur
© Centre Georges Pompidou

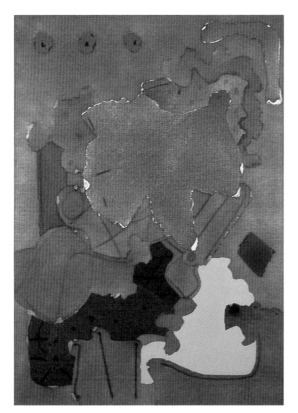

Christian Bonnefoi
Eureka IV, 1997
Collection of Dave and Nancy Gill, Columbus, Ohio
Photo: Bill Nieberding

Imi Knoebel
Odyshape I, 1994
Collection Six Friedrich, Munich
Photo: Nic Tenwiggenhorn

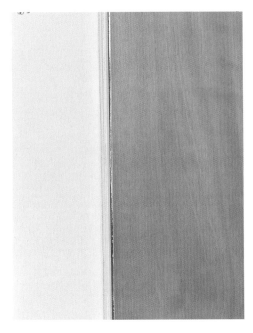

Imi Knoebel
Sandwich 2 (detail), 1992
Collection of the artist, Düsseldorf
Photo: Nic Tenwiggenhorn

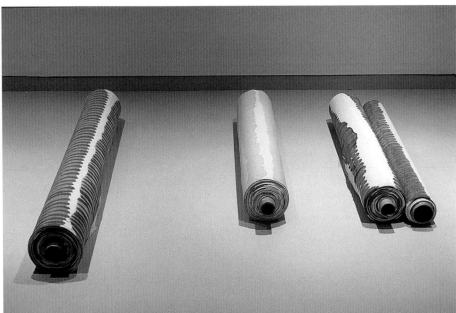

Polly Apfelbaum
Bones: Large, 1999
Courtesy the artist and D'Amelio Terras, New York
Installation view at Bowdoin College Museum of Art, Brunswick, Maine
Photo: Melvin McLean

François Rouan
Tressage quatre toiles, gris, rose, bleu et blanc, 1967–69
Courtesy the artist
Art © 2000 Artists Rights Society (ARS), New York/ADAGP, Paris

Donald Judd
Untitled, 1987
Courtesy Paula Cooper Gallery, New York
Photo: R. Wilson
Art © Donald Judd Estate/VAGA, New York

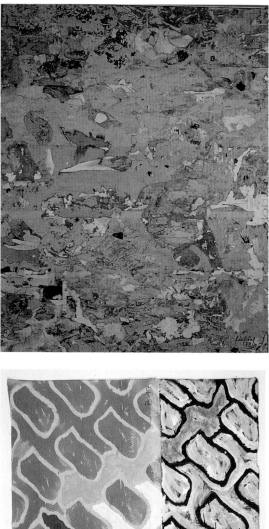

François Dufrêne
Où je perçois personnellement en perspective persane, 1973
Courtesy Galerie Véronique Smagghe, Paris
Art © 2000 Artists Rights Society (ARS), New York/ADAGP, Paris

Claude Viallat
Sans titre no. 130, 1997
Courtesy Galerie Daniel Templon, Paris
Photo © André Morain
Art © 2000 Artists Rights Society (ARS), New York/ADAGP, Paris

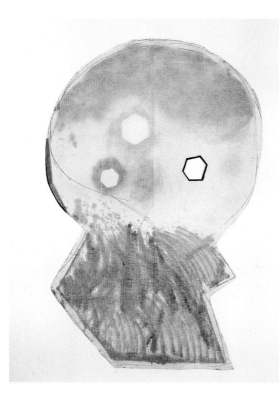

Daniel Dezeuze
Gaze découpée et peinte, 1980
Collection of the artist, Sète, France
Art © 2000 Artists Rights Society (ARS), New York/ADAGP, Paris

Jacques Villeglé
Plateau Beaubourg, 1960
Collection of Howard and Pamela Holtzman, Chicago
Photo courtesy Alan Koppel Gallery, Chicago
Art © 2000 Artists Rights Society (ARS), New York/ADAGP, Paris

François Rouan
Porta Latina, 1971–74
Collection Mrs. Maria Gaetana Matisse, New York
Photo courtesy the artist
Art © 2000 Artists Rights Society (ARS), New York/ADAGP, Paris

Gerhard Richter
I. G. (790-5), 1993
Private collection
Photo: Tore H. Røyneland

Mel Bochner
48" Standards, 1969
Courtesy Sonnabend Gallery, New York
Installation view at Sonnabend Gallery, New York
Photo: Lawrence Beck

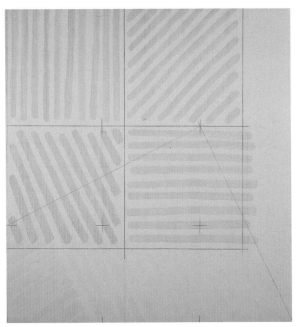

Martin Barré
74–75-D-113 × 105, 1974–75
Private collection, Paris
Photo © André Morain
Art © 2000 Artists Rights Society (ARS), New York/ADAGP, Paris

Agnes Martin
Untitled, 1962
Collection Museum of Contemporary Art, San Diego;
Museum purchase, 1976.18
Photo: Philipp Scholz Rittermann

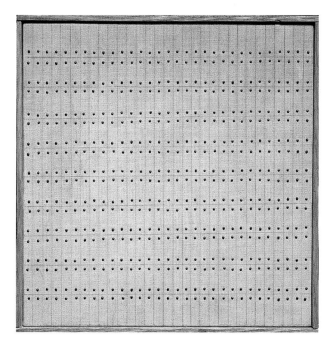

Jean Degottex
Pli x Pli III (recto), August 1980
Collection Marcelle and Maurice Benhamou, Paris
Photo: Patrick Müller
Art © 2000 Artists Rights Society (ARS), New York/ADAGP, Paris

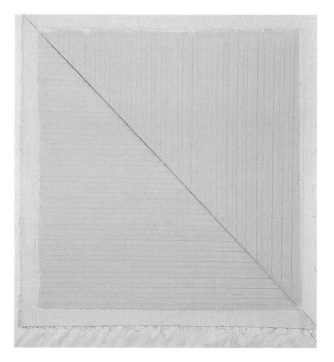

James Bishop
Untitled, 1974
Courtesy Galerie Jean Fournier, Paris
Photo: J. Hyde

Martin Barré
74–75-B-113 × 105, 1974–75
Private collection
Courtesy Galerie Laage-Salomon, Paris
Photo © André Morain
Art © 2000 Artists Rights Society (ARS), New York/ADAGP, Paris

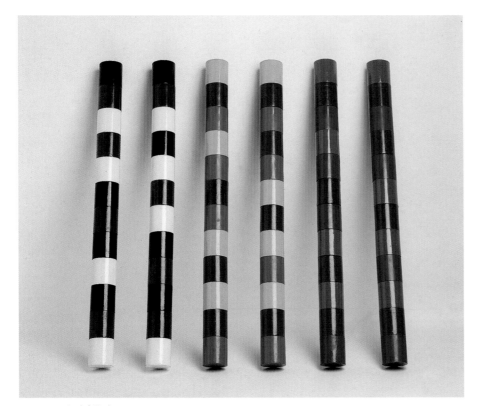

André Cadere
Six barres de bois rond, 1975
Collection Centre Georges Pompidou, Paris
Musée national d'art moderne/Centre de création industrielle
Photo: Philippe Megeat
© Centre Georges Pompidou

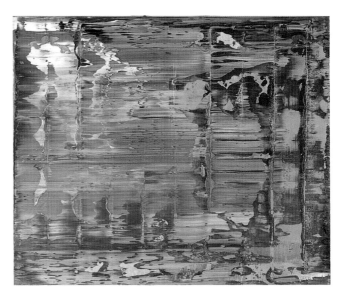

Gerhard Richter
Abstraktes Bild (825-10), 1995
Collection Mark H. Williams, Los Angeles
Photo: Friedrich Rosenstiel
Photo courtesy the artist

Gerhard Richter
I. G. (790-4), 1993
Private collection
Photo: Tore H. Røyneland

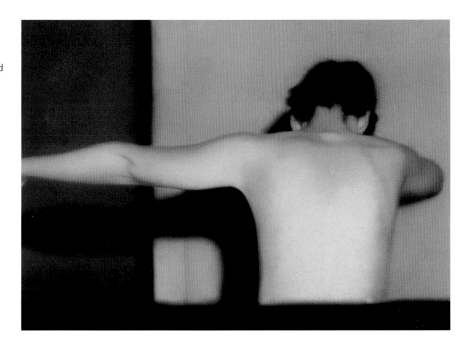

James Welling
IJWC, 1989
Courtesy the artist

38. Stanley Cavell, *The World Viewed,* enlarged edition (Cambridge: Harvard University Press, 1979; first published 1971), p. 103. The following quotations are taken from Cavell's chapter on "automatism" and the "excursus" on modernist painting.

39. The rewriting of an "instance" of the work in terms of its "ex-istence" is indebted to the writings of Jean-Luc Nancy, to whom we will return. For Nancy this rewriting entails a distinction between what he terms "presentation itself"—"the *praes-entia* of being-present"—and the "presentness" of a presence. As a gloss on "the *praes-entia* of being-present," Nancy suggests not only "the in-finity of a coming into presence, or an *e-venire*"; in a footnote, he also suggests that "one could say, for example, the event is not the execution of Louis XVI, but that the king becomes executable and the leader culpable." We are trying to register something of this difference in our discussion of seriality. See Jean-Luc Nancy, *The Sense of the World,* trans. Jeffrey S. Librett (Minneapolis: University of Minnesota Press, 1997), p. 126 and n. 130.

40. It is in the French context that this question of "failure" or sense of radical *loss* is most fully explored as an originary measure of painting's continuity: through strategic refusals to paint for extended periods of time (Parmentier, Hantaï); numerous appeals to a "degree zero" of painting as an initiating moment of its dispersion; attention to what Bonnefoi terms the "first painting," paraphrased by Jean Clay and Yve-Alain Bois as an attention to the "archi-tableau" (in the sense that Derrida will speak of "archi-writing"); or painting's claim to make a difference, which is thus exposed to the mark of the "indifference" (Georges Bataille) that it generates. When Cavell writes that each and every instance of the work "*calls*" for other instances, it remains a permanently inscribed possibility for painting that this summons or appeal may not be met. An early attempt to articulate this question is presented in Philip Armstrong, introduction to Christian Bonnefoi, *Ecrits sur l'art (1974–1981)* (Brussels: La Part de l'Oeil, 1997), pp. 5–24.

41. For further discussion, see Christian Bonnefoi's essay "The Objection That the Obscure Makes to Painting" in this catalogue. The terms of this analysis can also be read in many of Deleuze's early writings.

42. See Gilles Deleuze, *The Logic of Sense,* trans. Mark Lester, ed. Constantin V. Boundas (New York: Columbia University Press, 1990), pp. 36–41 and 48–51. For a more sustained discussion of serial thinking, see Deleuze's "A quoi reconnaît-on le structuralisme?," in *La philosophie au XXe siècle,* vol. 4, ed. François Châtelet (Paris: Marabout/Hachette, 1979), pp. 293–329. The essay was first written in 1967. For a compelling essay on serial thinking and form in reference to both Deleuze and Nancy, see Marie-Claire Ropars-Wuilleumier, "Forme et contreforme: L'invention du sérialisme," in *La forme en jeu* (Paris: Presses Universitaires de Vincennes, 1998), pp. 85–100.

43. Jean-Luc Nancy, *The Sense of the World,* pp. 124–25. Further quotations from Nancy's text are from the chapter "Art, a Fragment." Nancy's text takes up his and Philippe Lacoue-Labarthe's earlier discussion of fragmentation in *The Literary Absolute: The Theory of Literature in German Romanticism,* trans. Philip Bernard and Cheryl Lester (Albany: State University of New York Press, 1988).

44. There have been enough *illustrations* of Deleuze in recent years, at least in the context of an attempt to rejuvenate "abstract" painting, to make such a caveat all the more necessary.

45. See Melville's essay in this catalogue for further discussion of the way in which this question reopens Greenberg's notion of "self-criticism."

46. The implications of these terms are investigated further in Nancy's essay "The Vestige of Art," in *The Muses,* trans. Peggy Kamuf (Stanford, California: Stanford University Press, 1996), pp. 81–100. See also Yve-Alain Bois, "L'inachèvement," in *Martin Barré* (Nantes: Musée des beaux-arts; Tourcoing: Musée des beaux-arts, 1989), pp. 71–80.

47. As Nancy and Lacoue-Labarthe suggest throughout *The Literary Absolute,* the very concept of the theoretical "model" or object is an intimate aspect of the "literary absolute." A similar question can be raised about our earlier reading of Althusser.

48. One of the first consequences of this insistence on fragmentation will also be a radical transformation of those contemporary practices whose presentation is repeatedly offered through a simultaneous denegation of painting and the notion of tradition it is said to represent. It is worth recalling Nancy again at this point:

> "Happenings" and "performance art," and all of that which, within contemporary art, has revolved around the motif of the event (for example, Polaroid and video, the residual, the accidental, the aleatory, staining, interruption, and so on)—all of this seems to have either merely prolonged one posture or the other or merely continued to destroy, reduce, and shatter art. Moreover, the two gestures are not contradictory, and much seems to suggest that it is possible to say that art petrifies and fractures itself in the pose of its own end. Romantic irony, which Hegel saw as the element of this end, attained in this way its extreme of yawning subjectivity. (*The Sense of the World,* pp. 126–27)

Nancy is referring to the way in which, since romanticism, "little" or "marginal" works find their uneasy or confrontational match against "great works," "sovereign art," or the "grand style." The questions we might ask are whether the presentation of the work in *As Painting* remains irreducible to this form of romantic irony and what it might mean for painting today even to pose such a question, or sense its necessity.

Artists in the Exhibition

Polly Apfelbaum
Born 1955, Abington, Pennsylvania
Lives and works in New York

In 1995, the *Journal of Philosophy and the Visual Arts* devoted an issue to "Abstraction." It included contributions by philosophers and critics and work by some of the leading artists working in the "field" of abstraction. Except for Polly Apfelbaum, all of the artists included were recognizably painters. For the issue, Apfelbaum provided an essay titled "Varieties of Abstraction: A Partial Taxonomy," in which she describes her work as "flows, spots, heaps, fields, patchwork, pointillisms, wrinkles."[1]

This taxonomy recalls the lexicon that Daniel Dezeuze develops in writing about his work, both in its format and in the proximity of some terms (Dezeuze refers to point, stain, imprint, fold, and cut-up). The difference between Dezeuze's and Apfelbaum's uses of these terms is apparent in the description of her work as relative to two dominant limits of abstraction: painting and minimalism. "Abstraction" is a word that doesn't figure in Dezeuze's vocabulary. To find Apfelbaum's work in the context of *As Painting* is not to ignore the influence of abstraction. Located here, however, the work is dislodged so that the limits Apfelbaum mentions may add up to something not immediately contextualized within a discourse of abstraction.

Apfelbaum's work is most often included in exhibitions centered on questions of abstraction and painting, but her selection for *Sense and Sensibility: Women Artists and Minimalism in the Nineties* shifts this focus. Lynne Zelevansky, the curator, selected seven women artists who belong to a legacy of postminimalism she defines in three ways: a use of the basic tactics associated with minimalism (repetition, the grid, and geometric structure); a foregrounding of the "historical interplay" of the women's movement with postminimalism; and a move toward lighter and more "mundane" materials, as opposed to the heavy, expensive materials and processes associated with minimalist works.[2]

In terms of seriality and repetition, Apfelbaum's materials and processes derive from her interest in the patterned practices of "rote and routine" that develop logically from her concept of a nonmechanical standardization of seriality. She stains, cuts, folds, places, and piles fabrics, from common sheeting to pseudoluxurious synthetic velvets. Sometimes she shows these works in or on cardboard boxes or tubes, materials present during her rudimentary dyeing process.

The Somnambulist of 1988 represents work that precedes Apfelbaum's explorations with fabric. The prevalence of the heavier materials and the structured repetition of the work's individual wood discs are indicative of her minimalist grounding. When Apfelbaum then introduces a less-structured material to her practice, she states in her taxonomy: "the work is structured not around a simple opposition of supple and erect, but instead provokes questions about the structurality of the unstructured itself." This comment challenges the interpretation that many of her materials and processes are specifically tied to questions of femininity. In her insistence on the "structurality of the unstructured itself,"

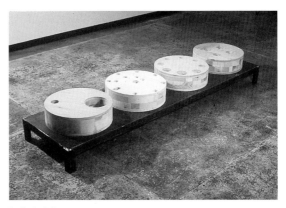

Polly Apfelbaum
The Somnambulist, 1988
Wood on steel base
11 × 20 × 79 in. (28 × 51 × 201 cm)
Courtesy the artist
Installation view at Loughelton Gallery, New York

Polly Apfelbaum
Compulsory Figures, 1996
Velvet, dye
Dimensions variable
Courtesy D'Amelio Terras, New York
Installation view at Dalarnas Museum, Falun, Sweden
Photo © Ollie Norling

destructuring impulse found in feminist discourse and an alternative feminine voice such as that theorized by Luce Irigaray (whom Apfelbaum quotes in her taxonomy) can keep a play of limits alive without retreating into an essentialized difference.

Spill literally gathers flat sheeting into heaps or mounds. As crushed form, it reserves as many of its colored spots as it reveals. Even a work as clearly based on a systematic grid as *Enigma Machine* can be collapsed into another version of itself. The mutability and mobility of the stacks of color-coded patches represent Apfelbaum's interest in displacing structure. Again, her work thus finds commonality with other works in *As Painting,* notably Cadere's batons and their "error," Dufrêne's torn posters and their "underneaths," or Hantaï's paintings and their blind folds.

Polly Apfelbaum
Spill, 1992–93
Courtesy the artist and D'Amelio Terras, New York
Installation view at Heiligenkreuzerhof, Vienna
Photo: Pello Irazu

we begin to see the rapport between Apfelbaum's work and that of other artists included in the exhibition, notably Viallat, Dezeuze, and those artists interested in the "unstructured" as a challenge to the conventions of painting's support-to-surface relationship. Whereas the artists associated with Supports/Surfaces derived the use of fabrics, nets, and rope, as well as the dyeing or staining of materials, from their interest in artisanal or archaic crafts, Apfelbaum's introduction of supple materials emerges from an interest in the patterns or rhythms of habit or the everyday.

Her introduction of color and supple materials into the systematic layout of *Compulsory Figures* reflects the dislodging of the systematic toward fluidity. Neither the urge toward fluidity nor the introduction of color should be seen as based on a desire for the aestheticization of minimalist or postminimalist practices, or as a return to pleasure or beauty, a reading frequently collapsed or essentialized into a form of feminine intentionality. As Apfelbaum cautions, reading her work as belonging to the feminine too often ignores her interests in structure. It remains to be seen whether the

Polly Apfelbaum
Enigma Machine (open), 1993–95
Courtesy the artist and D'Amelio Terras, New York
Photo: Adam Reich

Polly Apfelbaum
Enigma Machine (closed), 1993–95
Courtesy the artist and D'Amelio Terras, New York
Photo: Adam Reich

Apfelbaum deploys color and systematicity as "fields" that move between, and are transformed by, the disciplines of sculpture and painting. The combination of grids or geometric systems and folds or crushed structures hinges her work to the range of limits explored by artists influenced by minimalism, as well as those influenced by a different concept of structure. In this context, Apfelbaum recognizes the insights offered by writers closely associated with structuralism. Under the heading "pointillisms" in her taxonomy, she quotes French art historian Jean Clay on Pollock, Mondrian, and Seurat: "The pigmentary mass 'unfolds' itself in a certain number of imbricated strata that, between them, offer sufficient similitude to form a system."

Beginning from a specific system of color and arrangement, her "pointillisms" are most prevalent in her large floor pieces begun in 1996, which consist of hundreds of cut-out stained spots of color laid out on the floor in patterns that form a fluid system. Her "still-life" works are a kind of micropointillism. The precision of the cut-out spots and their decisive positioning on the colored rectangles at once still and activate the pigmentary flow or "mass." As Apfelbaum notes in the titles, some of the "still-lifes," (i.e., *For Blinky and Imi*) invoke a sense of what it might be like to walk through a Palermo or Knoebel.

When Apfelbaum mobilizes color and system into spaces, the sites for her works become fluid grounds as color enfolds and transforms them. We might think of Knoebel's *Genter Raum* or Palermo's *To the People of NYC*, or even the simplicity of Palermo's blue triangle from which Sherrie Levine's *After Blinky Palermo* is made. One might also think of the displacement of Cadere's bars of wood into galleries and streets. Apfelbaum's play between the compact, rolled spots in *Bones* and the dispersion of the color in the "still-lifes" recalls the limits of intensity and extensivity discussed by Bonnefoi and reflected in the displacement and cut-out color of his wall collages and *Eureka* series. These various pieces are all a dispatching of color from painting into another place that extends painting's limits.

Polly Apfelbaum
Still Life: Green/Orange/Blue, 1997
Courtesy the artist and D'Amelio Terras, New York
Photo: Adam Reich

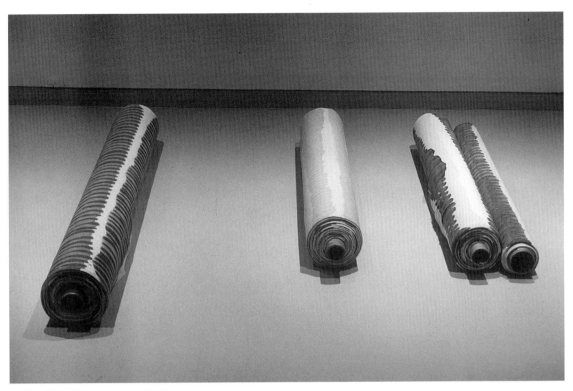

Polly Apfelbaum
Bones: Large, 1999
Courtesy the artist and D'Amelio Terras, New York
Installation view at Bowdoin College Museum of Art,
Brunswick, Maine
Photo: Melvin McLean

Apfelbaum's grounding in minimalism asserts the structure that a systematicity based on repetition and geometry offers for the mobilization of her vocabulary. In *As Painting,* her work is removed from the obscuring lens of abstraction. Instead, it is seen as traversing the terrain of painting's limits in light of the systematicity associated with minimalism and the impulse of work informed by its own destructuring.

L. L.

1. Polly Apfelbaum, "Varieties of Abstraction: A Partial Taxonomy," in *Abstraction,* ed. Andrew Benjamin, *Journal of Philosophy and the Visual Arts,* no. 5 (1995): 86–89.

2. Lynne Zelevansky, *Sense and Sensibility: Women Artists and Minimalism in the Nineties* (New York: Museum of Modern Art and Harry N. Abrams, 1994), p. 12.

Martin Barré
Born 1924, Nantes, France
Died 1996, Paris

Martin Barré's object, from early in his career right through to the end, was the making visible of painting's particular or proper space.[1] Such an invocation of space may seem to have more to do with architecture than with painting, and so it may be of some relevance that Barré's initial training was indeed architectural. Certainly he came to see painting with ever greater explicitness as a peculiar modification of the wall, rather than as something that hangs on it—as if the wall were to cut itself out from itself, gaining a capacity for exposure to which it otherwise had no access. Conceived along these lines, the "space of painting" cannot be an illusion that simply arises within the painting but must appear as the very fact of its surface. *Affleurement* becomes perhaps the painter's favorite word for this; in the interviews with the artist included in this catalogue we have rendered it as "surfacing." *Affleurement* is frequently posed in terms of a relation to light and to air, so this notion of "surfacing" aims both at what a surface is as such and at the breaking through of something into a region different from that in which it was previously immersed (as something that has been under water surfaces). Surfacing has its violences, then, as well as its risks—above all, risks of exposure, the entering into an alien element. If the occasional cracking in the paintings is not entirely what Barré might have wanted, it is not foreign to his understanding of what a painting is—and the various drifts of the grounds away from their initial white is an inevitability he actively cultivated at times, a measure of their surfacing. Except for this interest in exposure, Barré stands relatively apart from the "materiological" interests so prominent in the work of a number of the other French painters in *As Painting*, and he is likely to strike the viewer as oriented to a certain asceticism and "purity." (One may be reminded of Mallarmé's aspiration to write a poem that would be on, or rather in, its page the way a watermark is in a sheet of paper.)

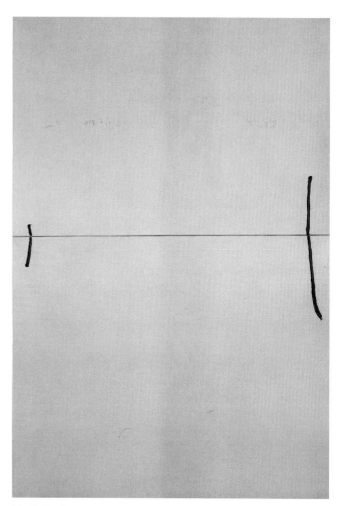

Martin Barré
61-T-15, 1961
Private collection, Paris
Photo © André Morain
Art © 2000 Artists Rights Society (ARS), New York/ADAGP, Paris

Martin Barré
63-Z, 1963
Private collection, Paris
Photo © André Morain
Art © 2000 Artists Rights Society (ARS), New York/ADAGP, Paris

interested in overcoming oppositions of this kind. He works always off a white ground that remains indubitably a ground; sometimes it is complex and layered, but it is clearly there as what receives the marks, immediately legible as such, placed on it by his knife or tube of paint or spray can or brush. "Two-dimensionality" here amounts to the demand that this mark form an indissoluble whole with the ground that receives it. Barré's preferred name for this whole is *tableau,* the familiar French word for a fully achieved painting. The standard ways of understanding what underlies that achievement were from the outset not available to him, and he pursued throughout his career a number of "anti-compositional" strategies to keep traditional composition out of play—imposing arbitrariness on his own gesture, using stencils large enough to wholly hide the canvas he is working on, and developing abstract grid systems from which a particular painting is realized only as an arbitrary selection. "Composition" has

Barré spoke of wanting to make paintings that would be purely two-dimensional, an ambition that both is and is not what Clement Greenberg meant when speaking, in the American context, of "flatness." Greenberg's sensitivity was to a certain "opticality," a visual presence proper to painting and borrowing none of its effects from the ways things are visually present in the world. Such opticality entailed the defeat of anything that worked to establish one element of the painting as figure over and against a ground that would count, however abstractly, as the space in which that figure stood; thus, Greenberg tended to emphasize Pollock's way of turning line toward all-over composition and away from the bounding of a figure. Barré is never

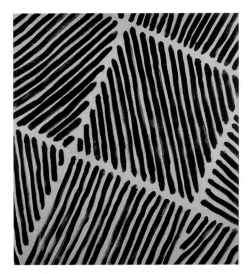

Martin Barré
72–73-F-108 × 100, 1972–73
Private collection, Paris
Photo © André Morain
Art © 2000 Artists Rights Society (ARS), New York/ADAGP, Paris

Martin Barré
74–75-D-113 × 105, 1974–75
Private collection, Paris
Photo © André Morain
Art © 2000 Artists Rights Society (ARS), New York/ADAGP, Paris

nowhere to arise except from the very contingency of the mark as the becoming visible of the painting's surfacing. But this entry into exposure can only happen so long as the mark appears as if constitutive of the ground at the very same moment that it is placed upon it—as if the mark were nothing more or other than the occasion of the ground's passage to figuration, to surface.

Typically in the work of the sixties, the tube paintings and the early sprays, Barré works at this in two primary ways: by, in effect, asking the mark to bare no more of its originating gesture than the time of its process, and by setting these marks in what feels as nearly as possible like a wholly contingent relation to the canvas. Most often this means the marks either roughly limn the canvas's borders or present themselves as if existing mostly outside the canvas and only accidentally intruding onto it. *61-T-15* is unusual in part because it attempts to use this strategy to move the mark more firmly into its (divided) field. Both the amplified gesture of the so-called "Zebra" paintings of the late sixties and the shift, at roughly the same time, to using stencils that mask the actual limits of the canvas in a series of sprayed "Arrow" paintings do much to make the painting surface as a whole available to Barré while also maintaining it as marked by the particular way in which it stands out—or is cut out—from a larger whole.

At just this point Barré stopped painting for a time and turned to a series of conceptual and photographic explorations in which he appears to be working out several interlocking issues: questions of spatial displacement and questions of time, particularly as they are available to photography. This turn appears motivated by an interest in the peculiar integrity of the photographic surface, as well as by the close approach of some of the spray paintings to a photographic condition, both in their actual look and in their making as "projections."

The paintings Barré began making in 1972 clearly participate in his long-standing project while

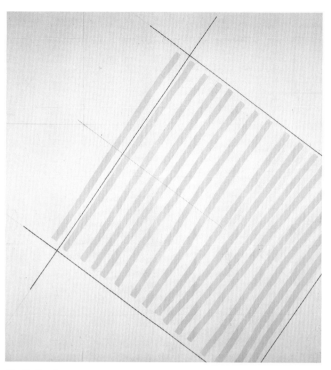

Martin Barré
75–76-B-174 × 164, 1975–76
Courtesy Galerie Laage-Salomon, Paris
Photo © André Morain
Art © 2000 Artists Rights Society (ARS), New York/ADAGP, Paris

Martin Barré
74–75-B-113 × 105, 1974–75
Private collection
Courtesy Galerie Laage-Salomon, Paris
Photo © André Morain
Art © 2000 Artists Rights Society (ARS), New York/ADAGP, Paris

also reformulating it in ways that could not have been easily anticipated on the basis of his work of the late sixties. In particular, the question of the contingency of the mark and the time of its making are knitted together by presenting the painting as cut out from a larger system of grids and marks, usually at an angle oblique to the axes of the painting itself. A "series" is now, in effect, the cutting out of several discrete canvases from a single such larger space, of which each completed painting is a particular "surfacing." Built up thinly out of successive effacements of layers of grid and mark, these paintings present themselves as nothing but the surfacing of something prior to them and not composed by them, something of which they are at once the realization and the effacing—say, the trace—but which also exists nowhere apart from them. Surfacing through themselves, they figure nothing but their ground.

S. M.

1. The fullest account of Barré's career is Yve-Alain Bois, *Martin Barré* (Paris: Flammarion and Centre national des arts plastiques, 1993). Additional useful material can be found in Martin Barré, *Martin Barré* (Paris: ARC—Musée d'art moderne de la ville de Paris, 1979).

James Bishop
Born 1927, Neosho, Missouri
Lives and works in Blévy, France

James Bishop has been living and painting in France more or less continuously since 1958. Throughout the sixties his work had a fair amount of visibility in the U.S., partly through direct exhibition and partly through reviews of his French exhibitions by such writers as John Ashbery and Annette Michelson, both early and articulate supporters of his work. Although the concerns informing his work are in many ways remarkably constant, it is hard not to mark a particularly significant step or break in 1966 (also the year of his first sustained return to the U.S.), when he began making the poured monochromes with which he is now primarily associated. Bishop has shown increasingly little in recent years and particularly rarely in the U.S.[1]

American painting of the fifties and sixties provides some ready references for considering the development of Bishop's work. His own frequently attested references are to what he calls "the quieter branch" of abstract expressionism—Robert Motherwell, Clyfford Still, Barnett Newman, and Mark Rothko, with these last two having the most sustained and palpable presence in Bishop's own work. But clearly Bishop is also to be located in relation to the work of such post-painterly colorists as Morris Louis and Kenneth Noland. Like Jules Olitski, Bishop finds his way from gesturally interested coloristic painting to a practice of the monochrome—although at the level of technique this is for Bishop a passage toward a form of stain painting (with oil strongly thinned with turpentine), while Olitski moves away from stain. And while Olitski undertakes a coloristic recovery of Pollock's linear all-over painting that negotiates with its limits in much the way Pollock's painting does, Bishop's painting moves always toward finding an inner articulation that makes itself out of those limits.

Because of this last feature, Bishop's work has frequently been compared with the early work of Frank Stella. But here one notes that Bishop's paintings do not open toward anything like the shaped canvases so prominent in Stella's work. Indeed, Bishop's acceptance of or insistence on the fixed format of a square canvas, 195 × 195 cm, is a key feature of his work. However responsive the inner articulation of Bishop's paintings may be to the initial condition of the support, that articulation always appears in the first instance as the working of color internal to them. Bishop thus appears closer to Louis, while the weight and texture of his interest in color is in some ways closer to Noland. And given what is sometimes described as the austerity of his painting and its careful working through of the possibilities within a distinctly limited set of means, it is hardly surprising that Bishop is frequently grouped with Robert Ryman and Agnes Martin.

All these references play their role in the French criticism as well, but they are often crucially extended by explicit comparison to Matisse, particularly the late cutouts, and a strong emphasis on Bishop's depth of historical knowledge and engagement.

A certain play between drawing and painting, between the work of line and the work of color, is evident from Bishop's earliest work, as is a tendency to rough geometric forms loosely answerable to the rectangularity of the canvas. As Bishop moves toward his fixed, square format, these forms coalesce into a distinct vocabulary—the square, the rectangle, the triangle, and the truncated triangle or trapezoid, with such allusions as they can carry (the window, the house, the mountain, a sort of emblem of recession). These forms and their allusions remain active across the whole of Bishop's work, capable of being variously awakened even in his most "reduced" and systematic works. The 1963 painting *Hours* is often taken to mark a particular step within Bishop's work on two counts: it is the first painting to make use of the pouring technique that becomes his primary means of making paintings, and it first brings into real focus the relation between the painting's ground and its structure that is the presiding problematic of the whole. Many of the paintings of 1963–64

James Bishop
Roman Painting IV, 1975
Collection of the artist
Photo courtesy Galerie Jean Fournier, Paris

James Bishop
Untitled, 1974
Courtesy Galerie Jean Fournier, Paris
Photo: J. Hyde

are built in the same basic way—a color field placed on, and so "framed" by, the white ground which may also re-emerge within or cut through that field (a few paintings explore this in reverse, setting fields of white ground within a painted frame). The link thus posited between the painting's limitation and its having the depth we point to in speaking of its "ground" sets the fundamental condition for Bishop's painting. A striking feature of a number of paintings from this time is that the dominant field often is presented as if torn along one of its edges—as if to block any reading of it as a figure in favor of seeing it as a collage-like repetition or re-marking of the ground it also covers.

The paintings Bishop began making in 1966 amount to a radical reinvention of this problematic.

Color is made both technically and visually continuous with the painting's ground, so that the canvas can no longer be considered as a *tabula rasa* on which a figure emerges or is projected. It is, as ground, always given over in advance to the color through which it comes to articulation. Bishop favors the colors in which we are most prone to imagine the condition of ground—the white of the canvas, the browns of the Old Masters, the grays that carry the force of the neutral, the possible: undecidables that do not lose touch with themselves and their reserves even as they fold themselves also into their own figuration.

These paintings begin on the ground, where their structure is sketched in (drawing is never expunged from Bishop's practice but continually reinterpreted by it; drawing itself remains a central concern and practice for him). The paint is poured and tilted, dammed and blotted where necessary, to form the characteristic seams of his grids. One might say that the task is to find in the painting—in its being both ground and on the ground—the articulations that will permit it to stand without betraying its fundamental groundedness. These articulations are rarely fully "abstract." They may carry something of the form and force of architectural post-and-lintel construction, as if supporting the painting that way, or they may appear as if rendering the painting a window on itself, or as if taking up into the painting the structure of the stretcher that is its literal support. The seams the color makes with itself may appear as edges or as blurrier overlaps, may feel like lines or folds or edges of solider elements that nonetheless can be neither abstracted from nor firmly located within the field that is both their context and condition. Critics have repeatedly remarked a certain "muteness" carried by the paintings, as if the work of color in them were to find within itself and its folding on itself the terms of its own articulation, and as if that articulation, when achieved, turned out to be a form of writing rather than speech.

S. M.

1. The best single source for Bishop's work is the catalogue of his 1993–94 retrospective, *James Bishop: Paintings and Works on Paper,* ed. Dieter Schwartz and Alfred Pacquement (Winterthur, Switzerland: Kunstmuseum Winterthur; Paris: Galerie nationale du Jeu de Paume; Münster: Westfälisches Landesmuseum, 1993–94), which includes a substantial selection from both French and American critical literature. Not included in this catalogue is Marcelin Pleynet's valuable essay "La couleur au carré, les rides, le dessein," for which see Marcelin Pleynet, *Art et littérature* (Paris: Editions du Seuil, 1977).

Mel Bochner

Born 1940, Pittsburgh, Pennsylvania

Lives and works in New York

Since the mid sixties, the reception of Mel Bochner's work has turned on the ways the work rethinks minimalist practices by opening itself to forms of conceptual thought, including logic, systemic thinking, and linguistic and mathematical theory. In this sense, procedure takes priority over the finished work, conceptual thought takes priority over the work's material existence, and the work is thus exposed in radically new ways to questions of perception and experience.[1]

In light of this reception, it might come as a surprise not only that Bochner has produced objects since the eighties that are recognizably *paintings* but also that he considers his work a "continuous investigation" into painting, in particular into those objects that offer themselves as a question of the conditions under which we are capable of *recognizing* paintings *as* paintings. In the interview with James Meyer in this catalogue, Bochner claims that "without the history of the practice of painting as the background for all my work, it becomes a series of disparate gestures." Bochner further claims "it's the absence of painting" that gives "definition" to his most well-known work such as the *Photo Pieces,* the *Measurements,* and the *Theory of Boundaries,* works that "all circulated around that missing signifier." And referring to the *48″ Standards,* he notes: "It was important for me in early pieces like *48″ Standards* that this question [of painting] take place in the *space of painting.* The sheet of brown paper had to be hung 'as if' it were a painting. I meant it to function as a proposition: what would it mean if this were a painting?"

Bochner's statements suggest an interrogation of painting's "functions and meanings," conventions, and the "theoretical constructs" that allow painting to be rethought as a "tool" to think with.[2] Bochner thereby exposes the irreducible difference between painting as such and an object situated "as if" it were painting. We might even say that he opens painting to a "theory of painting," thus demonstrating that the signifier /painting/ is never a stable category but a structural hinge around which Bochner's other work is opened to its simultaneous coherence and dispersion.

Bochner equally insists on questioning painting's limits and the "boundaries" that define it. This questioning demands a rigorous analysis of the language in which these boundaries are articulated, where articulation is understood as both phrasing and hinging. In the same interview, Bochner also speaks of a "bracketing and *unbracketing,*" a phrase that appeals to a phenomenological reduction informing his thinking since the mid sixties and the play of articulation in which painting now finds itself exposed.

But what is the "space of painting"? One of the wagers of *As Painting* is that Bochner's work might find itself in a space in which this question is renewed, particularly when the work is situated in rapport with other work from different traditions (both philosophic and artistic) in which this same question has also been posed since the mid sixties. A sense of this rapport can be gauged when comparing Bochner's frequent use of grids or geometrical structures—as in *Perspective Insert (Collapsed Center)* or *F-4*—with similar structuring impulses in other works, including Viallat's nets, Dezeuze's ladders and cubes, Bonnefoi and Dezeuze's tarlatan, Barré's serial hatchings, Degottex's geometrical grids, Rouan's *tressages,* Hantaï's structural foldings, and Valensi's O*bjets d'analyses.* This work shares a number of similar concerns, including questions of the "space" (and not installation) of painting, and of the wall or floor as a material dimension of the work's visibility. Also shared is an insistence on a structural hinging that includes a reference to architecture and spatial extension. In short, these commonalities reflect a continual exploration of painting's physical limits as a theoretically, structurally, and conceptually informed object.

Here, too, we can remark how the grid or measured structure in Bochner's work is never fully separated from the work's materiality. In one description, he notes that the *48″ Standards* are taken from standard

Mel Bochner
48" Standards, 1969
Courtesy Sonnabend Gallery, New York
Installation view at Sonnabend Gallery, New York
Photo: Lawrence Beck

Mel Bochner
Theory of Painting, 1969–70
Blue spray paint on newspaper on floor
Dimensions variable
Collection The Museum of Modern Art, New York
Installation view at Kunstnernes Hus, Oslo
Photo © Leif Gabrielsen
Photo courtesy the artist

measurements of building materials and that "these measurements are so deeply imbedded in our experience that they regulate our perception, yet remain completely invisible." Yet this recognition also forces Bochner to acknowledge that the weight of the paper and "the paper's materiality led me to other ways of thinking with it . . . the way it folds, the way it wrinkles, the way it crumples, the way it rolls and unrolls."[3] His description might apply to any number of other works included in *As Painting,* in which the work's materiality is a condition of its visibility and the structuring of the space it opens.

The spatial extension that characterizes much of Bochner's work is also indissociable from its intensive structuring. This intensive movement is also the play of folding and unfolding, of a pliability within extension, like the crumpling of a perspective "insert" that collapses the center of certain photographs, reinforcing the optical "physics" of photographic light as a distortion of the photograph's material surface in its very making. One thinks also of Bochner's photographs of shaving foam, vaseline, or mineral oil, in which the subject of

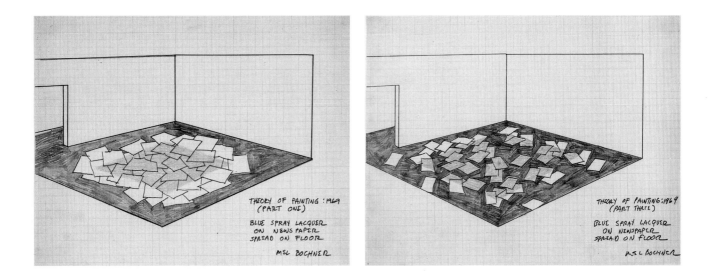

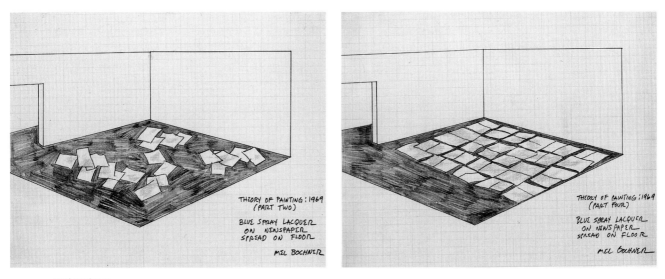

Mel Bochner
Studies for Theory of Painting (One–Four), 1969
Collection Sarah-Ann and Werner H. Kramarsky, New York
Photo: Peter Muscato

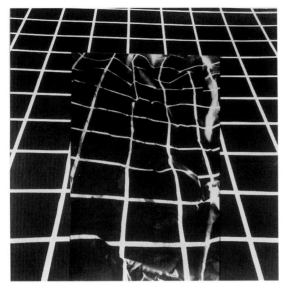

Mel Bochner
Perspective Insert (Collapsed Center), 1967
Courtesy Sonnabend Gallery, New York
Photo: Lawrence Beck

the photograph repeats and displaces the chemical transformation for which the photograph is both the trace and material expression. In a number of small drawings, permutational series of numbers fold back into themselves rather than unfold sequentially, and there are numerous figures of rotation, spiraling, and visual palimpsest in which the work folds and unfolds into and out of itself (the way one enters into and out of *The Domain of the Great Bear,* Bochner's collaborative project with Smithson from 1966).

The appeal to rethinking perspective in Bochner's work (an appeal that is also prominent in much of the work associated with Supports/Surfaces, as well as that of Knoebel) suggests that the inescapable element of illusion is not denied but turned back on itself, its conventions exploited and exposed through calculation and measurement. Bochner's appeal to perspective, grids, and geometrical forms is above all an insistence on a temporal rather than spatial dimension, a shift in emphasis that is clearly registered in his recent paintings, among them *Rome Quartet II*. This insistence on a temporal dimension—"to encode time"—coincides with the work's originary, serial motivation

Mel Bochner
F-4, 1966–67
Courtesy Sonnabend Gallery, New York
Photo: Pelka/Noble Photography

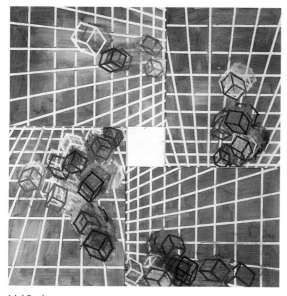

Mel Bochner
Rome Quartet II, 1992
Courtesy Sonnabend Gallery, New York

1. See the remarkable survey of essays in Richard S. Field, ed., *Mel Bochner: Thought Made Visible 1966–1973* (New Haven: Yale University Art Gallery, 1995).

2. It would be interesting to compare Bochner's reference to painting as a "tool" with Buren's notion of his own work as a "visual tool."

3. See Bochner's interview with Elayne Varian in *Mel Bochner* (Rio de Janeiro: Centro de Arte Hélio Oiticica, 1999), p. 55. Interestingly and significantly, one of Bochner's first pieces is a small painting that can be situated within the context of Dubuffet's materiological work.

and the articulations of opacity and transparency, continuity and discontinuity, that are also a measure of the work's temporal inscription.

The coincidence of seriate and temporally inscribed objects has been a decisive aspect of Bochner's work from the xerox copies used in 1966 for his *Working drawings* . . . to all the photographic pieces, and from the reproducibility of permutational variations and sequences to the recording of numerical measurements. In the context of *As Painting,* this serial and temporal dimension is inseparable from the play of extension and intension through which the work's serial existence continually (un)folds; it reopens the space of painting to an articulation or spacing, to what Bochner terms "a narrative of revisions which take place inside the object."

P. A.

Christian Bonnefoi
Born 1948, Salindres, France
Lives and works in Paris and Montargis, France

> This infinitely small (almost nothing) which defines the interstice of collage resonates with Mallarmé's "nothing will have taken place but the place" in "Un Coup de Dés."
>
> —Christian Bonnefoi

Christian Bonnefoi began his career by studying and publishing on architecture. A student of Hubert Damisch and Jean Louis Schefer, he worked closely with Yve-Alain Bois and Jean Clay around the journal *Macula* in the mid seventies. His background in art history, architecture, and archeology is also apparent in his published essays on subjects including Albers, Mondrian, Picasso, Barré, Ryman, Robert Mallet-Stevens, and Louis Kahn. The breadth of insight he brings to painting from philosophy, literature, art history, and theory is also evident in his theoretical texts such as "The Strategy of the Tableau" and "Collage," in his various interviews, including "A Propos of the Double Bind" and "The Apparition of the Visible," and in his essay translated for this catalogue, "The Objection That the Obscure Makes to Painting."[1]

In this last essay, Bonnefoi suggests that the problematic of collage is intimately tied to painting as a conceptual and structural arena. Beginning from cubist collage, he recognizes its "extension" into the world as well as its critical "return *toward* the surface"—its "intensivity." These two impulses produced by collage constitute Bonnefoi's central concept of "extensive intensity." And it is between these impulses that he locates an "interstice," an interval or intermediary space that can be seen as organizing not only his critical writings, but also his own work. As he writes: "The sense of cubist collage lies in the interstice, the non-disjunctive spacing between glued elements, between what comes from elsewhere, from the future, that which cannot be figured, and what comes upwards from underneath, from the ground. The interval is the site of expectation—of the event, and of enigma."

His first works, a series of collages called *Occasions*, represent his interest in the interval. The works are made by gluing various sheets of paper—construction paper, newspaper, tissue paper—onto a page in a sketchbook. He draws between and on top of some of the layers in black felt pen or pencil. In *As Painting*'s *Occasion*, the newspaper has been laid down slightly askew and covered by several layers of tissue paper, which unevenly obscure its legibility. The layers have been torn away throughout the process of addition, and remnants remain adhered at various levels in the depth of the collage. Incised cut marks around the perimeter, reiterated by drawing on some of the edges of the rectangle, seem simultaneously to adhere and divide the rectangle from the rest of the page, from which it is never fully cut. It is as if the image or figure that is the collage has come "upwards from underneath,"

Christian Bonnefoi
Occasion, 1974
Collection Jan and Ben Maiden, Columbus
Photo: Bill Nieberding

Christian Bonnefoi
Hyperion 2, 1977
Courtesy the artist
Installation view at Galerie Ricke, Cologne
Photo: Wolfgang Keseberg

even though it is made out of a myriad of intervals of applied glue and papers, producing a surface of veils, interstices, and thickness.

Bonnefoi's interest in an interstitial space is also evident in his writing on architecture. For example, he argues that Louis Kahn "resolves a question of construction in a manner that is both structural and formal through the *invention,* in the plastic sense of the word, of an intermediary element: the cantilever beams, structurally joined to hollow columns." Drawing an analogy between the "intermediary" element invented by Kahn and a problematic of minimalism that he terms "hanging," Bonnefoi suggests:

The hanging of a canvas or the positioning of a sculpture, an operation that previously was neutral or purely technical, becomes the very moment of plastic investigation. The most exemplary painter in this regard is Robert Ryman. In his work, the pictorial process is the sum of possibilities of marking the (subject) matter on the canvas and then from the canvas or other support onto the wall, or ultimately of marking upon the wall directly. Here the pigment plays the role of a transitory and intermediary, structural-formal object, a role which, in the architectural system, is assumed by the cantilever beams.[2]

The "transitory" object akin to the cantilever beams in architecture is a crucial component of Bonnefoi's concept of "extensive intensity," which produces a temporal conversion of space. Furthermore, it is what distinguishes the *tableau*—a "modality of the plane, time and the invisible"—from painting: "an art of surface, space and the visible."

The "transitory" in Bonnefoi's own painting is manifest in several materials consistent in his practice,

Christian Bonnefoi
Acuto, 1997
Installation view at Galerie du Dourven, Côtes-d'Armor, France
Photo courtesy the artist

notably tarlatan or gauze, as well as acrylic paint, which he divides into its binder (glue) and pigment. The tarlatan is a material that is semitransparent and open in weave so that the paint both passes through it and becomes caught in its mesh. *Hyperion 2* is a work on tarlatan, through sections of which one can see its metal chassis. Some of the surface is masked with rice paper, accentuating the experience of looking into and across the painting. The painted divisions on the surface echo the chassis below and create an effect of depth or intensiveness inside the surface; they also extend out onto the wall or floor, as in other works from the *Hy-*

perion series, including his most recent wall collages such as *Acuto.*

Bonnefoi's inventions of a series of relations or limits that belong to painting's structure, including the wall, are animated by his concept of the "division of the division." This concept is close to "extensive intensity" in its double impulse to identify a moment of division across as well as into a surface. This moment assures "intensive points of appearing," like the points of adhesion (pins or glue) on the wall or paper of the collage work, as well as the temporality essential to Bonnefoi's concept and creation of the *tableau.* His vocabulary of divisions is broad and articulates the numerous and ongoing interweavings of series that he has sustained since the beginning of his career.[3] For example, the divisions in the *Babel* series are established through dividing the gestural drawn lines that are then re-fused into the tarlatan by the glue of the paint. The paint's pigment, divided from the glue, is dispersed in sections of the painting. Whereas the *Babel* series orchestrates cut divisions of drawing, the *Eureka* series is primarily characterized by divisions and displacements of color—color patches cut together to produce an effect of movement. Many works incorporate a double move or impulse of dividing the already divided, such as cutting divisional lines or displacing the placement of color. Likewise, the visual accessibility through the surface to the stretcher further divides the work by its own structural support, suggesting that painting begins and returns to its own dividedness.

Machine 78 takes us away from the named series within Bonnefoi's work and back to the event of Mallarmé's "place." The relationship of the limits of the dense blue surface, rusting chassis, and thin periphery of gauze constitutes the infinitely small—"almost nothing"—of an interstice or place that Bonnefoi makes for thinking painting. This early painting has compressed within it the objections, strategies, and double binds that necessitate the *tableau.*

L. L.

Christian Bonnefoi
Babel II, 1979
Courtesy Galerie Jacques Elbaz, Paris
Photo: Jean-Louis Losi

Christian Bonnefoi
Machine 78, 1978
Courtesy Galerie de France, Paris
Photo: Patrick Müller

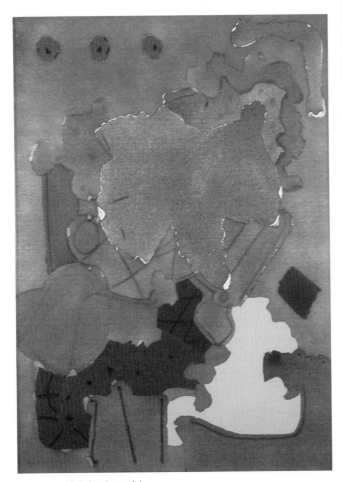

Christian Bonnefoi
Eureka IV, 1997
Collection of Dave and Nancy Gill, Columbus, Ohio
Photo: Bill Nieberding

1. See Christian Bonnefoi, *Ecrits sur l'art (1974–1981)* (Brussels: La Part de l'Oeil, 1997).

2. Christian Bonnefoi, "Louis Kahn and Minimalism," trans. Dan Cooper, *Oppositions* 24 (spring 1981): 3, 5–6. The translation has been modified.

3. On the relation of Bonnefoi's work to serial thinking, see Philip Armstrong, "Série(s) et apories: La peinture après le minimalisme," in *La Part de l'Oeil* 17 (2001).

Daniel Buren
Born 1938, Boulogne Billancourt, France
Lives and works in situ

Daniel Buren is well known in the U.S. as a conceptual artist engaged in a project of institutional critique. Without wishing to directly contest this characterization, *As Painting* takes a particular interest in how what Buren has come to call a "visual tool"—his signature striped fabric with one or more of the white stripes also painted white—originated from a concern for painting and continues to take some significant part of its sense from that starting point. Buren's own references and remarks are quite clear here: his recent essay on Robert Ryman (included in this catalogue) displays clearly enough his distance from the American centrality of minimalism, just as many of his early writings mark off a distance from the conceptualism into which his work was rapidly assimilated as it moved beyond France.[1] Closer to his own practice, Buren has frequently remarked on the early importance of the work of Hantaï and Villeglé. In common with many of the French painters in *As Painting*, Buren takes Cézanne as a central reference and shows little patience with or tolerance for Duchamp, as for example in this passage from "Standpoints," a text of 1971:

> But—and this is the crux of the problem—why can we say that a bottle-stand which is exhibited is art and not rupture with art? Duchamp made traditional art, adding a new form (without great consistency) to the multiples which make an art history possible. Why could and can this evidence pass almost unperceived and influence a number of artistic attempts, thus making them instantly sterile and regressive?
>
> We said that one of the questions posed by Cézanne's work was: is it possible to eliminate the subject in painting and to manifest only painting as painted—or paint itself—that is, to show a painting without a history other than its own, without illusion, without representation of the beyond, without perspective, without a framework other than the one on which this painting is inscribed—its support?

The earliest work that Buren still shows displays a clear affinity with *affichiste* collage or *décollage*, the white paint appearing partly as if imposed on the striped fabric whose order it disrupts and partly as if emerging where that fabric has been torn away. The work immediately prior to these paintings evidently involved building up layers of colored collage to a final white layer, which was then torn to expose the color underneath. By the time Buren began showing with Olivier Mosset, Michel Parmentier, and Niele Toroni, he had essentially settled on his visual constant—a support of vertical stripes 8.7 cm in width, usually with one or more of the white stripes also painted white—although the work is still exclusively stretched and shown as a painting. At the same time, the joint statement for these artists' first showing—in January 1967 at the Salon de la Jeune Peinture—ended by declaring "WE ARE NOT PAINTERS." Despite its emphatic capitals, the statement remains deeply ambiguous, poised between an unreserved condemnation of painting and a more qualified refusal of the current terms of making, exhibition, and criticism through which the statement defines painting. In fact, the second reading is consistently the more powerful in understanding the activity and subsequent careers of all four artists (Toroni is perhaps the only one who has come to seem fully at home in a broadly conceptualist context, but even his work remains consistently oriented to the painterly mark).

Buren has insisted on the consequential specificity of the marks or traces chosen by each artist. His own trace is profoundly anticompositional, in effect giving rise to a practice of painting (*peinture*) from which the *tableau* (any pictorial dimension whatsoever) is utterly expunged; he often stresses the difference of this from Parmentier's trace, which Buren sees as engaging a concern for the *tableau*, and particularly for

Daniel Buren
Peinture aux formes indéfinies, 1966
Courtesy Galerie Jean Fournier, Paris
Photo: J. Hyde
Art © 2000 Artists Rights Society (ARS), New York/ADAGP, Paris

the possibility of a last *tableau*. One might also note the contrast between Buren's starting point in collage and Parmentier's in the monochrome. The disjunction between painting and *tableau,* operated by the particular terms of his practice, opens his work to its various adventures beyond the stretcher. The core argument here is clearly laid out in an essay titled "Critical Limits," written to accompany a show of his paintings at Yvon Lambert in early 1971. The essay opens with a statement that reflects Buren's adherence to the Althusserian notion of a "theoretical practice": "The following text results from a specific practice or work which is meant TO BE SEEN. This text is only the demonstration, presentation of this work, and not its theory. It could be considered as an illustration of the work in question. It is dictated by the work itself and is not an abstract and purified image of some future project."

Polemicizing against a range of emergent alternative practices—including minimalist objecthood and the readymade and post-Duchampian conceptualism—the essay explores how painting opens beyond itself by virtue of the limits that define it and onto a field it inevitably reveals as both relational and contingent, exposed to, and so capable of exposing, the institutional and cultural limits within which it claims its presence. Buren's reading, turning on a view of painting as a covering of surfaces on a support, clearly understands this practice to find a certain explicitness in collage. The essay's accompanying diagrams demonstrate painting's limitation—the facts of its masking of and framing by its support—as the condition for its connection with the world, so also for its critical force. Where this finitude is refused or imagined as overcome, both painting and the critical force it brings into the world will be lost. Conversely, where painting can be broken free of the particular containment of the *tableau,* it becomes free to carry its problematic of masking and framing more directly into the world. "Painting" will appear there in shapes one may be tempted to call architectural or sculptural or perhaps to imagine as entirely free of

Daniel Buren
Peinture aux formes variables, 1966
Courtesy of Daniel Buren
Art © 2000 Artists Rights Society (ARS), New York/ADAGP, Paris

any concern with medium at all—but this will cost one the sense of Buren's enterprise.

If this enterprise offers an account of the particular nature of painting as a "theoretical practice," it is one that insists also on painting's (difficult) autonomy, an autonomy Buren tends to gloss by reference to his other major discursive reference, Maurice Blanchot, whose understanding of the impersonality constitutive of the work as such lies at the heart of Buren's practice. As Buren puts it in "It Rains, It Snows, It Paints," a crucial early text:

> The impersonal or anonymous nature of the work/product causes us to be confronted with a fact (or idea) in its raw form; we can only observe it without a reference to any metaphysical scheme, just as we observe that it is raining or snowing. Thus we can now say, for the first time, that "it is painting," as we say, "it is raining." When it snows we are in the presence of a natural phenomenon, so when "it paints" we are in the presence of an historical fact.

S. M.

1. See Daniel Buren, *Les écrits: 1965–1990,* ed. Jean-Marc Poinsot, 3 vols. (Bordeaux: capcMusée d'art contemporain, 1991); Daniel Buren and Michel Parmentier, *Propos délibérés* (Lyons: Art Edition; Brussels: Palais des Beaux-Arts, 1991); and Daniel Buren, *Au Sujet de . . .* (Paris: Flammarion, 1998). For Buren's early work, see Benjamin Buchloh, "Formalism and Historicity—Changing Concepts in American and European Art since 1945," in *Europe in the Seventies: Aspects of Recent Art* (Chicago: Art Institute of Chicago, 1977). Quotations in this entry are from Daniel Buren, *Five Texts* (New York: John Weber Gallery, 1973).

Daniel Buren
On Ash (Black), 1989
Wax and wood stain on wood
25 parts, 87 × 87 in. (221 × 221 cm)
Courtesy of Daniel Buren
Art © 2000 Artists Rights Society (ARS), New York/ADAGP, Paris

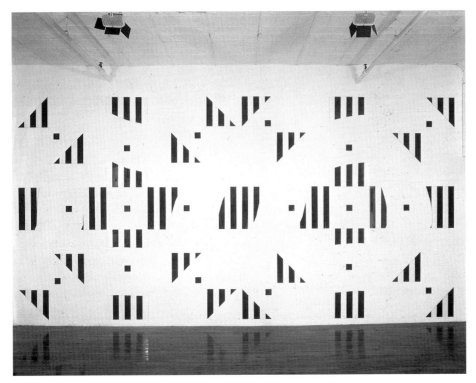

Daniel Buren
Through the Looking Glass (Corners in: bocour violet) and
(Corners out: bocour red), 1983
Paint on glass
Dimensions variable
Courtesy of Daniel Buren
Art © 2000 Artists Rights Society (ARS), New York/ADAGP, Paris

André Cadere
Born 1934, Warsaw
Died 1978, Paris

. . . a round bar of wood *is.*

—André Cadere

I want to insist on the fact that a bar of round wood contains within its structure all its own coordinates. In this sense, I am not a teacher and there is nothing to discuss or write. It is to be shown. I circulate everywhere with my work. If I felt I should offer no answers, mine would be a very old and traditional artistic attitude. What I do is really extremely simple, and I want to keep it that way; because of that, I have to speak when the situation allows me to. In this sense, speaking *for* my activity becomes extremely important.

—André Cadere

André Cadere's practice of speaking about—*for*—his work is only one of the strategies he developed for its circulation. Mobility, circulation, or displacement must be understood as a significant part of his practice, inseparable from the independent objects he made. By the early seventies he would consistently define these objects as "round bars of wood," painted segments of wood equal in length to diameter, where the segments are ordered based on mathematically derived permutations of primary and secondary colors, with a permutational "error" in each. His better-known strategies for circulation include publicly announced promenades or isolated walks toting a round bar of wood; participation in group shows, some invited, others not; and the use of art galleries as points of departure and sites with visible and permeable boundaries between everyday life and presentation. Here, however, we want to emphasize his strategy of circulating his work through speaking *for* it.

One of the situations in which Cadere spoke *for* his work was a lecture, *Presentation of a Work/Utiliza-tion of a Work,* given to the Faculty of Philosophy and Literature at the Catholic University of Leuven (Belgium) in 1974. For this presentation, Cadere sat in front of a chalkboard on which he wrote a code corresponding to the colored segments of the "round bar of wood" leaning against the wall to his side. In relation to painting and color, he suggested:

> In a strict sense, we can only see differently colored surfaces all around us. It is possible to say on this basic level, that painting (color applied to a surface) is an essential part of the artistic phenomena. To understand this work by how it looks, gives the work's appearance a privileged relationship. The painting that distinguishes the segments tries to show this relationship. The color is applied to a cylindrical surface. This work, unlike other paintings, does not have two sides. Being cylindrical it has neither a front or back.

This excerpt reveals the importance Cadere placed on painting and represents the context within which he worked throughout his brief career.[1]

When Cadere first arrived in Paris from Romania in 1967, he was influenced by op art and, later, by conceptual art. *Barre de bois carrée* of 1970 is particularly informative and unusual in that it marks the moment hinging his nonsystematic early painting—painted bars glued to a flat surface in optically complex organizations—and his fully conceptualized "round bars of wood." This work's playful nature is evident not only in the patchwork of multiple colors that wrap its three sides and fill its grooves but also in the differing lengths of the twelve square bars and the variety of their presentational configurations. Within two years, by 1972, Cadere came to draw decisive distinctions concerning the form and presentation of his work within the context of painting.

That we can see only "differently colored surfaces all around us" underscores the essential role color plays in the context of painting for Cadere. Color both

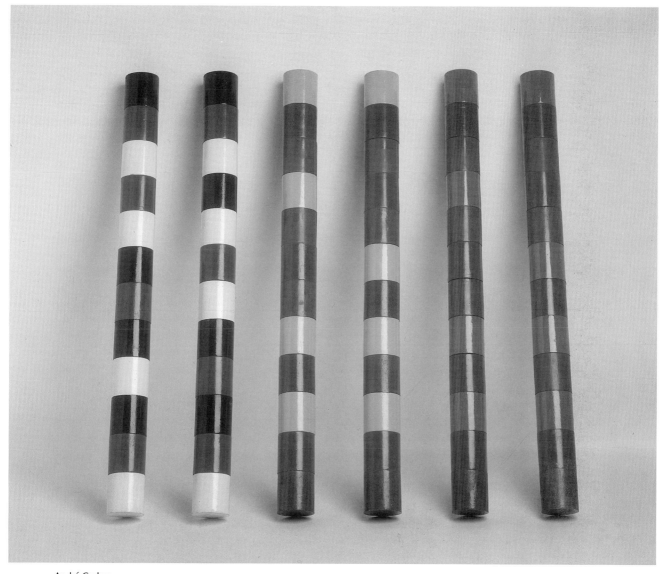

André Cadere
Six barres de bois rond, 1975
Collection Centre Georges Pompidou, Paris
Musée national d'art moderne/Centre de création industrielle
Photo: Philippe Megeat
© Centre Georges Pompidou

André Cadere
Barres de bois carré, 1970
Courtesy Galerie L. & M. Durand-Dessert, Paris
Photo: Adam Rzepka

differentiates objects from their grounds (i.e., the round bars of wood from their environment) and distinguishes the segments within the bars. "The essential function of color is to differentiate objects," he states. Like many of the artists in *As Painting*—notably Judd, Richter, Buren, Apfelbaum, Hantaï, and Parmentier—Cadere recognizes the capacity of color, like language, to "differentiate objects" and thereby displace and divide painting to test its limits.

Presentation and autonomy are coterminous in Cadere's work, and he argues for the significance of both the work's presentation and its existence: that "a round bar of wood *is.*" In the 1974 lecture, he states: "We have seen that this work has its own reality and is independent of any point of view or privileged space. It stays in the background, emphasizing the place in which it is situated and the person who is looking at it. A point of view is utilization." Each round bar of wood is unique at the same time that it marks the place in which—and the viewer to whom—it is presented. Cadere emphasizes that while he shows his work "towards and against everyone and everything," his "sole aim" is "the pieces themselves." In a closing comment at Leuven, he underscores this necessity of the work's presentation, as opposed to its mere utilization, by recalling a well-known anecdote about Cézanne: "It is obvious that on the hen coop Cézanne's painting was in use, but it was not presented. I hope the work presented here acts in a very different manner."

The clarity with which Cadere identified the relationship of the limits of his objects and the strategies of their presentation or circulation is evident in his instructions for the *Six barres de bois rond* included in *As Painting*. These state that the six bars of wood should be presented "in such a manner that one might not see from any point more than two at a time (however, it is perfectly possible only to see one of them)." With these instructions in mind, our placement of the bars aims simultaneously to present the work and mark the space of the exhibition—a space of painting—reflecting a relationship that Cadere enacted throughout his career. The criterion of viewing no more than two bars at once while still allowing for the viewing of an independent or single bar is an example of the rapport between presentational tactics and the existence of the bars as they present themselves. The dispersal of the bars implies work that is in circulation, like the circulation of the artist with his work. At the same time, Cadere's instructions for presenting *Six barres de bois rond* (which speak *for* the work) allow the work to exist independent of the artist's own presence—and thus maintain the criticality of a relationship of independence and presentation as limits for painting.

L. L.

1. The lecture text appears in *André Cadere: All Walks of Life,* ed. Carole Kismaric, Chris Dercon, and Bernard Marcelis (Long Island City, New York: Institute for Contemporary Art, P. S. 1, in association with the Musée d'art moderne de la ville de Paris, 1992), pp. 27–39. This useful book also includes letters Cadere wrote to his supportive gallery dealer, Yvon Lambert, in 1978, the last year of his life; the quotations used as epigraphs are from p. 21. Subsequent quotations are also from the lecture. In the same volume, Bernard Marcelis, "André Cadere: The Strategy of Displacement," pp. 40–75, and Cornelia Lauf, "A Tactic of the Margin," pp. 103–32, provide descriptions of the artistic and intellectual climate in which Cadere worked. See also André Cadere, *Histoire d'un travail* (Ghent: Herbert-Gewad, 1982), published posthumously.

André Cadere at Museum van Hedendaagse Kunst, Ghent, Belgium, 1977
Photo courtesy Galerie L. & M. Durand-Dessert, Paris

Jean Degottex
Born 1918, Sathonay-Camp, France
Died 1988, Paris

A pivotal moment in the early reception of the work of Jean Degottex centers on André Breton's claim from 1955 that his painting offers a compelling response to the demands of "automatic writing." If Breton's appeal to Degottex attempted to resolve a lacunae in surrealist aesthetics, it stemmed from a practice of painting that was already in place before Breton's intellectual patronage. Degottex's practice incorporates rapid movements of the brush in which, according to Breton, the gesture is the outcome of an unconscious automatism. Breton's description was equally informed by recent studies on calligraphy, a tradition that would come to play a determining role in Degottex's life and work.[1]

Degottex never belonged to the surrealist group, and his debts to oriental traditions became increasingly less pronounced in his paintings. But this initial encounter with Breton foregrounds the more difficult question of painting's relation to writing in general. For Breton's appeal to the early work as a form of automatic writing is but one episode within a more extended field of influences on Degottex's thinking, including calligraphy and oriental philosophies but also Wittgenstein, Mallarmé, and abstract expressionism—references that Degottex's occasional writings and interviews develop with some insistence.[2]

From this initial context, three related issues will be sustained in Degottex's work throughout his career. The first is an impetus to think of writing in relation to painting, not merely as a continuation of scriptural traditions but as *the space of inscription*. Writing is here understood as a temporal, nonnarrative, and nonmetaphorical mode in which the implication of writing and surface inscription is the measure in which the work (un)folds into visibility. The second issue involves the materials and techniques that constitute the work's physical conditions and limits. The third concerns the related question of process and temporality (for which automatism is but one form), where process is understood as a temporal transformation of the work's material inscription and not merely the visual demonstration of a specific technique.

Degottex always refused any notion of gesture as a form of subjective expression. Instead, his sense of radical detachment from the work insists on the "writing" of pictorial signs, with an emphasis on marking the surfaces on, through, or in which such writing becomes visible. This transformation from gesture to writing also displaces questions of composition and personal expression, reinforcing the claim (as Degottex notes, citing Barthes) that "art has a scriptural origin and not an expressive one."[3] Inscribing the space of the work also foregrounds a constant experimentation with questions of size, installation, and scale, which registers his debts to—and reading of—a specifically American exploration of painting since Pollock.

Associated with Degottex's shift from gesture to writing is his gradual transformation from using brushes to a wide array of tools. These tools are a measure of the multiple ways in which Degottex attempts

Jean Degottex in his studio
Photo courtesy Maurice Benhamou
Art © 2000 Artists Rights Society (ARS), New York/ADAGP, Paris

Jean Degottex
Lignes-Report, 1977
Collection Marcelle and Maurice Benhamou, Paris
Photo: Patrick Müller
Art © 2000 Artists Rights Society (ARS), New York/ADAGP, Paris

to inscribe a surface: through techniques of folding, sizing and scoring, collage, tearing and unthreading—techniques that necessarily include chance effects. A multiplicity of working surfaces coincides with his frequent working on the floor, eliminating the easel, and experimenting with further ways to write the space of painting after Pollock.

Degottex's emphasis on writing a space equally insists on the materials with which the painting is made. The work thus turns on an incessant exploration of textures and material resistances, especially with materials taken from his immediate surroundings, such as debris and rubble. These are remnants of things that once existed, were then demolished, and then get recirculated in and as the work. Degottex seems concerned less with the expressive nature of materials than with their energy, an energy that includes a sense of "suspension" or reserve, opening painting to a void or radical "negation"—"la voie négative"—of what the work of painting is or claims to be.[4]

The insistence on material transformation can also be seen in the ways Degottex recycles materials in a potentially endless process of conversion, dispersion, and displacement, circulating the remnants and residues from work to work (frayed edges from cut canvases glued back across the surface, powder from scraping bricks used as dry pigment, etc.). The making of the work redistributes different excesses that are not initially *in* the material but are produced by an action performed on it, an excess that is then taken back up either within the same work or into another.

This appeal to inscribing the space of painting is further reinforced by a recurrent emphasis on the work's divisions and limits. The operations of division include lateral divisions *of* a given surface (median lines and hand-drawn geometries, especially the oblique) and divisions incised *into* the surface (pulling threads from the weave of the support, applying tools to make imprints [*Lignes-Report*], or pasting glue from both sides of the canvas to create a sizing effect that is also a structural tracing of color [*Oblicollor*]). Divisions are

Jean Degottex
Oblicollor, 1983
Collection Marcelle and Maurice Benhamou, Paris
Photo: Karin Mancotel © Paris Musées
Art © 2000 Artists Rights Society (ARS), New York/ADAGP, Paris

Jean Degottex
Papier-Plein no. 7, December 14, 1975
Collection Marcelle and Maurice Benhamou, Paris
Photo: Patrick Müller
Art © 2000 Artists Rights Society (ARS), New York/ADAGP, Paris

The work of Degottex is not only a response to traditions of painting (oriental, abstract expressionist, the Ecole de Paris) but also to the appeals to minimalist reduction or theoretical/conceptual dispersion.[6] In consequence, writing the space of painting becomes a measure of what painting is able to transform, a temporal process that includes, as one of its most intimate (im)possibilities, the "work" itself. What we are "given to see" is thus, for Degottex, "anti-expressionist, anti-subjective, anti-formalist, anti-modernist, and yet at the point of a permanent modernity of non-knowledge and questioning."[7]

P. A.

1. Breton's 1955 text, "L'épée dans les nuages," is reproduced in facsimile with commentary in Jean Frémon, *Degottex* (Paris: Editions du Regard and Galerie de France, 1986), pp. 314–15.

2. See Renée Beslon-Degottex, "Notes on the Artist's Path," in *Degottex: Parcours 1970–1984* (Espace Fortant de France, 1997), pp. 12–13.

3. Degottex cites Roland Barthes's *L'empire des signes* in Frémon, *Degottex,* p. 255. See also Francine C. Legrand, "Peinture et écriture," *Quadrum* (Brussels), no. 13 (1962): 5–48.

4. See Maurice Benhamou, "Jean Degottex: Le 'faire' et le 'comment c'est fait,'" in *Jean Degottex/René Guiffrey* (La Seyne-sur-Mer, France: Villa Tamaris, 1998).

5. Jean Degottex, interview with Dominique Bozo, "A propos des Toiles-Report," in *Degottex: Toiles, papiers, graphiques, 1962–1978* (Paris: ARC–Musée d'art moderne de la ville de Paris, 1978), p. 20.

6. On the relation to minimalism, see the interview with Dominique Bozo, "A propos des Toiles-Report," and Bernard Lamarche-Vadal's discussion, "L'oeuvre de Jean Degottex et la question du tableau," in *Degottex* (Grenoble: Musée de peinture et de sculpture; Saint-Etienne: Musée d'art et d'industrie, 1978).

7. Quoted in Frémon, *Degottex,* p. 262.

also created by collage and *décollage* (*Papier-Plein no. 7*), where adhesive tape is stuck to the surface and then torn away, leaving traces of lacerations, and where the median line includes graphite traces of the edge of the tape both before and after the effects of adhesion and tearing, opening this play of surface inscription to a temporal dimension. Finally, we might note divisions that imply a folding or unfolding of surfaces, creating interior edges, folded reversals of material in closed and open positions, pleats, and traces of folded edges created by unfolded surfaces. These varying forms of folding reveal the work's surface in terms of a temporality that implies the past, present, and future, but in which the painting is never fully revealed, even when shown front and back (*Pli x Pli III*). The work is here held in permanent suspension, punctuated by reserves and voids, open to continual inversions between the recto and verso ("l'en-droit et l'en-vers") that are simultaneously visible and invisible.[5]

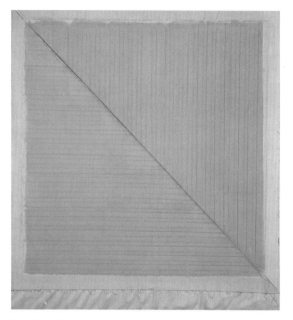

Jean Degottex
Pli x Pli III (recto), August 1980
Collection Marcelle and Maurice Benhamou, Paris
Photo: Patrick Müller
Art © 2000 Artists Rights Society (ARS), New York/ADAGP, Paris

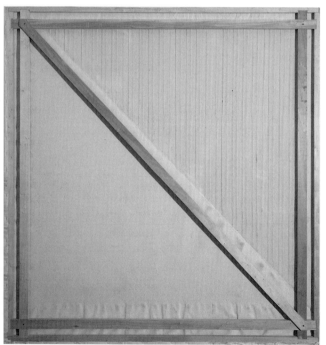

Jean Degottex
Pli x Pli III (verso), August 1980
Collection Marcelle and Maurice Benhamou, Paris
Photo: Patrick Müller
Art © 2000 Artists Rights Society (ARS), New York/ADAGP, Paris

Daniel Dezeuze
Born 1942, Alès, France
Lives and works in Sète, France

The text that Daniel Dezeuze contributed to the catalogue for his recent retrospective at the Musée d'art contemporain de Nîmes takes the form of a lexicon. It includes a brief explication of the following terms: "illusion, limit, gap, Simone Martini, Matisse, Malevich, Kline, Matta-Clark, Twombly, frame/stretcher, infinite space, language, historical perspective, geometry, sighting device, aims, ballistics, heroics, wood, nomads, grammar, nets/traps, butterflies, cloud, breath, Indian, work, deconstruct, density, eye."[1] The list is not arbitrary, nor is it arbitrary that Dezeuze's contribution to his own catalogue should take the form of a list. In fact, as early as in 1969, he writes:

> Starting from a very simple grammar (point, stain, imprint, fold, cut-up), numerous combinations are beginning to be organized. These come about through a well-tempered meeting between a support and some "marking" agent, with or without a medium. Considered from this point of view, painterly practice may, without necessarily being reductive, develop along different lines."[2]

The notion of a "simple grammar" that might allow painterly practice to develop along "different lines" reflects Dezeuze's manner of intellectually framing his own practice as one predicated on the identification of certain structural elements and their recombination. This grammar or lexicon reflects the gaps and linkages between his different series of works and is also reflected in much of the critical writing on his work. For example, Christian Prigent's seminal book on Dezeuze, *Comme la Peinture/Like Painting,* is divided into its own lexicon of sorts, including sections entitled: "like a geometry," "like a space," "like drawing," "like writing," "like frescoes," and "like a spectre."[3]

Dezeuze's work includes series of objects that can be variously categorized as weapons (arms), traps, and butterfly or insect nets. What connects these series to those represented in *As Painting* can be found in the contiguities of the categories, each more or less namable, of Dezeuze's lexicon. A lexicon operates in terms of its syntagmatic and paradigmatic sense or structure. The structure of painting, as operative in Dezeuze's practice, might similarly be found in the movement linking the grammatical units of the lexicon. And as Prigent reminds us in his contribution to this catalogue, the "as" or "like" of painting is its very "movement"—the "being of it."

The movement that is painting for Dezeuze exists between the grammar that he locates and displaces, between the mediums of painting, sculpture, and drawing. One of the founding artists of Supports/Surfaces in 1970, and one of the founding members of the journal *Peinture: Cahiers théoriques* in 1971, he resigned from both in 1972 and left Paris to teach in Nice. Just before his involvement with the intellectual and practical experiments associated with Supports/Surfaces, he exhibited stretchers covered in plastic, leaning against the wall. This formative work is by now recognized as the starting point of his (de)construction of the relationship between the support and surface of painting, where the symbolic and formal relationship is established between the grid of the stretcher bar and the perspectival grid of Western painting.

Dezeuze's ladders (including *Echelle de bois rouge et brune*) can be seen as an extension of this early work, though with some significant differences. Their pliability or suppleness allows them to unfold or roll over themselves, thereby enacting a counterperspectival gesture to that of the stretcher bar that had symbolized the window or grid of painting. As Alfred Pacquement points out, the most significant aspect of Dezeuze's work from 1968–72 is his revision of the stretcher (the "archetypal figure of painting") as the "image" of the stretcher, which, as Dezeuze states himself, captures the "world of meaning."[4] One can read these paintings' stretchers, along with the nets of Viallat and Valensi, as a sketching or "capturing of the world" in a loosened

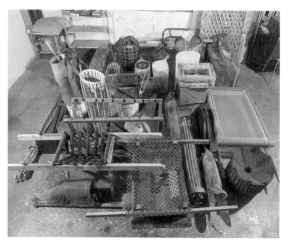

Daniel Dezeuze
La remise (objets variés), 1992–95
Mixed media
Dimensions variable
Courtesy Galerie Daniel Templon, Paris
Art © 2000 Artists Rights Society (ARS), New York/ADAGP, Paris

Daniel Dezeuze
Echelle de bois rouge et brune, 1975
Collection of the artist, Sète, France
Art © 2000 Artists Rights Society (ARS), New York/ADAGP, Paris

grid, one with as many holes as ligatures. Dezeuze's geometry is gestural and destructures painting's rapport with the grid as it restructures its relationship with a world. One can understand the later "traps" or harvesting and gathering devices—for example, *La remise (objets variés)*—as extensions of painting's support as a gridding or netting and as a movement of painting toward and away from its subjects.[5]

Dezeuze's move from the thin balsa strips of his ladders to working on gauze can be seen as a formulation in visual terms of (in Pacquement's words) "the

disappearance of the painted canvas, while—less paradoxically than one might think—remaining in the domain of painting."[6] *Gaze découpée et peinte* is representative both of this movement and of the consequent appearance of the wall, architectural context, and drawing. The conflation of surface weave and structural support is already present in the tarlatan. Without the necessity for additional support, Dezeuze draws onto the gauze with graphite or felt marker, sprays or stains the gauze with color, tapes off forms or shapes, and finally cuts out the overall shape, as well as the interior, hexagonal form (as can be seen in the detail). The appearance of the wall is evident in the framed interior holes, through the transparency of the tarlatan, and as a residual surface cut out by the overall shape. In this sense, the wall is captured and revealed through the cutting and netting of the tarlatan.

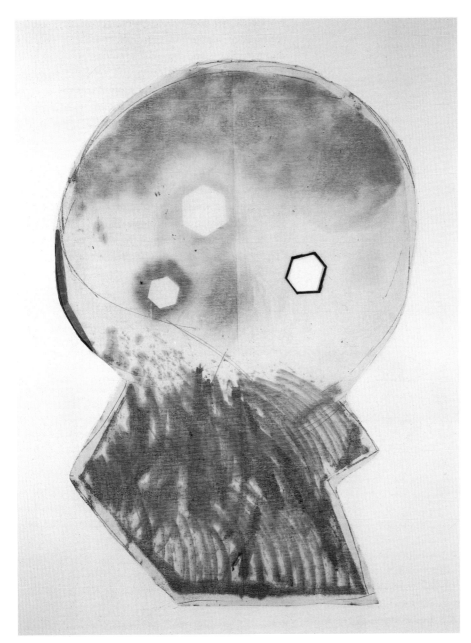

Daniel Dezeuze
Gaze découpée et peinte, 1980
Collection of the artist, Sète, France
Art © 2000 Artists Rights Society (ARS), New York/ADAGP, Paris

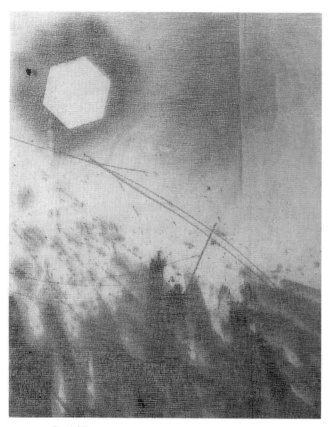

Daniel Dezeuze
Gaze découpée et peinte (detail), 1980
Collection of the artist, Sète, France
Art © 2000 Artists Rights Society (ARS), New York/ADAGP, Paris

work collapses down is no surprise and underscores the concepts of suppleness, gesturality, and condensation that carry his work toward a simultaneous generation and degeneration of painting. Elsewhere in this catalogue, Christian Prigent aptly summarizes the work of Dezeuze and other artists in *As Painting* as "both the institution of a form and a provocation to formlessness. . . . a taste for the infinite that exceeds finite forms, an attraction for the insignificant that hollows out sensible figures." That painting can attend to its specific grammar—without resorting to a reduction—in order to generate *painting* is reflected in the lexical structure of Dezeuze's practice. It is the movement or spacing between the elements of his lexicon that produces a permanent opening to—and within—the question of painting.

L. L.

1. See *Daniel Dezeuze* (Nîmes: Carré d'art, Musée d'art contemporain, 1999). The lexicon is a response to a request by Olivier Kaeppelin.

2. Reprinted in Joëlle Pijaudier, Alfred Pacquement, and Olivier Kaeppelin, *Daniel Dezeuze* (Paris: Flammarion, 1989), p. 110. For a useful collection of texts by Daniel Dezeuze, see his *Textes et notes 1967–1988* (Paris: Ecole nationale supérieure des beaux-arts, 1991).

3. Christian Prigent, *Comme la Peinture/Like Painting (Daniel Dezeuze)* (Paris: Yvon Lambert, 1983).

4. Alfred Pacquement, "The Supports-Surfaces Years," in Joëlle Pijaudier, Alfred Pacquement, and Olivier Kaeppelin, *Daniel Dezeuze,* p. 99.

5. Interest in archaic, artisanal, and preindustrial crafts is evident in much of the work of the artists associated with Supports/Surfaces. See the entry on André Valensi for more on Supports/Surfaces.

6. Alfred Pacquement, "The Supports-Surfaces Years," p. 100.

The interplay of condensation and dispersion is evident as well in *Cube,* a piece constructed of sheets of lattice that can potentially be extended into an open gridwork or compressed into dense, closed forms. Bolts hold several sheets of the lattice together to form a cube: not a closed volume like the cubes associated with minimalism but rather one that holds its form loosely, dispersing, even sketching its volume through the ligatures of the netlike, lattice panels. That all of Dezeuze's

Daniel Dezeuze
Cube, 1997
Fonds national d'art contemporain, Puteaux
Carré d'art—Musée d'art contemporain, Nîmes
Art © 2000 Artists Rights Society (ARS), New York/ADAGP, Paris

Moira Dryer

Born 1957, Toronto
Died 1992, New York

It is hard to look at Moira Dryer's work without thinking about her death at the young age of thirty-four. Perhaps an inability to make this separation has encouraged the many readings that emphasize the qualities of absence and pathos in her work, for, at first glance, it is undeniably lyrical, even emotive.[1] But these readings are in stark contrast to Dryer's own comments. For example, she writes: "I like paintings in the here and now, allowing for irritation, tension, a little anxiety and conflict." Or, again: "Conceptual/Minimal Art principles of my education have become integral in what I do and how I do it. I find fault with most of the people who paint or . . . ignore the implications [of conceptualism or minimalism]."[2]

Dryer's interest in agitation and respect for the principles with which minimalism and conceptualism broke a narrative of painting—displacing and distancing it from the artist—dispel the overly romanticized reading of her work. In addition, when asked if she felt a commitment to the idea of abstraction, Dryer replied: "Not abstraction as a religious activity. Not formalist or utopian abstraction where you look at it and are supposed to forget all of your troubles, like with drugs. That kind of abstraction is about amnesia. I like to think of my works as artifacts."[3] When we look beyond the overreading of her work in relation to her private biography and attend to its contribution in the context of *As Painting,* we might begin to understand more clearly some of her own premises and their relation to issues of painting after minimalism and conceptualism.

If, as Dryer claims, her work does not belong to a context of abstraction (despite her proclaimed debts to Ross Bleckner and Elizabeth Murray), what is it that extends the work from minimalism or conceptualism? Perhaps, simply stated, it is the interest Dryer takes in the object of painting and in the literalness of the work. This includes the literalness not only of the work's surface but also of references to objects in the world—including postage stamps, mirrors, headlines, props, title plates, fingerprints. Dryer's interest in literalness is particularly evident in the objects she makes besides her paintings: additions to the paintings themselves (like the "signature boxes" she places below several paintings as a reference to the title plates below objects in museums), as well as the sculptural objects she makes at the same time as the paintings. The influence of her background as a theater set and prop designer is evident in the relationship Dryer strives for her work to have to props, before and after the actors are on stage with them. As she describes, "the lighting would be there, and the tension and the audience would be there, but not the actors. The props had an incredible, provocative effect. I've been recalling and using that lately."[4]

In her interest in the object or "artifact," we can most clearly understand Dryer's work as stemming from minimalism and extending the limits of painting. The lessons of Judd's "specific objects" are evident in Dryer. The four grommets that pierce the lush black striped surface of *Wall of Fear* at its four corners give us access to the fact that the painting's support is a panel of wood, vulnerable to hardware. Consequently, we read its surface as a coating, covering, or staining of the wood, reminding us that painting is fundamentally a relationship of surface and support. *Untitled* shows one of the several ways Dryer borders her paintings. The edges are rimmed like a frame, and in combination with the trompe l'oeil water droplets that descend from the top edge of the work, they remind us that painting can only pretend to fool the eye. Dryer borders other paintings by cutting and scalloping the edges, painting a postage stamp pattern around the perimeter, reiterating the edges of the work. Her attention to the literal edges of her work in relation to its surface is an attention to the limits of painting.

Several other artists in *As Painting* work on wood, and, like Dryer, treat it as a surface that can be cut out or drilled into, a surface that is inherently patterned,

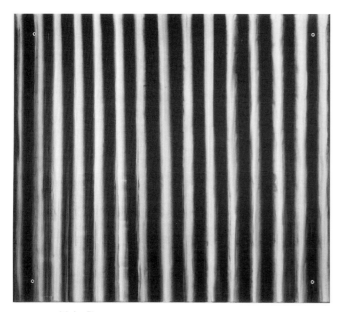

Moira Dryer
The Wall of Fear, 1990
The Estate of Moira Dryer
Courtesy Gorney, Bravin + Lee, New York

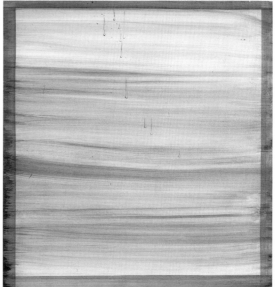

Moira Dryer
Untitled, 1991
Collection of The Newark Museum, Gift of Leonard Lieberman
in honor of Arlene Lieberman, 1996
Photo © The Newark Museum

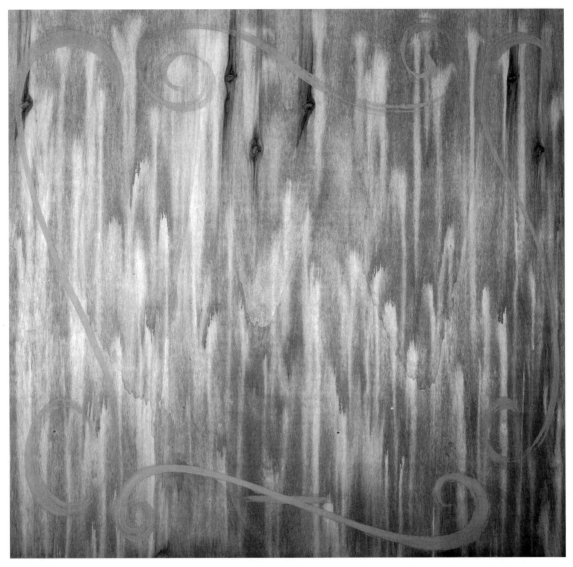

Moira Dryer
Headline, 1989
Collection Barbara Schwartz, New York
Photo © Zindman/Fremont, New York

already drawn or painted by its own grain. For example, we see Levine's response to the surface pattern of wood in her checkerboard graphite drawings on walnut, in her casein painting on mahogany (*After Ilya Chasnik*) and in the "knot paintings" of the mid eighties. Knoebel's *Sandwich 2* uses the grain of the wood on its primary surface panel, under and at the side of which he places the paint. Judd either paints the selected wooden planes of his plywood boxes or covers them in Plexiglas, thereby allowing access to the materiality and given pattern of the surface. And Dezeuze consistently stains or paints his wooden lath "ladders" or lattice panels in a way that does not obscure the fact of the wood.

As Dryer plays with the materiality of her work, she also plays at the margins of the image. *Headline* leaves the wood grain visible through the thinly applied blue and yellow casein washes, allowing the knots in the wood to arrest the surface (not unlike the grommets in *Wall of Fear*), while four lime-green flourishes border its perimeter. They read associatively, like the flourishes one might make under a signature. Other signlike images that appear on the surface of Dryer's paintings include f-holes, flower or leaf forms, traces from fingerprints, and border patterns. However, the visibility of the wood panel as surface and support returns any associative play of signs back to a relationship with the literalness of the object of painting.

The associative play of signs and the objectness of painting are not mutually exclusive interests, as the range in Dryer's work clearly demonstrates. Her works, like Frank Stella's early paintings, often situate a "particular emblem, drawn from the common repertory of signs—stars, crosses, ring-interlocks, etc.," and Rosalind Krauss's assessment of Stella's black paintings seems pertinent in this regard: "The real achievement of these paintings is to have fully immersed themselves in meaning, but to have made meaning itself a function of surface—of the external, the public, or a space that is in no way a signifier of the a priori, or of the privacy of intention."[5]

Dryer's recognition of the central problematic of the painting's surface includes both its literalness and the emblems or signs that are a "function of surface," a surface whose meaning is crucially associated with a public or external space—and thus distinguished from the prevalent interpretations in which it is seen only as a reflection of Dryer's self or loss of self.

L. L.

1. Jeremy Gilbert-Rolfe's essay "Beyond Absence" is one of the best for avoiding this reading; it is reprinted in *Beyond Piety: Critical Essays on the Visual Arts, 1986–1993* (Cambridge: Cambridge University Press, 1995), pp. 150–66.

2. The first quotation is from an interview with Klaus Ottman published in *Journal of Contemporary Art* 2, no. 1 (spring/summer 1989): 50–57. The second is from Dryer's artist's statement from 1984–85 reprinted in the exhibition catalogue for *After the Fall: Aspects of Abstract Painting since 1970* (Staten Island, New York: Newhouse Center for Contemporary Art, Snug Harbor Cultural Center, 1997), p. 126.

3. Peter Schjeldahl, "Remembered Life," in *Moira Dryer* (New York: Mary Boone Gallery, 1990), p. 1.

4. Interview with Klaus Ottman, *Journal of Contemporary Art*.

5. Rosalind E. Krauss, "Sense and Sensibility: Reflection on Post 60's Sculpture," *Artforum* 12, no. 3 (November 1973): 47.

François Dufrêne
Born 1930, Paris
Died 1982, Paris

Dufrêne's "underneaths" of posters were first exhibited in 1959, exactly ten years after Jacques Villeglé and Raymond Hains first declared that an anonymously lacerated poster from the street constituted a work of art. Through his own interest in posters and the practice of *décollage*, Dufrêne became one of the *affichistes*, the group that included Villeglé, Hains, and Mimmo Rotella and derived its name from the use of public posters (*affiches*) as primary material. But before the exhibition of his own posters, Dufrêne's primary interest was in experimental writing, public recitals, and performances. Between 1946 and 1953, he was a prominent member of the *lettriste* movement, along with Jean-Louis Brau, Gil Wolman, and Guy Debord. (In 1957 this movement became the Situationist International, but Dufrêne and the other *affichistes* did not join, in spite of their initial proximity.) As an active *lettriste*, Dufrêne presented unrehearsed versions of "concrete" music and poetry that he called *crirythmes*, which emphasized the repetition of phonetic automatisms and sonic interferences and included recitals of ready-made sources such as phone books and dictionary entries. Dufrêne also participated in all the activities of the *nouveaux réalistes* as well as in several Fluxus happenings in the sixties, continuing such performances until his death in 1982. A tribute to his work was organized by the Association Polyphonix at the Centre Pompidou a year later.[1]

Dufrêne himself acknowledged the difficult question of the exact rapport between his experimental writing, phonetic language games, and the visual practices for which he was also known. Alain Jouffroy suggests that a concern with the image rejoins Dufrêne's central preoccupation with sound by "exploring its underside (*l'en-deçà*) and applying equivalent operations to the image to those practiced on the voice and in writing."[2] In this sense, phonic, written, and visual language are exposed to their simultaneous articulation and disarticulation—a turning of words that is also a turning over of words. Just as his visual practices exposed the underneaths of posters, so his written and spoken work exposed the "underneaths" of language (its "material," its "concrete" utterance and iterability, the "glue" that holds words and sounds together), an appeal to language and its "unconscious" that became a decisive focus in numerous intellectual and creative contexts after the war. If Dufrêne insists on a radical displacement or *détournement* of all semantic and syntactical conventions, he does so by opening writing and its graphic analogy to forms of fragmentation that break apart the very possibility of analogical thinking and thus open language to further forms of rearticulation and invention.

Considering the underneaths of posters within the context of the *nouveaux réalistes* might also suggest that the "real" to which the public was exposed after the war—conspicuously, the space of advertising and consumer culture—has as its underside the surfaces that get effaced in the seduction of all spectacle culture. In this sense, Dufrêne opened the pictorial space in which the poster then found itself into a space that *interrupts* the real, radically suspending all knowledge derived from immediate forms of legibility and visibility. But this reading remains at once too literal and too metaphorical, and never fully adequate to the specificity of the work before us.

Dufrêne's *affichiste* practice also finds resonance in pop art. For any appeal to the space of popular and consumer culture is also an appeal to the ways in which words and images come together in order to assume for the urban pedestrian a charged signification. As a response to this culture, pop art can be characterized by its quotation of these signs, so that the actual painting of the surfaces is organized such that each element can be recognized as a code or metaphor, as an identifiable sign whose cultural significance and recognition is the measure of the work's critical success.

François Dufrêne
Où je perçois personnellement en perspective persane, 1973
Courtesy Galerie Véronique Smagghe, Paris
Art © 2000 Artists Rights Society (ARS), New York/ADAGP, Paris

Dufrêne's underneaths of posters have a fundamentally different appeal, whatever their initial rapport with popular or consumer culture. This is especially evident when we turn to *Où je perçois personnellement en perspective persane,* a title whose reference to seeing in "Persian perspective" already suggests a transformation in assumed perceptual conventions. The surface of the work enacts a series of reversals, resisting any reading or decoding of culturally inscribed signs—the very

François Dufrêne
Dessous d'affiche, 1962
Courtesy Galerie Véronique Smagghe, Paris
Photo: Ricci Gaillard
Art © 2000 Artists Rights Society (ARS), New York/ADAGP, Paris

reading for which the original poster is, of course, the paradigmatic occasion. Instead, the different layerings of colored scraps of paper meticulously scraped off walls show the color seeping through from the back (the once legible "front" of the poster pasted to the wall).[3] The color we see is always slightly effaced, bleached out, diffused, not only by the effects of sunlight or time on the poster but by the materiality of the paper itself. The degree to which the colored ink is effaced from its original saturation stems from the thickness of the support and the paper's degree of porousness. The mixture of the glue (first applied to the "back" of the poster when attached to the wall), combined with the saturation of colored ink mechanically printed onto (or into) the paper, determines the diffusion of the color and its subsequent layerings as it seeps through the paper's thickness. The perceptual effect is thus determined by the amount of glue originally applied, the degree to which it eats into the support and blends with the colored inks (through their shared acidity), the ways in which it transforms the paper's texture and dries the surface, and the supplementary effects of Dufrêne's regluing from behind the inverted surface and initiating this entire temporal, chromatic, and spatial transformation yet again. The glue also enacts the displacement between the recto and verso, so that the "original" glue is now, temporally, the first surface that we see rather than (as in both the original poster and in numerous collage practices) the first surface applied and the first effaced in the subsequent layering.

This description of technical process and materials demands a simultaneous transformation of the work's theoretical, perceptual, and conceptual implications. It also situates Dufrêne's work in proximity to Hantaï's painting, as well as to the play of recto and verso that appears in numerous places throughout *As Painting,* from Richter's figurative pieces to all the work that implicates the wall on which it is shown and which is the condition of that exposure—including that of Buren, Bochner, Ryman, Dezeuze, and Barré. The temporally and spatially inscribed diffusions of color and structure also recall the work of such artists as Apfelbaum, Bishop, Rouan, and Welling, but it is in the work and writings of Bonnefoi that this rethinking of the materials and theoretical implications of collage is most fully explored as a measure of painting's continued strategy of *détournement*. For that revolution, as Dufrêne insists, there are no models—no prescribed language games—that can be secured in advance of their permanent reinvention.

P. A.

1. The best introduction to Dufrêne's work is *François Dufrêne,* Cahiers de l'Abbaye Ste-Croix, no. 60 (Les Sables d'Olonne: Musée de l'Abbaye Ste-Croix; Villeneuve d'Ascq: Musée d'art moderne, 1988).

2. Quoted in a collection of commentaries put together by Véronique Smagghe, to whom we wish to express our thanks.

3. Dufrêne insists that this attention to scraping marks his difference from both Hains and Villeglé, who are concerned more with the appropriation of the poster from its original environment. The work of the *affichistes* is explored from a different angle in the entry on Villeglé.

Simon Hantaï
Born 1922, Bia, Hungary
Lives and works in Paris

Simon Hantaï first painted on a folded canvas around 1950, and the result was, as nearly as one can tell, inconsequential. The folded and unfolded canvases that he began making around 1960 are an entirely different matter, for he obviously discovered in them a territory capable of sustaining a practice of painting for nearly forty years now. The impact of his work on younger painters has been equally strong, giving a crucial impetus to a number of further practices, often quite sharply opposed among themselves.

Hantaï found his way to France from his native Hungary in the late 1940s and was rapidly drawn into the circle around André Breton. His exhibition catalogues date his break with Breton to 1954, occasioned by a deep disagreement about abstraction and the work of Jackson Pollock in particular. Hantaï is thus to be numbered among the earliest of Pollock's French audience. Although his work in the fifties does move strongly toward abstraction, the pieces that have been shown to date reveal little evidence of any direct attempt to take up the look or procedures of American abstraction. Hantaï's tendencies at this time seem appropriately qualified as calligraphic and residually biomorphic. Toward the end of the fifties, his experiments become increasingly engaged with questions of technique, and the techniques that most draw him are notable for the ways in which they all involve an extraordinary slowing down, even routinization, of painterly gesture—as if automatism, whether as imagined by surrealism or as one might think it at work in Pollock's painting, were being shifted to some entirely different ground. *Ecriture Rose* committed Hantaï to writing out the Catholic liturgy for each day of the year across the entire surface of an immense canvas that had little other development or incident. *A Galla Placidia* (the title is from 1997) made its demands differently: a canvas built up out of a certain play of form and color

was covered over with what amounted to a dark ground, and Hantaï then undertook to scrape his way back down to the underpainting, using as his distinctly awkward tool the bell of an old-fashioned alarm clock. A third painting one might consider as belonging to this same moment is a monochrome in gold leaf, another labor of patience and one in which the gesture that the other works variously routinize or render both difficult and repetitious is now all but completely effaced.[1]

If one takes these three works to constitute a single precondition for the emergence of folding as a method, certainly the first thing to notice will be the ways they seek an impersonal gesture within a certain protraction of time. One will also note that the three paintings seem to equate the impersonal and the all-over, albeit in distinctly different ways. None can be taken as purely formal exercises; all are in some sense spiritual exercises as well, and they are in this sense directly connected with the strong ethical force that has been a constant feature of Hantaï's work and its reception.

The first series of folded paintings—variously called *Mariales* or *Manteaux de la vierge*—breaks down into four subseries, an arrangement that reflects the breadth of Hantaï's experiments within what was not yet fully or clearly a medium for him. Some of these early foldings take the folds as a material fact to be preserved by the thick and stiff oil painting; others take a stronger interest in the flattened unfolding of what has been reserved from the applied paint. Some take folding as a way of working an essentially bare canvas; others take it as a way of reworking a prior act of painting (in some cases one will feel comfortable saying that Hantaï is using this procedure to address such figures as Picasso or Pollock); still others explore successive foldings and refoldings on a single canvas. Later series are more closely focused; the *Catamurons* of 1963–64 confine the folded part of the painting to a more or less central area, and the *Saucisses* (later called *Panses*) that follow them explore repeated foldings in and out of a fixed oval shape, allowing no area of the canvas to remain unpainted. The notably Matissean *Meuns*, from

Simon Hantaï
M.c.8, 1962
Collection of the artist, Paris
Photo: Sabine Ahlbrand-Dornseif

Simon Hantaï
Blancs, 1973
Collection Musée d'art moderne de la ville de Paris
Photo © Photothèque des musées de la ville de Paris

1966–68, are fully made out of the reserves created in the folding, bringing Hantaï to his primary understanding of *pliage* as medium in which "the unpainted paints." The works that follow continue to explore this proposition in various concentrated forms up through the *Tabulas*, in which folding is explicitly and operationally connected to the tying of a grid of knots that determines the final canvas as a grid of colored areas each of which contains its own more arbitrary unfolded articulation. In 1982, following an exhibition of extremely large, loosely stretched *Tabulas* in Bordeaux, as well as a major exhibition as the French representative to the Venice Biennale, Hantaï withdrew from exhibition altogether.

In 1998 and 1999, Hantaï re-emerged with three major exhibitions in rapid succession. The new work consisted of a distinctive further "unpainting" of the *Tabulas* shown at Bordeaux: the *Laissées*, or "Leftovers,"[2] as these new pieces are called, are made by cutting up the earlier works—which had spent some time being composted in Hantaï's yard—and then stretching them (with whatever restitching was necessary to doing so) as individual paintings. In retrospect, it is tempting to say that such cutting had been available to Hantaï's work since the *Meuns* and was deeply implied by everything in his practice that pushed toward the realization of painting's surface as all edge. Hantaï appears to have been able to take this up into the painting itself only through the radical caesura of his withdrawal from painting. The *Laissés* are thus the unfolding of a reserve at the heart of Hantaï's career. Like that created by the folding of the canvas prior to its painting, this is a reserve that articulates or rearticulates the whole.

The most curious moment of this late work is undoubtedly Hantaï's burial—and in some cases destruction—of elements of his past work, a moment to which he repeatedly recurs in the correspondence with Georges Didi-Huberman included in this catalogue. The least one can say here is that such treatment of the work is a constant in Hantaï's career—studio shots show still-folded canvases variously hanging on the wall or sitting on the floor with no particular care given them, and Hantaï repeatedly presents his painting of them as an essentially inattentive, even mindless, activity. The evidences of this rough or casual treatment are obvious in the finished work, markers of the way in which the operations that shape Hantaï's work are irreducibly material and reminders that the force within that work, which one may be inclined to describe variously as spiritual or ethical, imagines nothing beyond that condition: as if it is always the mantle of the Virgin and not the Virgin herself that Hantaï invokes.

s. m.

1. For Hantaï's work of the fifties see Anne Baldassari, *Simon Hantaï* (Paris: Centre Georges Pompidou, 1992). For Hantaï's own valuable notes on his work, see the catalogue for *Donation Simon Hantaï* (Paris: Musée d'art moderne de la ville de Paris, 1998).

2. Jacques Derrida's "Restitutions of the Truth in Pointing" actively works the relations among *laissées, laisser,* and *lacer* in ways pertinent to Hantaï's work. See his *The Truth in Painting,* trans. Geoff Bennington and Ian McLeod (Chicago: University of Chicago Press, 1987), and Jacques Derrida, *Le toucher: Jean-Luc Nancy, accompagné par des travaux de lectures de Simon Hantaï* (Paris: Editions Galilée, 1999).

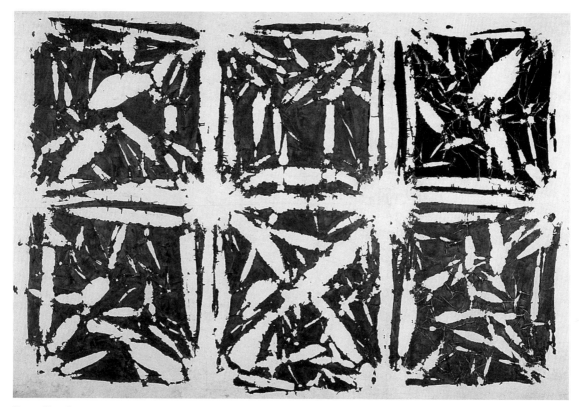

Simon Hantaï
Tabula, 1980
Collection of the artist, Paris
Photo: J. C. Mazur
© Centre Georges Pompidou

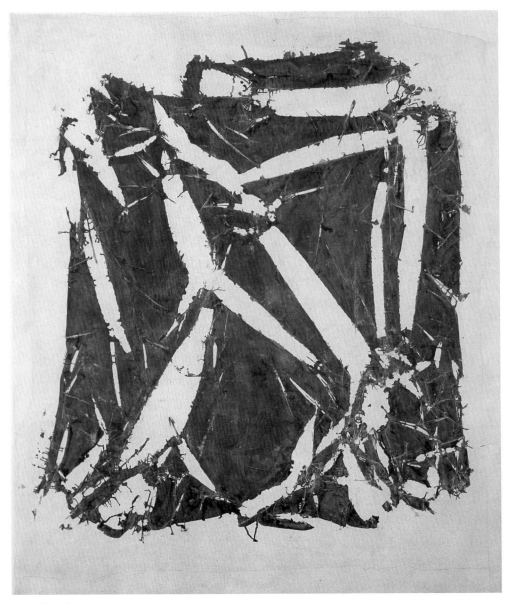

Simon Hantaï
Laissée, 1981–89
Collection of the artist, Paris
Photo: J. C. Mazur
© Centre Georges Pompidou

Simon Hantaï
Laissée, 1981–95
Collection of the artist, Paris
Photo: J. C. Mazur
© Centre Georges Pompidou

Simon Hantaï
Stèle (en mémoire de Denis), 1984
Private collection, France
Photo: J. C. Mazur
© Centre Georges Pompidou

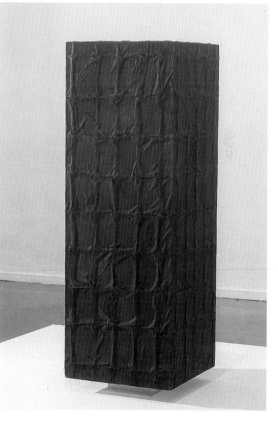

Simon Hantaï
Installation view at Westfälisches Landesmuseum für Kunst und
Kulturgeschichte, Münster
Photo: Sabine Ahlbrand-Dornseif

Donald Judd
Born 1928, Excelsior Springs, Missouri
Died 1994, New York

In a note of 1965 I wrote that form, which I don't like so much as a word, and color should be "intelligent" without being ordered.

—Donald Judd

In 1994, *Artforum* published Donald Judd's last essay, "Some Aspects of Color in General and Red and Black in Particular," as part of an issue to commemorate his death in February of that year. The essay opens with the claim that "material, space and color are the main aspects of visual art," continues with the passage cited above, and as its title announces, highlights Judd's preoccupation with color throughout his career.[1] This emphasis provides us with a lens through which to interpret not only Judd's writings but his work. Indeed, though many of his texts focus on the closures and possibilities of contemporary art, his own work demonstrates and emphasizes the intelligibility of color, material, and space, opening toward the accessibility of parts and wholes foregrounded in the celebrated essay "Specific Objects."[2]

On the fate of color in contemporary painting, Judd writes in the 1994 essay: "The achievement of Pollock and the others [Newman, Rothko, Still, Noland, and Louis] meant that the century's development of color could continue no further on a flat surface. Its adventitious capacity to destroy naturalism also could not continue. Perhaps Pollock, Newman, Rothko and Still were the last painters. . . . Color to continue had to occur in space." Judd's own movement to three dimensions is doubly motivated by an impulse away from the exhaustion of painting's space (its illusionism, compositional generalities, etc.) and from painting's inability to explore color in new ways. In retrospect, we might even understand this move as primarily motivated by the search for a space that can accommodate aspects of color exhausted by painting.

Several other developments can be traced through the evolution of color, as well as material and space, in Judd's work.[3] After abandoning the flat, two-dimensional space that limits painting, in the early sixties he made his first three-dimensional "specific objects" from plywood, which he painted cadmium red and black. He moved from plywood to metal in the mid sixties due to the uneven absorption of the paint on the plywood surface. During this time, he also introduced Plexiglas into the work, which allows one to see through to the structure and, at the same time, adds color. The Plexiglas, like the metallic surfaces, also introduces a level of gloss and reflection to the otherwise spartan structures.

In 1974 Judd returned to making works in plywood, mainly in order to better accommodate the increased scale necessary to pursue the relationship of his objects to architectural spaces, which provided him with a way to incorporate another kind of specific fact into his work. The return to plywood also provided a platform for some of his more experimental divisions of space. He created open boxes with variously placed internal planes, like the lid of a box that has slipped obliquely inside.

Though Judd's work attempts to be fully transparent to its structure, fully present or graspable, a listing of the materials, measurements, shapes, and colors does not completely take the measure of the work, despite Judd's own proclamations of the work's intelligibility. Instead, we find what Rosalind Krauss calls a "lived illusion" as opposed to a pictorial illusion—"an illusion that plays off the illusory quality of the thing itself as it presents itself to vision alone."[4] Our position in relation to Judd's objects, the proportion of their parts, their height on the wall and their color, all produce more than a listing of their attributes. To experience the specificity of a work by Judd is to realize that this specificity gives way to its insides, underneaths, and perceptual surplus. The surplus of color, material, and space that one experiences is dependent on the apparent simplicity of the work, an intelligible simplicity that is necessary to frame this perceptual excess.

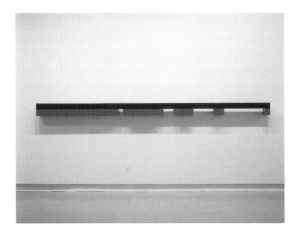

Donald Judd
Untitled (Progression), 1965
Collection Wexner Center for the Arts, The Ohio State
University; purchased in part with funds from the National
Endowment for the Arts
Photo: Lynette Molnar
Art © Donald Judd Estate/VAGA, New York

freed by color's ability to be material and yet still to produce obdurate and lived existence in three dimensions.

Judd's strategy is more complex in the four-unit wall piece, *Untitled* (1987). He plays with the placement of a single plane of plywood within each box, positioning it like a sliding door at different intervals from the sides and halfway between the front and back. An ensemble of shifting proportions is emphasized by the quantity of color exposed—in this case, the red of the Plexiglas that lines the back wall of each box. Moving left or right of center in relation to the piece reveals the

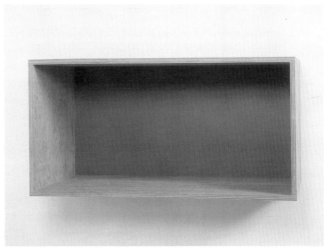

Donald Judd
Untitled, 1978
Courtesy Paula Cooper Gallery, New York
Photo: Tom Powel
Art © Donald Judd Estate/VAGA, New York

It is perhaps most surprising that *Untitled* (1978), the simplest of Judd's pieces in *As Painting,* can operate within these terms of "lived illusion," transforming a literal object toward a perceptual object within a highly reduced vocabulary of color and form. The brilliance of the cadmium red light paint on the back plane produces an exaggeration of the specificity of the whole through the saturated particularity of the color, itself focused and amplified by the decisively proportioned and "simple" plywood box. The color is fully intelligible, material and namable. This clarity exceeds apparent accessibility and literal specificity. And it is precisely this insistence on the specificity of color that we find repeated in his last essay: "Color is like material. It is one way or another, but it obdurately exists. Its existence as it is is the main fact and not what it might mean, which may be nothing." The meaning of the need for color in painting that so eluded Judd is

Donald Judd
Untitled, 1987
Courtesy Paula Cooper Gallery, New York
Photo: R. Wilson
Art © Donald Judd Estate/VAGA, New York

shifting combination of shadow added to the red coloration, as well as the changing proportion of the boxes' open and closed planes. The spacing between the four boxes derives from one of the dimensions, which returns any reference for the work to itself, without illusion or allusion to anything outside of it. And yet, in the mutability of color and shadow, the play of open and closed planes, and the spatial engagement created by the stacking and placing of the work on the wall, we have the productive collision of a "lived" phenomenology and positivism, of perceptual objects and specific objects.

Judd leaves us with a number of questions: If color is to "happen," does it have to happen in "space"? How might color be "differently intelligible" as painting? And, what does a "specificity" of color mean for painting? We find these same questions variously explored in two- and three-dimensional space elsewhere in *As Painting*, notably in the work of Richter, Knoebel, Apfelbaum, Cadere, Hantaï, Truitt, and Buren.

L. L.

1. Donald Judd, "Some Aspects of Color in General and Red and Black in Particular," *Artforum* 32, no. 10 (summer 1994): 70–79, 110–14.

2. See Donald Judd, "Specific Objects," in *Complete Writings: 1959–1975* (Halifax: Press of the Nova Scotia College of Art and Design; New York: New York University Press, 1975), pp. 181–89.

3. For a useful chronology of Judd's career, see Barbara Haskell, *Donald Judd* (New York: Whitney Museum of American Art in association with W. W. Norton & Co., 1988).

4. Rosalind E. Krauss, "Allusion and Illusion in Donald Judd," *Artforum* 4, no. 9 (May 1966): 26.

Imi Knoebel

Born 1940, Dessau, Germany

Lives and works in Düsseldorf

Schattenraum 4, a large, Masonite floor-structure standing opposite black monochrome panels on an adjacent wall, brings together several strands in the work of Imi Knoebel.[1] In its formal simplicity, the piece refers to the three-dimensional volume of sculpture and the two-dimensional surface of painting. The construction is taller than the viewer, and it is possible to walk through the gap between the structure and the panels. But there is no one position where the piece "coheres," and no position from which the monochrome panel can be faced fully from the front. The viewer's relation to *Schattenraum 4* is always anamorphic.

The black panels also refer to the monochrome in the history of painting and specifically to Malevich's *Black Square,* a consistent reference in Knoebel's work since the early sixties and the translation of *The Non-Objective World* into German. Yet the reference is perhaps less to *Black Square* as such than to its belonging to a "space," the installation of works in the famous *0.10* exhibition of 1915. The placement of the wall panels in *Schattenraum 4* is thus not only part of Knoebel's consistent reference to Malevich and to a Russian tradition but also a way of rethinking the "space" of painting after the absoluteness—the degree zero—that the monochrome and Malevich represent to the history of art.[2]

The title of *Schattenraum 4* further recalls Knoebel's early experiments with exterior and interior projections, such as *Innenprojektion.* In these early projects, we begin to see emerging an interest in the relation between the source of projection, the "space" of a projection, and the materialized and dematerialized surfaces on which the projection comes into view. As an extension of such work, *Schattenraum 4* projects areas of invisibility that structure what is visible. Situated in its interstitial space, our bodies also occupy the work's "shadow space," a proximity that is physical and si-multaneously unlocatable. This proximity is all the more disturbing in that the structure also figures here as a tomb or crypt.

The use of Masonite extends Knoebel's earlier *Raum 19,* an "installation" of Masonite structures and thus a dispersion and concentration of the most elementary materials of sculpture and painting.[3] With its pieces arranged so that the viewer is unable to enter the work, this three-dimensional space is thus framed more like a painting than an environmental installation. As Bernhard Bürgi has suggested, "*Raum 19,* though containing every aspect of sculptural installation, touches upon the essential questions of painting; this clarifies a collection of stretchers and their parts, which don't function as carriers of the picture, but refer to the absence of painterly craft."[4]

Both *Raum 19* and *Schattenraum 4* recall Knoebel's various projects with architectural spaces, projects that themselves recall different environments in the history of constructivism and de Stijl. In relation to *Schattenraum 4,* these references suggest the implication of sculpture in a pictorial space, of pictorial space in the volumetric space of sculpture, and of sculptural and pictorial space in and as the space of architecture. At the same time, the Masonite constructions suggest ways in which exterior architectural spaces become incorporated within exhibition spaces: a redefinition of interior space, as Johannes Stüttgen argues, in terms of its "pure exteriority." Painting and sculpture are thus exposed to their architectural dimensions, and architecture itself is now opened to "the concrete materialization of the pictorial." In Knoebel's work, this opening could be seen as constituting an extension of painting into its own radical exteriority, not the overcoming of painting in the environment of an installation. Extending this claim, we could say that his extraordinary *Genter Raum* is closest to what it might mean to inhabit the "thinking space" of painting *as* painting.[5]

Schattenraum 4 additionally evokes similarities with a number of minimalist exhibitions and simultaneously recalls Judd's notion of "specific objects" (a

Imi Knoebel
Schattenraum 4, 1988
Collection Centre Georges Pompidou, Paris
Musée national d'art moderne/Centre de création
industrielle
Photo: Adam Rzepka
© Centre Georges Pompidou

term frequently employed in discussions of Knoebel's work). However, Knoebel's interest is not, arguably, a movement *beyond* painting as much as an imagination of what remains of the lessons of Malevich or Mondrian after minimalist practices, and of what remains of Kelly, Stella, and Ryman after these same lessons. It is precisely through this history that Knoebel's exploration of color comes to the foreground.

Color is understood not as what covers the elements after they are assembled but as the hinge of the construction, what articulates the work *as* a structure, covering a surface but also lying behind or between two surfaces. A constitutive aspect of Knoebel's various series of "shaped" canvases (or of the permutations through which certain series unfold), color also inhabits the margins of painting, in both the *Sandwich* series and the *Odyshape* series, which takes up the use of aluminum begun in 1991.

In *Odyshape 1,* the center of the painting is a conspicuously worked red monochrome; the center of *Sandwich 2* equally foregrounds the texture of the

Imi Knoebel
Innenprojektion, 1969
Photo courtesy Carmen Knoebel

Imi Knoebel
Raum 19, 1967–68
Fiberboard and wood
Dimensions variable
Collection Dia Art Foundation, New York
Photo: Nic Tenwiggenhorn

Imi Knoebel
Genter Raum, 1980
Lacquer on plywood
459 parts, dimensions variable
Installation view at Dia Art Foundation, New York
Photo courtesy Carmen Knoebel

Imi Knoebel
Odyshape I, 1994
Collection Six Friedrich, Munich
Photo: Nic Tenwiggenhorn

Imi Knoebel
Sandwich 2, 1992
Collection of the artist, Düsseldorf
Photo: Nic Tenwiggenhorn

wood's surface. But in both cases, the initial face of the work is but one in a series of layers. Extensions of colored, structural forms extend beyond and behind the surface of *Odyshape 1,* as if a painting by Mondrian had been reconstructed in its sculptural thickness. In *Sandwich 2,* three sheets of wood are fixed to the wall with nails, but the colored sides of the work give it a sculptural dimension with multiple, anamorphic viewpoints. Only the parts of the painting that are nearly invisible have been painted—including the undersides of the two outer sheets and the front and rear surfaces of the sheet sandwiched between—so that the viewer sees paint only on the extreme edges of the inner sheets.

Knoebel's works refuse any notion of composition by stressing the structural articulation of the work as its simultaneous dislocation. As such, they foreground less the question of assemblage than the delineation of the work's space. Such work is not in pursuit of an autonomous form: it demands the rearticulation of line as edge, division, cut, shape, and experimental geometry and thus a constant rethinking of the limits that define the work's interiority as "pure exteriority." In presenting this possibility for painting, Knoebel's work is an invitation to imagine its delimitation as a measure in which color begins to assume its "space" and thus also an invitation to rethink painting's historical and structural limits. As Max Wechsler reminds us, such rethinking would now constitute a more just measure of the "picture's worldliness" within the (non)objective world we inhabit. If only ever anamorphically.

P. A.

1. On Knoebel, see especially *Imi Knoebel: Works 1968–1996* (Amsterdam: Stedelijk Museum and Cantz, 1996). I am indebted here in particular to the essays by Max Wechsler and Johannes Stüttgen.

2. For a further reading of Malevich in related terms, see Yve-Alain Bois, "Malevitch, le carré, le degré zéro," *Macula* 1 (1976): 28–49.

3. The title refers to the number of the studio given to Knoebel in 1965 by Joseph Beuys, his teacher at the Kunstakademie in Düsseldorf. He shared the studio with Imi Giese and, later, Jörg Immendorf and Blinky Palermo.

4. Quoted in *Imi Knoebel: Works 1968–1996,* p. 280.

5. The last two quotations are from Max Wechsler. *Raum 19* and the *Genter Raum* were both reinstalled at Dia in New York in 1987. See the interview with Johannes Stüttgen in *Imi Knoebel* (New York: Dia Art Foundation, 1987), pp. 26–32.

Sherrie Levine
Born 1947, Hazelton, Pennsylvania
Lives and works in New York

> Translatability is an essential quality of certain works, which is not to say that it is essential for the works themselves that they be translated; it means, rather, that a specific significance inherent in the original manifests itself in its translatability.
>
> —Walter Benjamin[1]

Sherrie Levine's reputation continues to be centered on her direct photographic reproductions of earlier photographic work, accounts of which are often offered without any particular reference to the work that both precedes and follows from this relatively early moment. This reading has its costs not only for any broader understanding of her strikingly various work but also for the appropriation work itself. *As Painting* brings together Levine's very early president collages, both as collage and in their original form as projection, with several more recent works—a wall piece after Blinky Palermo and one of two photographic series after Monet's paintings of the cathedral at Rouen—and offers them both as crucial elements in any understanding of Levine's work as a whole and as significant elements within the larger problematic of the exhibition.

The series of president collages sets a range of images of woman within the frame of an essentially masculine economy. The work depends on a peculiar form of "collage" in which one image (the presidential profile found on various denominations of U.S. coinage) is used to cut out the other. As collage this series is clearly closer to Matisse than to Picasso, but it's also finally closer to, indeed is a form of, silhouette cutting, a practice not usually described as collage at all. If the description of these works as collage seems fairly natural and unforced, it is undoubtedly because the pieces set two images in juxtaposition with one another such that the one is felt as if laid under or over the other.

But of course, this is not strictly true of these pieces; the actual play is between the bounding edge and what is markedly frontal within that edge. This edge is surprisingly complex, and as is so often the case in Levine's work, it can be hard to make out the exact limits of the intuitions the edge draws on: How much, for example, of the low relief of the coin's form does it carry with it? How far does the edge carry with it some echo of the coin's reversibility (and so, how far does this piece carry as one of its dimensions an implied obverse)? What exactly do we experience as "figure" and as "ground" when images are played through or across one another in this way? One's particular answer to the question

Sherrie Levine
Presidential Profile, 1979
Collection of the artist, New York
Installation view at The Kitchen, New York
Photo courtesy Paula Cooper Gallery, New York

Sherrie Levine
Untitled (President: 5), 1979
Collection The Museum of Contemporary Art, Los Angeles;
Purchased with funds provided by Councilman Joel Wachs

probably matters less than one's sense of its pertinence to the work's capacity to appear as it does.

The particular difficulty of these pieces is clearly a consequence of their photographic basis. This basis complicates, perhaps baffles, attempts to make out the nature of the "collage" in terms familiar from painting. The effect depends on a quasi-transparency: one image showing through another without either posing any direct visual obstruction to the other. This structure is rendered absolute in the appropriated images Levine began making in 1979. The president collages do much to make clear the exceedingly difficult job the edge is once again asked to do in these new works—marking the cropped continuation of the world in the original image and remarking that cropping in its appropriated repetition. One's sense of a shifting edge here is continuous with one's sense of an original photograph that is simply of its object and an appropriation that includes both that object and its photographer or viewer.[2] If asked what counts as "composition" in the original as contrasted with its appropriation, one will probably say that the original is composed across its surface and by the determination of the limits of that surface, whereas the appropriation is composed at right angles to that surface, in or as a consequence of the temporal depth that is the one's being "after" the other.

Levine's photographic reworkings of Monet's cathedral series take still further what is already a complex dialogue about transparency and opacity, time and depth, photography and painting, and the layerings and lacings that are variously proper to the one or the other and through which they are bound to one another. Like the earlier work, these prints are thoroughly photographic, making themselves out of the camera's time and its special way of making images "after" its object—both later than that object and, importantly, caused by it. Levine's prints after Monet's series pull apart the layers indissolubly joined in the painting, sending the color to one destination and the work of drawing to another. In so doing, the prints also separate out two sequences fused within Monet's practice—one

Sherrie Levine
After Ilya Chasnik, 1984
Collection of the artist, New York

Sherrie Levine
Cathedral: 1, 1995
Courtesy the artist and Margo Leavin Gallery, Los Angeles

ordered to a reduced and abstracted system of color, the other oriented to light and shadow and the repetition of gesture—as if performing a kind of semiotic analysis of both the individual paintings and their claims to individuality within the series they constitute. Like the appropriated images, the *Cathedrals* use the camera to discover a seriality grounded in contiguity—the photographic prolongation of the work opening up in it what is already beyond it—rather than in the process of substitution, of standing for, that we more standardly take

Sherrie Levine
Romulus and Remus, 1998
Graphite on walnut
2 panels, 12 $^1/_4$ × 7 $^1/_2$ × $^7/_8$ in. (31 × 19 × 2 cm) each
Private collection
Photo: Adam Reich
Photo courtesy Paula Cooper Gallery

Sherrie Levine
After Blinky Palermo, 1996
Courtesy the artist
Installation view at Städtisches Museum Leverkusen,
Schloss Morsbroich, Germany, 1996
Photo: Nic Tenwiggenhorn

to model abstraction and representation alike. In Levine's hands, repetition never returns to the same but instead makes visible a work of displacement, always profoundly temporal. The camera plays a crucial role in making this dimension of repetition clear, but once it has become clear, Levine's work is no longer bound to photography and opens, as in *After Blinky Palermo*, on to a more general practice that is irreducible to mere ironic quotation: Palermo does not cease being a radical colorist and painter in Levine's repetition of him, but his work is taken up into a logic of repetition and displacement that now appears as a part of its initial condition.

S. M.

1. Walter Benjamin, "The Task of the Translator," trans. Harry Zohn, in *Selected Writings, Vol. 1, 1913–1926,* ed. Marcus Bullock and Michael W. Jennings (Cambridge: Harvard University Press, 1996), p. 254.

2. Howard Singerman, Levine's best critic, offers a much more detailed version of a closely related argument in "Seeing Sherrie Levine," *October* 67 (winter 1994): 78–107. Levine's collage work is usefully seen in relation to Gilles Deleuze's remarks at the close of the preface to *Difference and Repetition,* trans. Paul Patton (New York: Columbia University Press, 1994). These remarks are especially interesting given the interest Deleuze takes elsewhere in the work of both Bonnefoi and Hantaï.

Agnes Martin

Born 1912, Maklin, Saskatchewan, Canada
Lives and works in New York and Galisteo, New Mexico

Untitled (1962) remains unusual in Agnes Martin's career, for it is one of only a few works produced between 1957 and 1963 that incorporate "found" objects. The brass nails punctuating the surface are usually considered part of an early experiment, a practice that Martin definitively put aside by 1963, when she found such constructions "too indebted to material reality."[1] This decision to abandon reference to the material world reinforces a narrative that seeks to efface all reference in her work to material reality (including landscapes) in favor of an increasing emphasis on "abstract" qualities. It is as if the very materiality of the "found" object is what must be overcome in our contemplation of the work's path toward absolute, if unattainable, "perfection." The frequent exhibition and reproduction of *Untitled* in recent years might thus suggest a permanent measure of the material world that Martin's paintings attempt to overcome in their drive toward a spiritual ideal. But it is precisely this use of nails that opens another reading of the painting, one that remains irreducible to this privileged narrative.[2]

    Untitled appears to embody all the elements associated with a painting by Martin: the coincidence of a monochrome surface with graphite lines, the "dissonance" between the square format and the drawn rectangular grid, a nonhierarchical relation between elements, and a systematic sense of reduction toward what is essential. The grid does not exist prior to the placement of the nails but is part of an established equilibrium, drawing the various elements together into an enclosed, unifiable whole. The painting thus appears to confirm Martin's frequent claim that her work aspires to a timeless, "classical" ideal.

    Seen in close proximity, the symmetry of the painting is effaced, and we are drawn toward the materiality of its surface—to the luminous transparency of the priming, to the exquisite precision and tracing of

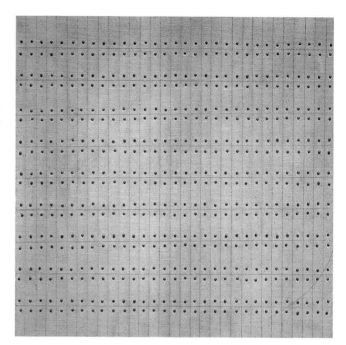

Agnes Martin
Untitled, 1962
Collection Museum of Contemporary Art, San Diego;
Museum purchase, 1976.18
Photo: Philipp Scholz Rittermann

the graphite line as it picks up the irregular weave of the support. This initial proximity to the painting's textures gives way to a more kinesthetic relation as we move back and view the painting from a distance. A prominent feature of Martin's paintings, this movement away from the surface opens "sequences of illusions of textures that change as viewing distance changes."[3]

    The placement of the nails is anchored by their lateral arrangement, with the surface organized so that we remark the symmetry of the nails *within* and *across* the modular repetition of rectangular boxes. Our eye is drawn laterally across the surface as part of a visual rhythm whose intensity is both heightened and contained by the relatively intimate size of the painting. But their placement also suggests a permanent disorientation of the rhythm in which the eye moves laterally across the surface by implicating this lateral movement *into* the material of the support itself.

In this sense, we begin to notice the different ways in which the painting faces us, exposing us to the surface in its lateral extension, the recto *on* or *against* which the nails appear. In the painting's frontality, the only opacity is the layer of acrylic priming blocked by the nails. But as they pierce the surface itself, the nails also imply a movement *into* or *through* the surface, so that we sense but cannot see an opacity that is deeper than what is simply blocked by the nails. The opacity opens the surface into the weave of the canvas and the real depth in which the nails hold themselves in place. The nails thus imply a transverse passage that is perpendicular or intensive to the surface rather than syntagmatic or lateral, opening this same surface to the space of a *between*. Traversing the support, the nails also imply a nonillusionistic or virtual thickness that is deeper than the furrows in the weave of the canvas, and deeper than the support's real thickness, even as this virtual thickness remains, paradoxically, the painting's own surface. Reinforcing this sense of thickness, the nails show us the surface that we face and demonstrate that the surface has not only a space *between* but a *back*, a hidden verso that faces us by facing away to the wall, the very wall on which this painting nevertheless hangs, exposed and exhibited.

Donald Judd first recognized the significance of this shift in emphasis in Martin's work. In a review from 1964, he suggests that if, in her earlier paintings, "the small horizontal and vertical marks were only marks on a surface," then in the later work "the marks usually have the effect of being incised and so incorporate the surface."[4] Our reading of *Untitled* suggests a similar way in which the nails "incise" and "incorporate" the surface, informing it in such a way as to give the painting a sense of having a "body" with a sculp-

tural dimension (a "crushed volume"), a surface that has a front and a back and an in-between, and all at once. And it presents itself so that its thickness is a prior condition of that surface and its exposure, a materiality that is precisely what gives the painting its visibility and *not* what is dialectically *overcome* in the pursuit of abstraction.

This transformation of surface effects—the way in which the nails "incorporate" the surface—invites a further reading of the later paintings (opened by Rosalind Krauss) in which scale is often coincident with the viewer's own body. Martin's use of the nails also questions the view that abstraction is "a means of penetrating to the unseen but palpable truths beneath surface appearances," not only because the use of the nails suggests the painting remains irreducible to this positing of

Agnes Martin
Untitled, 1975
Collection Herb and DeeDee Glimcher, Columbus, Ohio
Photo: Richard K. Loesch

truth (and its associated and gender-specific metaphors) but because the nails reopen the same painting to issues of thickness in which such metaphors find the measure of their own displacement.[5] *Untitled* does not find its place in terms of a tradition of abstract expressionism or the sublime, nor in relation to the form of minimalist reduction with which Martin's work has so often been situated. Read in light of its incision and incorporation of a surface, *Untitled* begins to find critical resonance instead in relation to a number of marginal practices, part of a shared experiment in which the materiality of painting and its visibility are thought differently: in Bonnefoi's use of "pins,"[6] in the grommets punctuating the surface of Dryer's *The Wall of Fear*, in the traces of incisions made by nails in paintings by Degottex, and in Ryman's supporting metal brackets holding the work to the wall.

P. A.

1. Barbara Haskell, "The Awareness of Perfection," in Barbara Haskell, ed., *Agnes Martin* (New York: Whitney Museum of American Art, 1992), p. 103.

2. For an incisive questioning of this narrative, see Jacques Schmitt, "Agnes Martin," *Peinture: Cahiers théoriques* 8–9 (1974): 51–53.

3. Kasha Linville, "Agnes Martin: An Appreciation," *Artforum* 9, no. 10 (June 1971): 72. Linville's reading figures prominently in Rosalind Krauss's essay "The /Cloud/," reprinted in *Bachelors* (Cambridge: MIT Press, 1999), pp. 75–89.

4. Donald Judd, "In the Galleries," in *Complete Writings 1959–1975* (Halifax: Press of the Nova Scotia College of Art and Design; New York: New York University Press, 1975), p. 112.

5. See Barbara Haskell, "The Awareness of Perfection," p. 7. The question of metaphorical readings of Martin's work is explored further in Anna C. Chave, "Agnes Martin: 'Humility, the Beautiful Daughter. . . . All of Her Ways Are Empty'," in Haskell, ed., *Agnes Martin*, pp. 131–53.

6. See Yve-Alain Bois, "The Pin," in Christian Bonnefoi, *La stratégie du tableau* (Madrid: Alfredo Melgar Editions, 1992), pp. 14–17.

Michel Parmentier
Born 1938, Paris
Died 2000, Paris

The genesis, asceticism and foundations of his work reveal both a comprehensive knowledge of the artists he admires, such as Bram van Velde and Hantaï, and a desire to explore in depth what Blanchot called "the literary space," the space to be painted and that of painting. Parmentier's genuine familiarity with the writings of Louis René Des Forêts, Blanchot and Lévinas has also greatly influenced his approach. Nevertheless, Parmentier is by no means a "literary painter"; I know of few other works less likely to fit such a category. Nonetheless, his "way of being" in the world has always been shaped by the philosophical and intellectual debates that arose during that time.

—Bernard Blistène

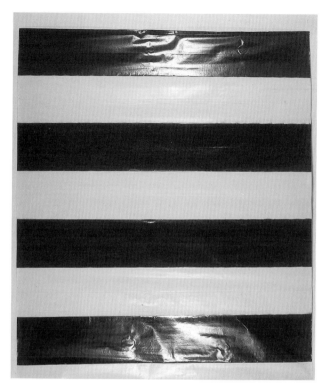

Michel Parmentier
5 octobre 1966, 1966
Collection Bénédicte Victor-Pujebet, Paris
Photo: Philippe Simon

In this comment from 1992, Bernard Blistène emphasizes a crucial aspect for any understanding of Michel Parmentier's work: his "approach" or "way of being" an artist.[1] Informed by this philosophical background, Parmentier's deep interest in Maurice Blanchot's concept of "literary space" encompasses the complexity of a space that includes its own absence, reserve, and necessary silence. Such a space sets itself apart from the author in order to produce an experience that requires a turning away in order to see or apprehend it.[2] If Parmentier is not a "literary" painter, it is precisely because the challenge of his work is to approach this "literary space," not to represent it. His approach to making work, which includes decisive moments of inactivity or refusal to work, is indissociable from a reflection on the experience of "literary space," but also from the notions of reserve, restraint, and silence that suggest an ethics of painting as an approach to painting.

Looking at the trajectory of Parmentier's career, we see that he exhibited in 1966, 1967, and 1968, then not again until fifteen years later. In a letter in 1972, he explained why he ceased working: "The limit-trace should cease to be produced, and in ceasing, it denounces and avows its situated limits (it denounces and avows the limits where it situates itself), it preserves—as much as possible—its subversive quality."[3] This comment reflects the provocative position Parmentier maintained since 1967 when he worked with Daniel Buren, Olivier Mosset, and Niele Toroni. The group staged four "manifestations," each meant to demonstrate their collective position against lyrical and gestural painting in France at the time, as well as against

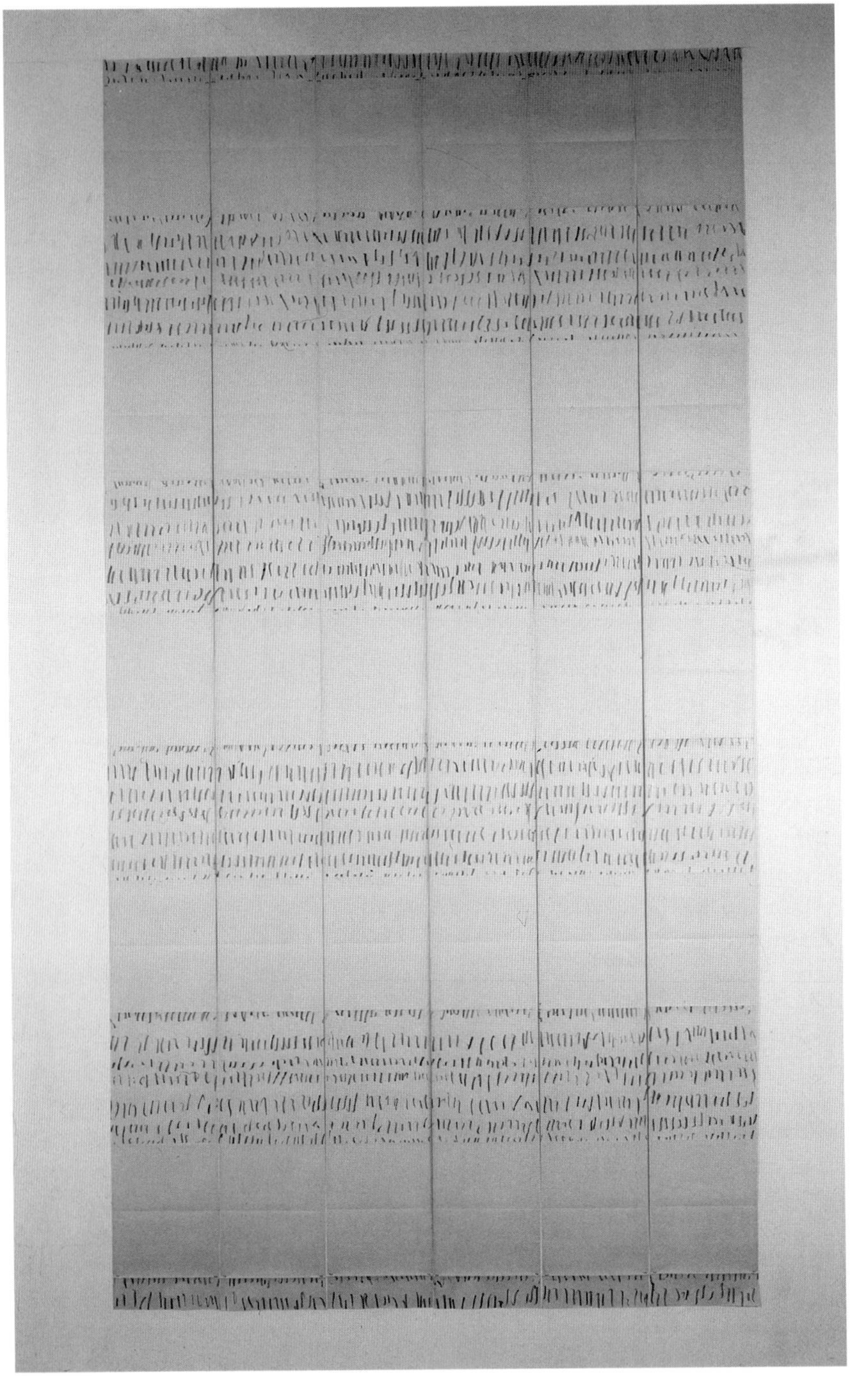

Michel Parmentier
12 août 1988, 1988
Pencil on paper
121 $^{11}/_{16}$ × 65 in. (312 × 165 cm)
Collection Bénédicte Victor-Pujebet, Paris
Photo: Philippe Simon

the art establishment. Later in 1967, rejecting the proposal that group members make each other's paintings, Parmentier defected, claiming that a distinction should be made between depersonalizing painting and making a depersonalized painting. This suggests his commitment to painting as a "praxis," in which the concept does not precede language but is formed through its practice. In his essay for this catalogue, he argues for the "inseparability of ethics and praxis," which includes both an essential doubt and an incessant reflection on painting's limits.

The works Parmentier began making in 1966 reflect his earlier interest in hiding and revealing the surface of the painting through the use of masking adhesives and stencils. He folded the canvases in such a way as to enfold alternating horizontal bands (38 cm in width) that remain shielded from the paint that he later applies to the exposed surfaces. He created an apparent monochrome by spraying lacquer in a mechanical and impersonal manner, thereby effacing any sense of gesture. The folded, monochromatic canvas was then unfolded to reveal 38 cm of unpainted stripes of white canvas alternating with the lacquered stripes. Residual traces of the staples that held the folds in place are evident along the edges of the painted bands; also visible is the faint crease of a supplementary 19-cm fold, a structural necessity for making the original 38-cm folds.

This method of folding in order to produce a reserve in the surface is consistent throughout Parmentier's work. One might argue that he begins painting by folding, that his work is constructed in relation to a surface that he understands as containing a depth, a reserve, and a temporality that is invisible during much of the process of making the work. For Parmentier, to continue painting was to continue to address this reserve, a void that must be acknowledged as a part of all substantial philosophical and visual experience. His approach to painting was driven fundamentally by an interest in the limit-experience of the invisible.

Michel Parmentier
detail

After ceasing in 1968, Parmentier returned to painting in 1983 by making black stripes. Earlier, each successive year was signified by a different color—blue in 1966, gray in 1967, red in 1968—as well as by the date Parmentier stamped on the back of each piece to mark the work's completion and serve as its title. In conversation, he claimed that 1988 was the "beginning of the disappearance." That "disappearance" is most dramatically apparent in a change of materials and overall effect, which might be summarized as much more recessive than in the earlier work. He began working with semitransparent paper and crayon, which allowed the folds to be more visible as crisp edges and made the marking or filling of the exposed faces less pronounced than the lacquered surfaces. The hatching of the black crayon and, later, white oil pastel appears diffused and recedes on the surfaces of the folds as opposed to the visual demand of the colored stripes in the earlier work.

The stripes covered with hatching are filled in a completely banal manner, with the type of marks one makes while talking on the phone or simply passing time. They achieve a kind of temporal duration not evident in the stilled sense of the earlier sprayed works. What appears as an additional supplement on this thinner support is the interruption that the crease from the folded edges underneath the surface makes in the marking system (as seen in the detail view). In this way, evidence of a surface within a surface and a set of internal divisions appears. As in the earlier work, the final mark made was the stamping of the date of the work's termination.

Parmentier's critical approach to painting maintains an interest in limits, including an interest in the "bête"—what in English might be translated as both a dumbness and muteness—the "impoverished" mark, and the necessary doubt (despair) that is essential to making any work at all. Likewise, the works themselves, their broken pattern over time as "limit-traces," face us with the desperate question that so absorbs and interests Parmentier in Blanchot's *Space of Literature:* "What would be at stake in the fact that something like art or literature exists?" As Parmentier's late work proceeded toward literal invisibility, that question pressed even harder.

L. L.

Michel Parmentier
15 mars 1994, 1994
Oil stick on paper
119 ⁵/₈ × 121 ¹/₄ in. (304 × 308 cm)
Installation view at 123 rue Marconi, Brussels, 1997
Collection Herman J. Daled, Brussels
Photo: Philippe de Gobert

Michel Parmentier
20 novembre 1999, 1999
Installation view of Galerie Jean Fournier, Paris
Courtesy Galerie Jean Fournier, Paris
Photo: Philippe Simon

1. See "An Interview with Bernard Blistène," in *Individualités: 14 Contemporary Artists from France,* ed. Roald Nasgaard and Marie-Claude Jenne (Toronto: Art Gallery of Ontario, 1990), p. 25–26. Although they participated in this exhibition, Parmentier and Daniel Buren wrote an artist's statement that attacked its premise and thus renewed the often militant stance that characterized much of their earlier work. For a thorough selection of historical and critical texts on Parmentier, see Alfred Pacquement, *Michel Parmentier* (Paris: Centre national des arts plastiques, 1988).

2. Maurice Blanchot, *The Space of Literature,* trans. Ann Smock (Lincoln: University of Nebraska Press, 1982).

3. The letter was written to François Mathey, the curator of *Twelve Years of Contemporary Art in France, 60/72,* and is reprinted in Daniel Buren and Michel Parmentier, *Propos délibérés* (Lyons: Art Edition; Brussels: Palais des Beaux-Arts, 1991).

Gerhard Richter
Born 1932, Dresden, Germany
Lives and works in Cologne

> But this completion without end—or rather, this *finite finishing*, if one attempts to understand thereby a completion that limits itself to what is, but that, to achieve that very thing, opens the possibility of another completion, and that is therefore also *infinite finishing*—this paradoxical mode of per-fection is doubtless what our whole tradition demands one to think and avoids thinking *at the same time.*
>
> —Jean-Luc Nancy[1]

Of the work in *As Painting*, Gerhard Richter's undoubtedly has the greatest general currency and is further distinguished by its explicit reference to pop art, including its early participation in the "capitalist realism" that is most often presented as the German incarnation of pop. The work thus carries a number of features—perhaps most notably an engagement with representation and a question of irony—that seem to set it apart from much of the other painting in this exhibition. Likewise, technique in Richter's painting seems to be almost entirely an instrumental matter as distinct from the fundamental status it is accorded by many of the French painters in particular.

At the same time, there are a number of features in Richter's work that do seem easy to connect with concerns active in *As Painting*—the relation to photography would certainly be one, and a certain recurrent engagement with mirrors might be another—but presumably one would want some fuller account of their exact pertinence before accepting that connection as anything other than a happy accident.

One way to move toward such an account is to back off from the attention to particular features in favor of some attempt at a characterization of Richter's work as a whole. Here there is little choice but to begin from the work's most obvious feature, its variety. Our

selection includes two very similar photo paintings, an *Abstract Picture*, and a freestanding mirror piece; any attempt to fully represent Richter's work as a whole would also need to include his gridded color charts as well as his gray monochromes (and this still leaves aside the extraordinary photographic body of *Atlas*). At least two things can be said right away: The first is that painting evidently does not happen for Richter apart from an engagement also with other practices, most obviously photography but also sculpture. The second is that painting clearly has no one place in which it finds its essential form but is permanently given over to a dispersion across a number of "genres." A related dispersion is evident within the photo paintings, which are highly transparent to traditional genre distinctions. The thought then follows that this practice of painting—as something both holding a particular place within a larger system of the arts and internally structured by a further such system—is answered or supported by a fundamental orientation within the

Gerhard Richter
Shadowpicture I, 1968
Calotype
23 ½ × 25 ⁷/₁₆ in. (60 × 65 cm)
The Saint Louis Art Museum; Museum Shop Fund

Gerhard Richter
Doppelglasscheibe (416), 1977
Collection Musée départemental d'art contemporain de
Rochechouart, France
Photo: Freddy Le Saux, Le Vigen, France

paintings to what we have variously characterized
throughout this catalogue as finitude, reserve, blindness, and so on. In other words, however different
Richter's historical bases may be from the basis that *As
Painting* primarily draws upon, the logic of his work
follows the same broad lines sketched out for the exhibition as a whole.

"Reserve" appears to take two forms in or in relation to Richter's work. One would be a distinct modification of the irony that certainly underlies his earliest
work, and "reserve" would be the best name for what
becomes of that irony as Richter becomes increasingly
willing to identify his work with "the daily practice of

painting."[2] This reserve, which one may feel as the difficult determination of the *Abstract Pictures* to be no
more than their collective name designates (their way of
holding themselves within themselves, generating no
imagination of deeper meaning or self behind them and
likewise showing no tendency to make themselves more
expansive than their support), is perhaps most thoroughly evident in Richter's various ways of speaking
about his work. The second form of reserve is most evident in the way his paintings repeatedly build themselves around some form of internal gap. Although one
may rightly feel that this internal gap is carried in much
of Richter's work, including the *Abstract Pictures*, by
the strongly registered mediation of the camera, it also
takes distinctly concrete form in, for example, the play
of paint and mirrors in his mirror work generally and
very specifically in the mutual engagement of the mirrors in the 1977 *Double Pane of Glass*, or in the interval between foreground object and projected shadow in
Shadow Picture 1, or in the presentations of I. G. that
strangely foreground the gap between the posed figure
and the background against which it stands.

The paintings of I. G., like the extraordinary
1988 painting of Richter's daughter Betty, involve a figure importantly turned away from both painter (or photographer) and viewer. The contrast with the frontality
of Warhol's equally mediated portrait images is striking:
where Warhol turns the fully presented image of the self
over to an unlimited irony, Richter, in paintings like
these, grants his subjects a space in which to withhold
themselves within the mediation of their presence (even
as he also grants them no exemption from such mediation—a position markedly similar to the one he takes up
in his interviews). Just as this space does not escape mediation, so it does not escape its condition as painted: it
appears not as a psychological space about which we
might more or less successfully speculate but, more
simply, as a withholding that has no more depth than
that of the hybrid surface on which it appears. There is
nothing concealed in these paintings—there is no temptation to look "around" the figures that appear in them,

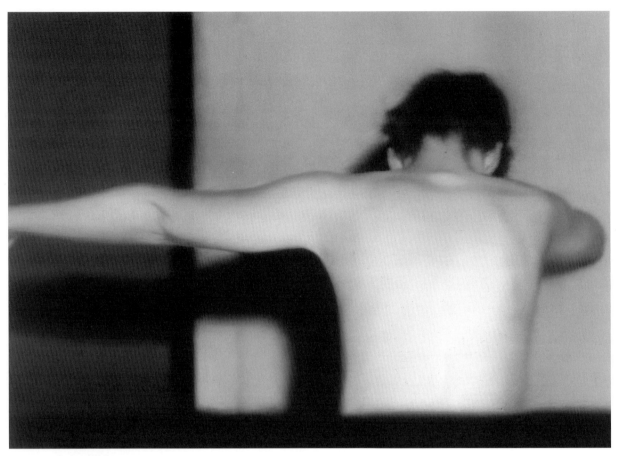

Gerhard Richter
I. G. (790-4), 1993
Private collection
Photo: Tore H. Røyneland

Gerhard Richter
I. G. (790-5), 1993
Private collection
Photo: Tore H. Røyneland

grounded in *As Painting* and another way toward questions of openness and closedness, candor and reserve, is perhaps a way of remarking how Richter's work stands in *As Painting* as one of its inner limits: a place where the thought of painting emerges into or finds itself within another idiom, folding through itself into the renewed complexity of its practice.

S. M.

Gerhard Richter
Abstraktes Bild (825-10), 1995
Collection Mark H. Williams, Los Angeles
Photo: Friedrich Rosenstiel
Photo courtesy the artist

and "nothing" is in fact concealed in the paintings and so appears at no particular place within them while nonetheless being actively at work in their structure.

If these characterizations seem just, then one may want to further explore the thought that with Richter the particular fact of painting that we have repeatedly put in terms of "exposure" and "visibility" and "showing" is definitively inflected into a question of "facing" as something painting does. "Facing" would be a name for the structure or action of painting as a surface, a way of claiming and displaying a depth inseparable from it. It would be something that does not happen without reserve, and so might well be taken as a qualification or revision of what Stanley Cavell claims as the "candor" of Morris Louis's *Unfurleds*—paintings that unfold themselves in crucial relation to the earlier series of *Veils.*[3] That we find ourselves here with Louis's work pointing one way toward a range of techniques fore-

1. Jean-Luc Nancy, "The Vestige of Art," in *The Muses,* trans. Peggy Kamuf (Stanford: Stanford University Press, 1996), p. 87.

2. See Gerhard Richter, *The Daily Practice of Painting: Writings and Interviews 1962–1993,* ed. Hans-Ulrich Obrist, trans. David Britt (Cambridge: MIT Press, in association with Anthony d'Offay Gallery, London, 1995).

3. See Stanley Cavell, "Excursus: Some Modernist Painting," in *The World Viewed: Reflections on the Ontology of Film,* expanded edition (Cambridge: Harvard University Press, 1979).

François Rouan
Born 1943, Montpellier, France
Lives and works in l'Oise, France

One way to approach much of the French work in *As Painting* is in terms of a shared and quite variously pursued ambition to find a way to let painting be the showing of its ground. "Showing" here would have to mean something like passing into articulation without ceasing to be ground, without coalescing into something that stands over and against it as figure. Barré, Bishop, Bonnefoi, Degottex, Hantaï, and Parmentier all participate at one level or another in this ambition, and it is tempting to think of many but not all of these artists as faced with an initial choice between collage, with its capacity to remark the ground, and the monochrome as that ground's pure repetition. Shifting the emphasis slightly, one can cast this initial choice as between the force of all-over composition as realized above all by Jackson Pollock and the rather different lesson of Matisse's cutouts (and lurking behind both these choices, one might discern the still powerful figure of Picasso).

François Rouan's work arises at a point where these varying phrasings come to a particular point and are complicated by his deep attachment to drawing.

In 1965 and 1966 Rouan made collages, clearly influenced by Matisse, out of colored paper that has been partly cut up into discrete squares and partly cut into so as to form a roughly orthogonal grid through which one sees a similar second layer. Each layer by itself would be monochrome but for the cuts that open it to a ground beneath, and the clear intention is that nothing should emerge as figure over and against this process of opening into the ground. The tension necessary to open the interior cuts to what lies beneath inevitably creates here and there small foldings of the paper against itself. To the extent that something like figure persists in these early collages, it is typically set beneath a more nearly all-over final layer. The ambition is to make something that would be the painting, or its ground, by being its showing through itself.

Rouan's practice of *tressage*—the weaving together of two or more separately painted canvases on a single stretcher—as it emerges in 1966 certainly interprets the earlier work this way, taking on the thought that painting can only show itself this way if it also interferes with itself as it does so. The question can no longer be put in terms of figure and ground but is directly a matter of a painting whose visibility is explicitly a function of a materiality that also binds it to concealment. "Beneathness" now becomes an explicit dimension of the painting, an integral condition of its surface. Every other concern of painting is submitted to the presiding structure of a mutual interference that is the holding open of the painting.

Tressage is "anticompositional" insofar as composition as something worked across the surface of the painting is put out of play in favor of what arises from the painting's particular material thickness. Hubert Damisch, Rouan's strongest early supporter, is inclined to see *tressage* as a radical interpretation of Pollock's all-over composition, making explicit the ways in which Pollock's work is ordered less by a complexity of line that undoes its figurative force than by a layering of paint as real thickness. This amounts to defeating the lingering hold of perspective over even abstract painting and finding instead a more materially responsive understanding of painting's complex supports.[1] Unlike the similarly "materiologically" oriented artists within Supports/Surfaces, Rouan maintains an active interest in questions of composition, of making a painting or a *tableau*, and not simply analytically dismantling the general practice into its separable components.

Although a certain practice of collage opens for Rouan the possibility of *tressage*, this new technique itself clearly cannot be fully assimilated back into collage. Having found its way into the canvas itself, it intends a claim on painting as such, bidding to redescribe the painting's surface as essentially deep or thick—more nearly a system of knots or cuts than an ideal plane analyzable as a grid or system of points. This redescription is not a matter of thick paint but of remaking the sur-

François Rouan
Papiers gouachés et découpés, 1965
Courtesy the artist
Art © 2000 Artists Rights Society (ARS), New York/ADAGP, Paris

face as everywhere punctuated or interrupted by its depth—a project whose most powerful early form is found in the *Portes* of 1971–76 and which Rouan then pushes into increasingly complex positions.

Because of the way *tressage* interprets painterly depth as a structural fact of surface, the practice has been particularly ripe for psychoanalytic understanding. Such an understanding has played an important role in Rouan's reception, particularly insofar as his practice seems to intersect interestingly with various models advanced by Jacques Lacan. The discussion set off by Lacan's somewhat cryptic notes for Rouan's 1978 show at the Musée Cantini in Marseilles is particularly striking for the way it addresses the major difficulty facing Rouan in the wake of the *tressage*s—that is, how to fully take up that work's claim on painting as painting. Stripping the argument to its most schematic essentials, Lacan implicitly claims that weaving—as opposed to his favored figure of the Boromean chain and associated braid—can do no more than replicate the logic of narcissism; Damisch, in rejoinder, argues that the painting of the woven canvas is precisely what makes a braid of it and enters the painting into a properly psychoanalytic region—that is, a region in which the autonomy of the individual is crucially supported by a contradiction that exceeds and escapes it. It is difficult to know what exactly to make of the extension of psychoanalytic models into the region of painting along these lines, but the exchange is useful in recalling the extent to which painting is conceived by many of the French artists in this exhibition as a theoretical activity, a form of thinking or working through. It also offers a rough way of thinking about the various resources Rouan draws on as he abandons the practice of literal *tressage* for one of direct painting—his use of mirrors, his interest in photography, and the search for an adequate return of the subject or figure in a practice of painting that would continue to link its visibility to a systematic Unconscious bound up in its materiality. For Rouan, these questions of visibility open also a question about drawing, which continues to be an essential

François Rouan
Tressage quatre toiles, gris, rose, bleu et blanc, 1967–69
Courtesy the artist
Art © 2000 Artists Rights Society (ARS), New York/ADAGP, Paris

François Rouan
Tressements de 4 surfaces, 1967–69
Collection of the artist
Art © 2000 Artists Rights Society (ARS), New York/ADAGP, Paris

François Rouan
Porta Latina, 1971–74
Collection Mrs. Maria Gaetana Matisse, New York
Photo courtesy the artist
Art © 2000 Artists Rights Society (ARS), New York/ADAGP, Paris

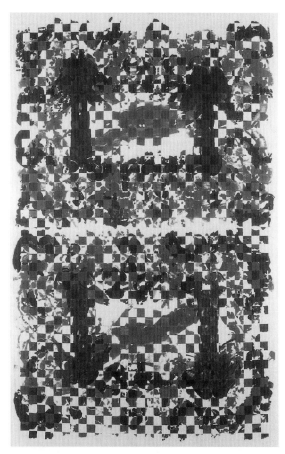

François Rouan
Queequeg III, 1999
Courtesy the artist
Art © 2000 Artists Rights Society (ARS), New York/ADAGP, Paris

part of his practice, capable of carrying with it a series of encounters with the art of the past and most particularly a sustained engagement with Picasso before it is further transformed by his turns toward, first, photography and then, the bodily imprint.[2]

S. M.

1. See Hubert Damisch, "La peinture est un vrai trois," in *Fenêtre jaune cadmium, ou les dessous de la peinture* (Paris: Editions du Seuil, 1984), and Yve-Alain Bois, "Painting as Model," in *Painting as Model* (Cambridge: MIT Press, 1990). Also useful are Denis Hollier's two studies, *Rouan: La figure du fond* (Paris: Editions Galilée, 1992) and *Epreuves d'artiste: Photographies de François Rouan* (Paris: Editions Galilée, 1996), as well as the catalogue to Rouan's 1984 retrospective, *Rouan* (Paris: Centre Georges Pompidou, 1984). See also François Rouan, "Circling around a Void," trans. Rosalind E. Krauss, *October* 65 (summer 1993): 77–88.

2. Another valuable context for considering Rouan's later work and its reception is provided by the repeated critical and theoretical appeals to Balzac's short story "Le chef-d'oeuvre inconnu." See Hubert Damisch, "Les dessous de la peinture," in *Fenêtre jaune cadmium;* Georges Didi-Huberman, *La peinture incarnée* (Paris: Minuit, 1985); and the collection *Autour du chef-d'oeuvre inconnu de Balzac* (Paris: Ecole national supérieure des arts décoratifs, 1985). Dore Aston's short book *A Fable of Modern Art* (Berkeley: University of California Press, 1991) provides an interesting contrast here.

Robert Ryman
Born 1930, Nashville, Tennessee
Lives and works in New York

In his essay for the 1993 Ryman retrospective, Robert Storr remarks that up until that point, Ryman's work was "far better known and more highly regarded abroad than in his own country."[1] Given this background, one might expect that other work included in *As Painting* bears the trace of Ryman's earlier reception in Europe, especially in the work of those artists whose careers were beginning in the sixties and seventies. At this level, his inclusion in the exhibition has historical as well as critical interest.

Ryman's work has also become a standard reference for any discussion of painting's situation after abstract expressionism (his acknowledged debts to Rothko are key in this regard), and the proximity of his work to questions raised by minimalism and postminimalism has been frequently noted and debated. If the inclusion of Ryman's work in *As Painting* attempts to do something different than these narratives suggest, it stems from his proximity to artists who were not only exposed to his work early on but whose sense of its importance to an understanding of painting is perhaps unusual in an American context. In particular, this distinctively European reception refuses to situate Ryman within an evolutionary history of painting in which his work represents a particular endpoint, a narrative of abstract painting pushed to its exhaustion and thus the license for pursuing abstraction through other means, notably pop art. Nor does this reception argue that his painting coincides with a form of minimalist "reduction" or conceptualism.[2]

Critical discussion of Ryman has predominantly emphasized the materials and techniques that inform the work's specificity. These material and technical aspects are then considered to be what the work is about, a reading that Ryman has acknowledged with disarming simplicity in his various interviews and statements, including his famous claim that the question is not "what" to paint but "how" to paint.[3] Thus, beyond the signature exploration of "white" paint, we now possess extraordinary lists of the different materials used since the beginning of Ryman's career in the mid fifties (materials used for the supports, applied to the supports, or used to hang the paintings), as well as any number of technical details about his procedures and processes. We also possess meticulous discussions of the painted surfaces, an attempt to approximate the pictorial experimentation that takes place in what Yve-Alain Bois has aptly termed "Ryman's Lab."[4] In the attempt to approximate the work, enumerating the various materials and technical details will always fall short of the effects fully produced by the work itself (a situation acknowledged by the repeated apologia that our language is

Robert Ryman
Stretched Drawing, 1963
Collection of the artist, New York
Photo courtesy Pace Wildenstein
Art © 1963 Robert Ryman

always inadequate to our perceptual experience and that any experience of the work is never fully capturable through photographic reproduction).[5]

The exact rapport between the materials and techniques and the painting of which they are the outcome remains a difficult question. By including Ryman's work in *As Painting,* our hope is that such attention to materials and techniques demands a fundamental transformation of these terms and their implications for painting. This transformation includes a radically different sense of painting's material conditions in relation to its exposure. It also includes a way of demonstrating how the material and technical implications of Ryman's work demand their simultaneous theoretical, historical, and conceptual re-elaboration.

This transformed reception of Ryman's work is evident in the writings of Christian Bonnefoi, one of the painters whose work in the seventies was deeply informed by Ryman's early reception. (Bois has suggested that Bonnefoi has understood the "lessons" of Ryman "perhaps better than anyone else in France.")[6] Bonnefoi argues that Ryman's work enacts a rupture with all the givens and traditions of the pictorial object, in which every element of painting is now put into question. As the title of one of Bonnefoi's essays—"The Destruction of the Surface Entity"—suggests, the work embodies a radical "destruction" or "disarticulation" of every aspect of painting (materials, processes, techniques, installation), not in order to efface painting or secure a reduction but in order to resituate it in terms of its infinite possibilities of articulation (and thus a radically different sense of painting's limits).

Emphasis is now placed not on the painting's surface but on the "destruction" of the surface entity, part of the painting's refusal of all "a-priority." It is not a question of promoting surface effects (which amount to nothing more than "formal" or "pedagogical" inquiry), nor is it a question of assuming that the surface is an "evidence" on which the white pigment becomes a "sign" for painting or a signature for Ryman. The surface is not a space where "the sign fastens and comes

Robert Ryman
State, 1978
Collection Albright-Knox Art Gallery, Buffalo, New York;
George B. and Jenny R. Mathews Fund, 1979

to rest," and thus a condition of the work's visibility. Rather, the application of the white is an opening of the surface to a temporal dimension or "thickness," with attention now paid to the aleatory effects of how pigment flows, dries, or adheres, refusing to become an entity "in itself." Attention is also paid to the position of the artist's body in relation to surface inscription (questions of horizontality and verticality, the "gift" of the body to "matter").

For Bonnefoi, this shift in emphasis constitutes a complete reconversion of abstract expressionism (with the literal, metaphorical, and theoretical painting of signs on a given surface). For if the surface is not a *given* for painting, "this signifies that to paint is first of all the invention of a surface (of this surface) and that the *tableau* is the result of this operation, plus its surface effects; thus, forms and colors etc. as supplements to the constitution of thickness." The supplementariness of color and form to the surface (in its temporal dimension as thickness) simultaneously demands a rethinking of painting's limits (Bonnefoi cites Buren in this regard as well as Ryman), opening painting to a radically new field of inquiry, a different sense of "ligature" (of divisions and displacements), the "place of its decision."

P. A.

1. Robert Storr, "Simple Gifts," in *Robert Ryman* (London: Tate Gallery; New York: Museum of Modern Art, 1993), p. 22.

2. The question of Ryman's reception is also foregrounded in Daniel Buren's essay in this catalogue. It coincides with what Buren sees as "the hegemony of American propaganda" when it comes to exporting its artists.

3. See the interview with Gary Garrels and the statements collected in *Robert Ryman* (New York: Dia Art Foundation, 1988).

4. See Yve-Alain Bois, "Ryman's Lab," in *Abstraction, Gesture, Ecriture: Paintings from the Daros Collection,* ed. Peter Fischer (Zurich: Alesco AG and Scalo, 1999), pp. 105–21 and "Ryman's Tact," in *Painting as Model* (Cambridge: MIT Press, 1990), pp. 215–26. In his essay for the 1993 retrospective catalogue, Storr provides a "Glossary of Technical Terms."

5. The question is discussed at length in Thierry de Duve, "Ryman irreproductible," reprinted in *Ecrits datés I: 1974–1986* (Paris: La Différence, 1987), pp. 119–58.

6. For Bonnefoi's discussion of Ryman, see "A propos de la destruction de l'entité de surface" and "Louis Kahn et le minimalisme" in *Ecrits sur l'art (1974–1981)* (Brussels: La Part de l'Oeil, 1997). Further quotations are taken from these two essays. The first essay was initially published in the "Dossier Robert Ryman," edited by Yve-Alain Bois and Jean Clay, in *Macula* (Paris), no. 3–4 (1978): 113–85. The "dossier" remains one of the most extensive critical explorations of Ryman's practice. Yve-Alain Bois's comment on Bonnefoi appears in "The Pin," in Christian Bonnefoi, *La stratégie du tableau* (Madrid: Alfredo Melgar Editions, 1992), p. 16.

Robert Smithson
Born 1938, Passaic, New Jersey
Died 1973, Amarillo, Texas

Robert Smithson's *Untitled (SF Landscape)* of 1966 shows a large matrix of interlocking cubes set into a dark, presumably hilly landscape on which a number of small figures labor to pull some kind of large cargo ship ashore. The matrix appears to have been drawn onto or perhaps pasted into its setting, and, as with many of Smithson's photographic works, the relation between positive and negative shifts across various sections of the image. Those familiar with Smithson's work are likely to find a whole nest of recognitions unfolding from this sketch: the interlocking cubes look very much like his early freestanding gallery works, quasi-minimalist pieces like *Plunge* and *Alogon* (also from 1966). At the same time, set into this landscape, the cubes suddenly look like geometrized versions of his later poured landscape pieces like *Asphalt Rundown* or *Glue Pour* (and the 1969 and 1970 drawings related to these pieces frequently play strongly geometrized rocks off against the pour that submerges them). And then it may suddenly be striking that the photostat does not so much offer a perspectival rendering of the gallery pieces as they appear as materializations—like *Pointless Vanishing Point*—of what reads in the image as its uneasy interest in perspective. This recognition may lead finally to the further recognition that this passage of perspective into the real has the entropic drift, the deep irrationality, of the poured pieces.

What one can see in this piece is very near the heart of Smithson's artistic intelligence—an intelligence that sets itself to work always in displacements: of the two-dimensional into and out of the three-dimensional, of the crystalline into and out of the liquid, of the gallery work into and out of the landscape, of vision into and out of its own blindness and density. This intelligence holds itself together only by displacing itself always toward other objects. That this piece is itself both photographic and montage marks Smithson's in-

Robert Smithson
Untitled (S. F. Landscape), 1966
Photostat
8 × 12 in. (20 × 30.5 cm)
Collection Estate of Robert Smithson
Photo courtesy James Cohan Gallery, New York
Art © Estate of Robert Smithson/VAGA, New York

terest in displacement and already touches on the role photography will play in his later work. The most natural figure for the coherence of what exists only in or as its own displacement—certainly the figure that holds Smithson's attention early and late—is the spiral, both opening always away from itself and turning back on itself as a vortex that can only consume the forms that also structure it.[1]

Glass and mirrors have repeatedly offered compelling images for painting. In Smithson's hands the transparency of glass turns into the complexity, the shifting opacity, cloudiness, and reflectivity put into play by his various *Glass Strata*. The moment of self-recognition and securable identity promised by the mirror is turned against itself so that it instead captures its object, taking it up into a chain of displacements. The "mirror trails" that accompanied the initial showing of *Slantpiece* at Cornell University ultimately give rise to the successive displacements operated by mirror and

Robert Smithson
Untitled, 1966
Collection Whitney Museum of American Art, New York; Gift of
the Estate of Robert Smithson, 92.2.3
Art © Estate of Robert Smithson/VAGA, New York
Photo © 2000 Whitney Museum of American Art

Within the context of *As Painting,* Smithson's
work charts an imagination of surface as irreducibly
deep and thus always submitted to the conditions of
three-dimensionality without ever fully giving itself
over to its terms. One could say that sculpture is always
experienced as having some defining relation to either
an interiority it apparently expresses or, more compelling, to an exteriority out of which it makes itself
wholly and without reserve. However, Smithson's work
never accepts either possibility, and instead actively
transforms the limits such possibilities more simply assume and portion out among themselves. If sculpture's
claims are likewise always divided between the instant
it renders and the permanence of that instant, Smithson's work takes up again and again the instant as already somehow beyond itself, caught up in its next
moment even from within the one it otherwise claims to
occupy. It's not clear that work made in these ways, out
of these refusals, is properly described as sculpture.

Smithson's experience of viewing the proposed
site for a work at the new Dallas–Fort Worth airport is
often taken as pivotal for making out the sense of his
work—as if there he learned or relearned and revised
the crucial informing facts of his work: that a surface is
the legible record of a history of breaks and surges and
flows variously from below and from what is adjacent
to it. (Imagine that this broad area is the melting of a
mountain, this thickly hatched passage the shivered
breaking of a crust.) In each instance a composition un-
furled across a certain space is dissolved back into a
work and record of time operating at another angle or
set of angles that tie that time to depth and take both as
the necessary structure of a surface.

It's uncertain whether one will be willing to call
Smithson's *Mono Lake Non-Site (Cinders Near Black
Point)*—or any of his other works shown in *As Painting*—a "painting." The temptation is to say that such
work addresses painting from somewhere adjacent to it
(as, one might imagine, the bins in *Mono Lake* address
the map placed on the wall). But this would be to miss
the way in which Smithson's work repeatedly appears

camera and text that end by binding nine scattered sites
in the Yucatan to the pages of *Artforum.* Means and
models of visual lucidity, glass and mirror reinterpret
and divide their sites, opening within sight a moment of
nonsight, on which sight depends and which does not
appear as a discrete darkness opposed to it, but as
something closer to its inner lining.

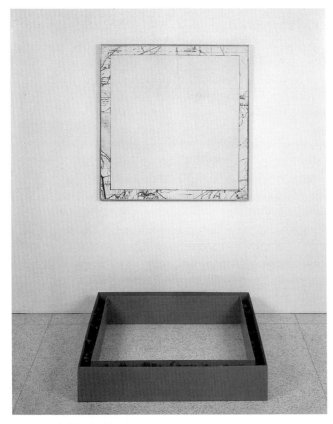

Robert Smithson
Mono Lake Non-Site (Cinders Near Black Point), 1968
Collection Museum of Contemporary Art, San Diego; Museum purchase, 1981.10.1–2
Art © Estate of Robert Smithson/VAGA, New York

as a remaking of painting out of its adjacencies, unfolding its surfaces into their proper depth. This "depth" is not the spatial fact of one thing behind another but the inherently temporal fact of the displacements through which a surface maintains its contact with itself and at the same time remains essentially exposed. The "concreteness" of Smithson's work, as well as its indifference to any straightforward opposition between abstraction and representation, is an effect of his refusal of metaphor, or of his submitting what feels like metaphor to the prior exigencies of metonymy, the continuing flight that is at once the doing and undoing of presence. The openness of Smithson's work to writing, the possibility of its finding some crucial continuation there, is one further effect of the structure of displacement that determines the work as a whole.

If Smithson's work exceeds painting, it does so in ways that are inseparable from the reserves proper to it; this inseparability of excess and reserve is the structure that determines painting's appearance always *as* painting, answerable to a problematic that is also its permanent placing in question.

S. M.

1. The Smithson literature is now immense. One might start with *Robert Smithson: The Collected Writings,* ed. Jack Flam (Berkeley: University of California Press, 1996), and Gary Shapiro, *Earthwards: Robert Smithson and Art after Babel* (Berkeley: University of California Press, 1995).

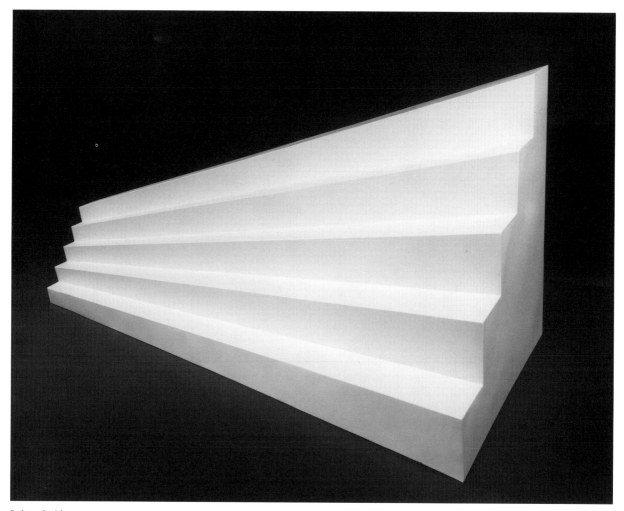

Robert Smithson
Pointless Vanishing Point, 1967
Collection Herbert F. Johnson Museum of Art, Cornell
University; Gift of Virginia Dwan, 86.122
Photo: Emil Ghinger
Art © Estate of Robert Smithson/VAGA, New York

Robert Smithson
Slantpiece, 1969 (original)/1976 (reconstruction)
© Allen Memorial Art Museum, Oberlin College; Gift of the
Buckeye Trust in memory of Ruth C. Roush, 1980
Art © Estate of Robert Smithson/VAGA, New York

Anne Truitt
Born 1921, Baltimore, Maryland
Lives and works in Baltimore

Still another artist who anticipated the Minimalists is Anne Truitt. And she anticipated them more literally and therefore, as it seems to me, more embarrassingly than Caro did. The surprise of the box-like pieces in her first show in New York, early in 1963 (at Emmerich's), was much like that which Minimal art aims at. Despite their being covered with rectilinear zones of color, I was stopped by their dead-pan "primariness," and I had to look again and again, and I had to return again, to discover the power of these "boxes" to move and affect. Far-outness here was stated rather than merely announced and signaled. At the same time it was hard to tell whether the success of Truitt's best works was primarily sculptural or pictorial, but part of their success consisted precisely in making that question irrelevant.

—Clement Greenberg

Anne Truitt
Grant, 1974
Courtesy Danese, New York
Photo: Zindman/Fremont, New York

Since her first solo exhibition in 1963, Anne Truitt has maintained a steadfast commitment to the introduction of color to form. Over the years, her colors have ranged from the subtle variations apparent in the light lavender, gray, and cream of *Grant* (1974) to the heightened palette of *Elixir* (1997) and *View* (1999). Her forms have varied as well: from the earliest, simplified fence forms or plinths to broad volumetric planes and a consistent use of the column or stele. She often grooves the surfaces, thereby producing divisions within the forms that, in addition to literal edges or corners of the structures, provide arenas between which to construct her varying color proportions.[1]

In a review of *Black, White, and Gray,* a 1964 exhibition at the Wadsworth Atheneum, Donald Judd criticized Truitt's use of color for being too close to the dark colors of Ad Reinhardt but without the changes and divisions that occur in his paintings.[2] This criticism raises a number of questions posed by Truitt's work: What are the criteria for the relationship of color and form in sculpture or three-dimensional work? And, in the case of the comparison between Reinhardt and Truitt, what is the difference between and significance of their colored divisions? As Lucy Lippard points out, the rules were "fortunately" still open in the sixties for creating relationships of color and form in sculpture.[3] In the same period when Judd wrote his criticism of Truitt, he himself moved to three-dimensional work in order to continue an investigation of color that he felt was no longer possible in painting. In effect, where Truitt introduces color to form, Judd introduces form to color.

Truitt's coupling of a rectilinear structure and a logic of dividing color around the form creates a color discontinuity, where colors are always held in reserve. Without a clear starting or ending point, the color in reserve is continually displaced as one circles the work. Through this treatment of three-dimensional form as a kind of accordion of successive colors, Truitt achieves

Anne Truitt
Elixir, 1997
Courtesy Danese, New York
Photo: Zindman/Fremont, New York

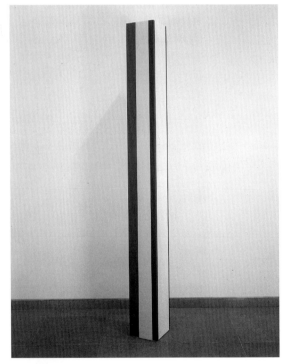

Anne Truitt
View, 1999
Courtesy Danese, New York
Photo: Zindman/Fremont, New York

her stated goal of taking "paintings off the wall, to set color free in three dimensions for its own sake."[4]

Truitt applies her colors after her structures have been manufactured by cabinetmakers. She layers the colors smoothly, sanding between each application of paint to make the color as "independent of materiality as possible."[5] Truitt's work is an experience of a surface rather than the presentation of color as substance. That experience depends on a proportional play of color underlays, abutments on the surface, and reserves of color held around every corner.

To begin with one of the faces of *Elixir,* one sees a strong magenta-hued plane bounded on its right edge by a thin vertical strip of lighter pink that wraps the corner into a full plane of the same color. When one turns the corner, a striking pistachio-green panel—nearly the pink's chromatic opposite—suddenly appears. This panel too is bounded by a thin, vertical strip of pale pink. The quantity and boldness of the once-hidden green is a significantly shocking punctuation in the evolution of the color logic, especially when compared with the simplicity of the columnar form. The fourth and final panel of the structure begins from the narrow band of pale pink that bounds the pistachio-green panel and expands to fill the majority of the final panel, except for a narrow band of strong magenta at its far right edge, which leads around the corner to the magenta panel where we began. The top of the column is bounded by a continuous narrow band of lavender, which is capped by twice its width of bright yellow. These bands function as a "counterpoint," a vertical elevation, in opposition to the circulation of color around the vertical simplicity of the column.

As Truitt states, her interest is in the ability of color not just to be a "counterpoint" to form but to hold "meaning all on its own."[6] This comment suggests an interesting asymmetry between her aspirations for color and those of Judd. Truitt's color depends on its divisions and layering for material independence and meaning; Judd's color depends on specificity and clarity for its own independence, or what he calls "obdu-

rate existence." If Truitt aspires to taking "painting off the wall, to set color free in three dimensions for its own sake," Judd aspires to setting color free from painting in three dimensions, also for its own sake.

The differences and similarities between Truitt and Judd are remarkable, yet no conversation was ever sustained between the two. Truitt's friendships with David Smith and Kenneth Noland stand out for her as the most significant, while Clement Greenberg's support was short-lived. Truitt has spent the majority of her career living and working near Washington, D.C., as opposed to New York. In addition, her own extensive writings take the form of diaries as opposed to criticism. In retrospect, it seems only too significant that her name is excluded from the caption for the photograph accompanying Judd's review of *Black, White, and Gray.*

Installation view of *Black, White, and Gray* at Wadsworth Atheneum, Hartford, Connecticut, 1964, which accompanied Judd's review: the caption mentioned "works by Ad Reinhardt, Robert Morris, Barnett Newman, Tony Smith and others," although the work in the center is by Truitt.
Photo courtesy Wadsworth Atheneum Archives, Hartford

What remains remarkable in Truitt's work is the relationship between sculpture and painting that turns around the *mobility* of color. The ability to actually tuck a color around a corner or under a fold in three dimensions is something that in two dimensions can only ever be a trace. The mobility of color is clearly evident in the reserves and thicknesses that are prevalent in Hantaï's paintings, as well as in his *Stèle*, in Cadere's interest in systematic color and the "error" in his *batons*, in Apfelbaum's heaps and rolls of interiorized and exteriorized stained colors, and in Knoebel's *Sandwich* pieces. Such approaches to color offer painting a thought beyond its own notions of space, pictorialization, and opticality.

L. L.

1. For an introduction to Truitt's work, see Jane Livingston's essay in *Anne Truitt: Sculpture 1961–1991* (New York: André Emmerich Gallery, 1991). The epigraph for this entry is from Clement Greenberg, "Recentness of Sculpture," in Maurice Tuchman, ed., *American Sculpture of the Sixties* (Los Angeles: Los Angeles County Museum of Art, 1967), p. 25.

2. Judd's review of "Black, White, and Gray" is reprinted in *Complete Writings: 1959–1975* (Halifax: Press of the Nova Scotia College of Art and Design; New York: New York University Press, 1975), p. 118.

3. Lucy Lippard, "As Painting Is to Sculpture: A Changing Ratio," in *American Sculpture of the Sixties,* pp. 31–34.

4. Anne Truitt, *Daybook: The Journal of an Artist* (New York: Penguin Books, 1982), p. 81.

5. Anne Truitt, *Turn: The Journal of an Artist* (New York: Viking Press, 1986), p. 57.

6. Anne Truitt, *Daybook,* p. 81.

André Valensi

Born 1947, Paris

Lives and works in Saint-Rémy, France

The title of André Valensi's *Objet d'analyse* makes clear its claim to be an "epistemological object," a term central to the work and expositions of the short-lived group Supports/Surfaces. Other works by Valensi from the time of his participation in the group, many sharing this title, would include stacks of cut and painted corrugated cardboard, knotted or braided cords, and stained and folded wall pieces. The difficult questions raised by this work have to do with both the apparent heterogeneity of these objects and their relation to the larger circumstance of Supports/Surfaces.

The short history of Supports/Surfaces as an exhibiting group was stormy and is still capable of provoking heated dispute. At least two moments can be distinguished: The first is centered around Coroaze, in the south of France, and gave rise to the group's essential theoretical formulations and to a body of work characterized, in part, by a markedly artisanal approach to production and an active interest in moving out of the gallery so as to make the work's literal, material exposure a part of its condition. Such production continues to be a significant feature in the work of the artists who participated in this southern branch of Supports/Surfaces; these artists prominently include Vincent Bioulès and Patrick Saytour in addition to Dezeuze, Valensi, and Viallat. Supports/Surfaces' second major moment is centered in Paris and entails a notable expansion of the initial group, as well as its coming more or less under the theoretical aegis of the journal *Tel Quel* and Marcelin Pleynet in particular. The new Parisian members (Louis Cane and Marc Devade are the most prominent) tended to work closer to received forms of painting and to bring in a more explicit interest in questions of color and pigment—questions that arise for them in part through a reception of the American color-field painting.

It remains unclear whether the work of the members of Supports/Surfaces necessarily entails some form of collective showing. On balance, it seems fair to say that the works remain resolutely individual and that their particular force as engagements of "painting" becomes most explicit when they are set into a broader field of mutual engagement. The particular clustering of Dezeuze, Valensi, and Viallat within *As Painting* is intended to loosely renew this situation.

Supports/Surfaces was directly, and copiously, a theoretical enterprise, and the journal it founded, *Peinture: Cahiers théoriques*, sustained itself for a number of years after the multiple fractures that dissolved the group as an exhibiting force in 1971. The particular theoretical formulations by individual members of the group are somewhat various: Dezeuze, for example, favored a kind of quasi-semiotic analysis that broke painting down into sets of tools, gestures, and supports capable of various kinds of combination. Viallat's analyses turned more directly on questions about the ability or inability of a surface to support itself. All the artists can be said to have shared a belief that traditional painting—the painting of a canvas stretched over a rigid support—laid itself open to a deep misrecognition of its actual material terms, and that it was therefore necessary to refuse and analytically dismantle that system of painting with a view to recovering a materially more adequate account and practice.[1]

Valensi's *Objet d'analyse* takes on its sense and weight within this general field. As a weaving, it is a display of the structure of the canvas itself, rendering visible in its colored warp and weft the intermittences—the passages over and under—that are the actual structure of the painter's surface. The size of this piece is, in the absence of any additional support, determined only by the lengths of the rope of which it is composed and so the piece comes, in the absence of the rigidity provided by such a support, to rest on the floor rather than the wall. Taken together, these features amount to a display of the unavailability of this surface as the support for any kind of projection. This critical point

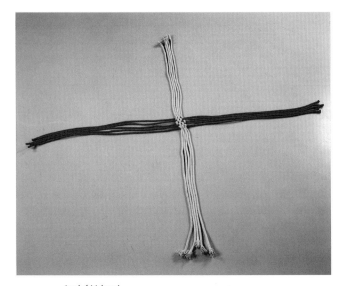

André Valensi
Objet d'analyse, 1970
Collection Musée d'art moderne de Saint-Etienne;
Gift of Vicky Rémy
Photo: Yves Bresson

recurs throughout the work and writing of the Supports/Surfaces group as a whole, particularly in its "southern" aspect, and informs its perhaps surprising sense that, even in an age of abstraction, painting must still struggle against perspective and, more particularly, against the support perspective finds in the treatment of the material facts of painting as, in effect, a screen.

S. M.

1. Supports/Surfaces has been the subject of several relatively recent retrospectives with very useful catalogues, most notably *Supports/Surfaces 1966–1974* (Saint-Etienne: Musée d'art moderne, 1991) and *Les années Supports/Surfaces dans les collections du Centre Georges Pompidou* (Paris: Galerie nationale du Jeu de Paume and Centre Georges Pompidou, 1998). Marie-Hélène Grinfeder's *Les années Supports/Surfaces* (Paris: Edition Herscher, 1991) takes a broad view of the group and other artists working in visible relation to it. Catherine Millet's *L'art contemporain en France,* first published by Flammarion in 1987 and now advanced through several editions, remains an indispensable resource for the work of many of the French artists in *As Painting,* including Valensi.

Installation view of the exhibition *Travaux de l'été 70* at Galerie Jean Fournier, Paris, April 1971, showing works by Dezeuze, Saytour, Valensi, Viallat
Photo: J. Hyde

Claude Viallat
Born 1936, Nîmes, France
Lives and works in Nîmes

There can be something frustrating, even faintly disturbing, about trying to choose works by Claude Viallat for an exhibition of this kind. You stand in his studio and look on as one piece after another appears on the floor before you and then is whisked away or just vanishes beneath the next. Many of Viallat's own exhibitions offer an experience not that different from this moment in his studio: pieces hang on the walls or free of them, are spread out on the floor or draped here and there, or they sit in neatly folded stacks or quietly rolled or in a crumpled heap. And they are all in some sense the same—a signature shape repeated across a surface. There are some things that do not fit in—tondo shields; drawings of various kinds, including perfectly straightforward renderings of bulls and bullfights (there are bullrings in southern France, and Viallat is an aficionado; some photos show him handling his pieces in ways distinctly reminiscent of a matador's handling of a cape); knotted nets and other knotted things; hanging pieces based on weathered wood and rope. . . . The ellipsis that is the only way to close this list is what the list itself is trying to master: one thing after another, always the same and always different. There's no accompanying patter of "problem solving" or progress, no account of how one thing leads to another, which would let you orient yourself in the midst of these things. You might imagine that, given time, patterns of particular concentration, recurrent strategies, or increasingly complex issues might indeed be found. However, faced with the sheer quantity of work, you're likely to have trouble seeing the determination of such patterns as a task that could actually be performed, and you're also likely to be extremely uncertain about its ultimate value.

To present Viallat as if choices were not difficult in this way, as if the selected pieces were single examples outstanding for their quality or their particular clarity about process or meaning or status, would play the work fundamentally false. This peculiar endlessness and ad hoc–ness of the work is certainly one of its leading features, its orientation to "bricolage"—a nonengineered, noncalculated bringing together of things at hand in order to get a given job done or a given thought formed. One might equally speak of its engagement of a certain nonromantic nomadism, a life of taking what one finds and offering it in exchange somewhere further down the line. Like the nomad's objects, Viallat's works are both portable and subject to exposure—the early pieces were shown outdoors and bear the marks of sun or rain; others visibly bare their history, their use before they came into Viallat's hands and the wear of the various places they've been and ways they've been stored.

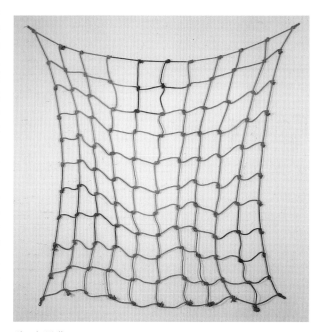

Claude Viallat
Filet, 1970
Courtesy Galerie Daniel Templon, Paris
Photo © André Morain
Art © 2000 Artists Rights Society (ARS), New York/ADAGP, Paris

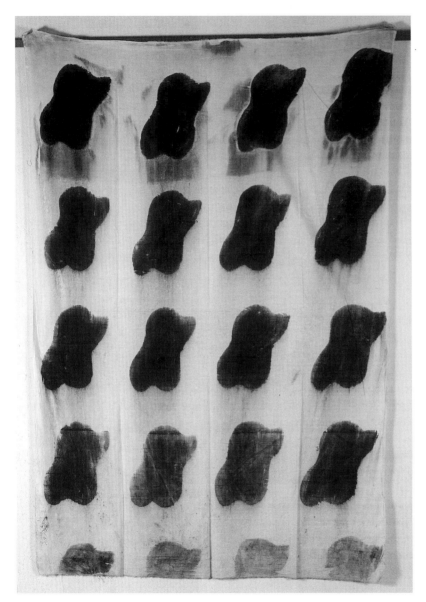

Claude Viallat
Untitled, 1971
Courtesy Galerie Jean Fournier, Paris
Photo: J. Hyde
Art © 2000 Artists Rights Society (ARS), New York/ADAGP, Paris

It can seem as if what one sees in Viallat's studio and exhibitions amounts to a sustained effort to display every sentence that can be said within his particular language. Coming away with what you can remember of a conversation is not exactly like choosing something, but it may be what the work demands and even imposes.

If one stays with this model of language—and it's certainly one that has mattered to Viallat—then one will describe the work's most characteristic element, the bean shape that repeats across so much of his work, as neither form nor figure but as signifier, a thing that has no sense apart from the relations it entertains first of all with other signifiers (including its own repetition) and, through them, with what will then appear as its signified. Repeated within ever-shifting constellations of support and pigment and spacing, the bean shape will in one place signify "form" and invite imagination of its content: an emblem of the artist's palette, so perhaps also of Viallat's abandonment or transformation of that palette; the form of the household sponge used, where Viallat grew up, to (among other things) paint walls; the shape cut out by a knotted net hanging under no greater tension than that provided by the natural pull of its knots, or not that shape but the void it delimits and that is a part of the net's truth. But with this last remark we are coming close to taking this form to be that often assigned to the signifier within a broader theory of language as a differential and relational whole.

In another place or piece, this same shape may seem more nearly to signify "figure" or perhaps "ground," and each of these readings will entail some more or less grammatical shift in one's sense of that shape—as "figure" it stands alone, if also repeatedly alone, against some broader and more continuous field, while as "ground" it would be a site, among others, through which an underlying continuity repeatedly shows and before which Viallat's characteristic shape surrenders its proper presence.

Claude Viallat
Sans titre no. 130, 1997
Courtesy Galerie Daniel Templon, Paris
Photo © André Morain
Art © 2000 Artists Rights Society (ARS), New York/ADAGP, Paris

Following these flights of the signifier across Viallat's work, one inevitably retraces certain intersections that belong both to the shape and to the larger grammars it engages—for example, the interplay of net and knot, as well as the relations that interplay sets up between presence and absence, void and plenum. The first of these is perhaps the theoretical and material center of Viallat's work, where the act of knotting opens mere rope into possibilities of both volume and surface and determines the support for that surface through the tension engendered by those knots. Similarly, Viallat's "stretched" works, his tondo shields, are made of supple wood curved back and bound upon itself, holding both itself and whatever is stretched within it open only through the internal play of forces it sets up. Viallat offers this dialectic of support and surface over and against the more familiar tensioning of a canvas otherwise devoid of support on a rigid stretcher that is itself also not a tensioned whole but something cobbled together simply to hold the canvas. Painting that is autonomous in Viallat's way—holding itself together out of a play of internal binding and knotting—evidently does not lend itself to the imaginations of autonomy we are accustomed to (there's nothing of the *tableau* here). Viallat's practice does not naturally generate single works firmly contained within their frame (the kinds of works we know how to choose), but instead yields pieces visibly in flight beyond themselves. Viallat's knots, folding continuous rope against itself, bring the rope out of itself and into relation, discovering or generating discontinuities, gaps, and voids as a part of its new structure. To see this is to begin to understand what is properly elliptical and excessive in this work, the shape of its partiality and of its ambition to totality.[1]

S. M.

1. For more on Viallat, see above all Christian Prigent, *Viallat: La main perdue* (Metz: Musées de la Cour d'Or; Montigny-lès-Metz: Voix Richard Meier, 1996), as well as *Viallat* (Paris: Centre Georges Pompidou, 1982) and *Claude Viallat* (Vienna: Museum Moderner Kunst Stiftung Ludwig Wien, 1995).

Jacques Villeglé
Born 1926, Quimper, France
Lives and works in Paris

Jacques Villeglé and Raymond Hains first tore down anonymously lacerated posters in 1949 and presented them as works of art, thus becoming the first *affichistes* (from *affiche*, poster) or *décollagistes* (registering an opposition to collage as assemblage by tearing away the surface).[1] Their work immediately intervened within a number of discursive contexts: legal, sociopolitical, and aesthetic. The lacerated posters were already the result of vandalism against private property, according to the "law of 1881" still governing publicity space in France, and the site of the artists' activity carried its own iconography of political propaganda and postwar consumer culture and commodity display. Aesthetic components of their action might include avant-garde strategies of intervention and attempted appropriations or perversions of "spectacle" culture, the displacement of individual expression into a collaborative process involving anonymity in production and mechanically reproduced or defaced imagery, and collisions of established picture-making techniques with mass culture. These works might also suggest that we are looking at what Walter Benjamin terms a "document of barbarism," but it is still difficult to pinpoint the exact source of the *violence* of which the lacerated poster, repasted and stretched up, remains the simultaneous trace and expression.

Just as unsettling when confronted by a work by Villeglé is its seduction, its uncanny ability to both recall and transform any number of art historical practices and avant-garde strategies, all of which were well established by the late forties. Thus, a piece such as *Plateau Beaubourg* can be further situated as a continuation of surrealist ideas (the chance encounters of "automatic writing" or the "exquisite corpse," the fascination with urban environments), as a Duchampian readymade, or as an extension of dadaist practices (from the work of Kurt Schwitters, Raoul Hausmann,

Alfred Baader, or the late surrealist Léo Mallet, who coined the term *décollage*). It can also be considered as a continuation of cubist collage—related less to cubist paintings themselves than to the widespread publication of cubist reproductions after the war—as well as the appropriation of both surrealist and collage image/text juxtapositions in the unprecedented growth of postwar publicity. Further references include a transformation of Matisse's *papiers découpés,* also from the late forties, or Arp's torn bits of paper or Brassaï's and Dubuffet's appeals to urban graffiti. Finally, the paintings can be seen as a radical redefinition of abstraction: lacerated posters as reworkings of Monet's *Nymphéas,* fauve coloring, variations of biomorphic abstraction, or urban "action" painting, with the ritual photographic appearances of Villeglé pulling down posters as a streetscape variation on Hans Namuth's photographs of Pollock in his studio. When we turn to a piece like *Métro St.-Germain-des-Prés,* we might also see a continuation of the radical displacements of syntax and semantics in forms of experimental writing (in Lautréamont's juxtapositions, so crucial to the surrealists, or Villeglé's association with Camille Bryen and the work of the "*Ultra Lettres*"), in the theatrical language inventions of Jarry and Beckett, in dada sound poetry, in Apollinaire's ideographic *Calligrammes,* and in Joyce, Artaud, and Mallarmé. All these names and practices have been evoked in the context of the work, either by Villeglé himself or in the now extensive critical commentary on his work. Indeed, few practices involving such economy of means have been able to open up such an expansive range of art historical and literary references.[2]

Villeglé would also play a pivotal role among the *nouveaux réalistes* when those artists first exhibited as a group in 1960. As the term suggests, "new realism" announced a new perspective on "reality" and a rupture with the art of the past, notably with the values of painting and gestural expression represented by the different generations of the Ecole de Paris. Villeglé and the other *affichistes,* however, shared in addition an abiding

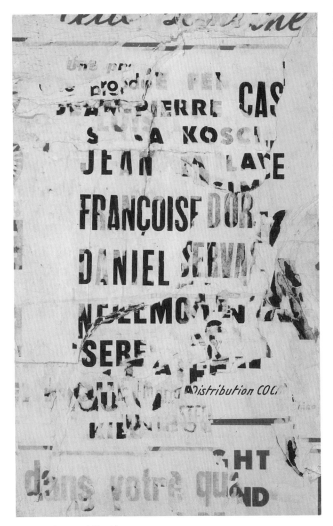

Jacques Villeglé
Métro St.-Germain-des-Prés, 22 September 1964, 1964
Courtesy Zabriskie Gallery, New York
Art © 2000 Artists Rights Society (ARS), New York/ADAGP, Paris

concern that the avant-garde strategies associated with their work had lost their former critical significance—indeed, had become appropriated as pictorial strategies informing much of the very publicity they were finding in the streets. Although the Situationist International began as a continuation of experimental practices with which the *affichistes* were initially associated, Villeglé and the other *affichistes* turned away from any participation in it. This rejection further supports the claim that their ambitions for a "new realism" were matched by an overwhelming sense that effective intervention in postwar urban and consumer culture was becoming increasingly compromised. As Didier Semin and Benjamin Buchloh have both insisted, the "conservative scepticism" and disenchantment of the *affichistes* thus demands a more nuanced acceptance of the discontinuities their work represents (rather than merely its con-

Jacques Villeglé
Plateau Beaubourg, 1960
Collection of Howard and Pamela Holtzman, Chicago
Photo courtesy Alan Koppel Gallery, Chicago
Art © 2000 Artists Rights Society (ARS), New York/ADAGP, Paris

tinuations of various avant-garde practices) and a more nuanced understanding of the conjuncture in which it first operated.[3]

In light of this recent criticism, it is possible to outline three ways in which the work of Villeglé finds its place in *As Painting*, three ways to further explore his place within what Buchloh has termed the "dialectics of painting's dispersal."

First, the lacerated posters share with much of the other work in *As Painting* a refusal to read collage in terms of either assemblage or composition and an attempt to see in it instead a temporally inscribed layering or thickness. The play of recto and verso evident in numerous pieces registers already in the difference between Villeglé's lacerated posters and those of Dufrêne, as does the sense of temporal layering implied in any notion of "appropriation" (for which the collage practices of Levine are the most clearly marked).

Second, Villegle's posters share with many exhibited works an appeal to writing, and in particular to writing as the space of inscription. Writing is understood here as the "already-written" or "already-read," as the production of a pictorial space in which writing not only is inscribed or materialized but constitutes the permanent "re-marking" of that space. This space of inscription finds echoes in Hantaï's and Parmentier's folds, as well as in works by artists as seemingly different as Richter, Degottex, Rouan, and Welling.

Third, and inextricably, Villeglé's practice of removing anonymously lacerated posters from the street and using them as material for his work foregrounds the questions of fragments and fragmentation, of the relation of parts to wholes and interior to exterior spaces, which are also pertinent to the work of Smithson, Cadere, and Buren. This appeal to fragmentation reopens the work of art's relation to its own autonomy, structure, or identity, simultaneously forcing a rethinking of the context in which it now finds itself exposed. In sum, the hope is that Villeglé's work will open a different sense of "dispersal," for which its divisions and displacements remain, arguably, its structural (and nondialectical) condition.

P. A.

1. The best introduction to Villeglé's work is his own writings and interviews, in particular the collection *Urbi et Orbi,* ed. Alain Coulange (Mâcon, France: Editions W., 1986). A useful recent reference in English is the interview in *Jacques Villeglé: Décollages 1950–1998* (Chicago: Alan Koppel Gallery, 1998). Anybody writing on Villeglé today is indebted to the writings of Benjamin Buchloh, from which this entry draws extensively. See in particular "From Detail to Fragment: Décollage Affichiste," *October* 56 (spring 1991): 99–110, and "Hantaï, Villeglé, and the Dialectics of Painting's Dispersal," *October* 91 (winter 2000): 25–35.

2. Perhaps only Warhol's late abstractions have been able to magnetize and "cite" so many art historical references while simultaneously emptying them of any of the critical hold they once seemed to possess.

3. See Didier Semin, "Le palimpseste," in *François Dufrêne,* Cahiers de l'Abbaye Ste-Croix, no. 60 (Les Sables d'Olonne: Musée de l'Abbaye Ste-Croix; Villeneuve-d'Ascq: Musée d'art moderne, 1988), and the essays by Benjamin Buchloh cited above.

James Welling

Born 1951, Hartford, Connecticut
Lives and works in New York and Los Angeles

Since the early seventies, James Welling has continually explored the materials and mechanics that constitute the medium of photography. This attention to the mechanics and "physics" of the medium is both the subject matter of Welling's practice and its matter, where matter is understood as the physical and chemical aspects of the medium typically effaced in any attempt to emulate painterly effects or pictorialism. Irrespective of the genres to which Welling refers (documentary, architectural, landscape, experimental abstraction), the emphasis on (subject) matter is visible in the different cameras he uses (the engines of visualization), the variety of techniques he employs, and the mediums with which he works. The sense of matter included in Welling's subject matter is also visible in the materials he photographs: gelatin, draped fabric, tiles, stone, paper and ink, light, crumpled foil.

A compelling example of this attention to the "physics" of photography is the series of *Degradés* (including *IJWC*). Since these photographs were made without a camera, what we see is not a photograph of color, or a photograph that represents the color of something else; it is a photograph that is colored. In this sense, the *Degradés* are made out of the "physics" of light and color and photographic paper, where color is not so much reproduced as "captured at the very moment of its production."[1] Production is understood here as color's temporal transformation as the photograph is made, a transformation that is registered through the chromatic transitions of color itself, such as the shifts from orange to brick red. This transformation has nothing to do with an attempt to make photography analogous to the qualities of a Rothko. It is the color of photography that matters here, the way color appears in and as the photograph. The prominence of the white frames for the *Degradés* reinforces this sense of color captured incessantly at the moment of its production.

James Welling
IJWC, 1989
Courtesy the artist

James Welling
LIV, 1988
Collection The Museum of Contemporary Art, Los Angeles;
Gift of Peter and Eileen Norton, Santa Monica

There have been two ways of responding to Welling's various experimental practices. The first suggests that the appeal to the mechanics of photography is metaphoric, part of an attempt to identify the specificity of photography as a medium. Thus, Ulrich Loock argues that Welling's series of draped fabrics (including *LIV*) fill the space of the photograph to remove spatial depth and so may be read "as a metaphor for the physical picture surface," with the velvet "a metaphor for the various manifestations of photographic grain."[2] The metaphoric relation between the materials photographed and the surface then demonstrates something "intrinsic to the medium," where the referent reflects back onto the materiality of the photographic support: "the essence of the photographic . . . is exposed photographically, by the structured exposure of photopaper." Extending this reading, Welling's photography is not only an analytic exploration of the medium's possibilities but "self-reflexive"—"photography of photography." This self-reflexivity is confirmed by the analogies between the nineteenth-century world of factories and trains that is the subject of several of Welling's series and the fact that photography was itself a nineteenth-century, industrial invention.

The second response to Welling's experimental practices has argued that his photography is irreducible to forms of self-reflexivity, irreducible to making the assumed transparency of the photographic image into an opacity, and then making that opacity a metaphor of the medium's specificity. Thus, referring to Welling's *Gelatin Photographs,* Rosalind Krauss argues that

> the gelatin is the enabling matrix of the photographic medium, the emulsion in which the silver salts are both held in suspension and bound to the two-dimensional support of the film. Yet it is important to stress that though this reflexiveness echoes that auto-referential concern of modernist painting to articulate the image by simultaneously displaying its own conditions of possibility, it is a reflexiveness with entirely different aims in sight.[3]

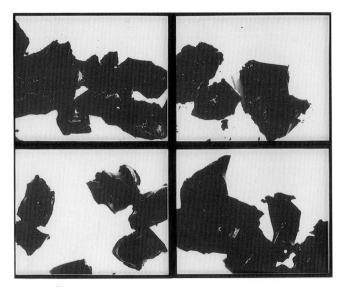

James Welling
Gelatin Photographs, 1977–80
Collection Frac Bourgogne, France

James Welling
Diary/Landscape #199 and *Diary/Landscape #178* from *Diary of Elizabeth and James Dixon (1840–41)/Connecticut Landscapes*, 1977–86
Courtesy the artist

Against a modernist reading, the "reflexive fold" is read as an experience of what Lacan terms the "missed encounter" or an absence of recognition, a "delay" between "seeing the image and understanding what it [is] an image of."

A refusal to secure Welling's photographs as examples of modernist self-reflexivity can also be examined in light of the temporal dimension of surface effects. In Krauss's reading of the *Diary* photographs, "the logic of the work, as opposed to its contents, [centers] around the fold of the book's binding and the pages' disappearance into and reappearance out of that fold. The fold seem[s] to express the logic of a single sheet bent over to become a double and therefore to mirror itself, to serialize itself, to create a system of recurrence. The fold [is] the topological expression of recurrence."[4] The surface is opened to a temporal dimension that breaks open any attempt to secure an identity between what is photographed and the material support of the photograph itself.

This sense of recurrence is investigated further in several recent essays in which photography's metaphoric identity with its medium-specificity is subject to a metonymic displacement from itself as a measure of its relation to the world.[5] What binds and unbinds photography to itself and the world is registered in Welling's series of *Light Sources* (such as *Lousianne*). For light is not just the "source" of these photographs, in the sense of their subject matter "in the world." It is indissociably its *matter* (light and shadow), what the photograph produces and is produced by, both the cause and effect of photography's "physics." The photographs of light suggest that the light sources are not about securing some metaphorical identity between the light of the world with the light

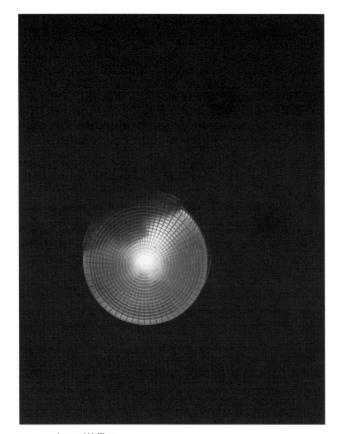

James Welling
Lousianne, 1998
Courtesy Donald Young Gallery, Chicago

surfaces; in reflexive folds that are irreducible to self-reflexivity, metaphor, or flatness. The relation of Welling's photography to the painting included in the exhibition does not suggest, for example, that the folds of draped fabric are analogous to the folds in the work of Hantaï, and thus another attempt to emulate painterly effects or pictorialism. For the limits that define Welling's practice are situated in their adjacency to painting, metonymically and not metaphorically. With luck, their proximity might open another way in which the medium of painting exposes itself—*as* painting.

P. A.

1. I owe this formulation to Hubert Damisch, "Concert (Portrait of an Artist as Michael Snow)," in Michael Snow, *Panoramique: Photographic Work and Films 1962–1999* (Brussels: Société des Expositions du Palais des Beaux-Arts de Bruxelles, 1999), p. 27. The essay turns around photography's *matière*—both matter and subject matter.

2. Ulrich Loock, "Photography and Non-Portrayability—James Welling," in *James Welling* (Lucerne: Kunstmuseum Luzern, 1998), p. 46.

3. Rosalind Krauss, "Photography and Abstraction," in *A Debate on Abstraction* (New York: Bertha and Karl Leubsdorf Art Gallery, Hunter College, 1989), p. 67.

4. Ibid., p. 66.

5. This transition is explored in Michael Fried's essay, "James Welling's *Lock,* 1976," in Sarah J. Rogers, ed., *James Welling: Photographs 1974–1999* (Columbus, Ohio: Wexner Center for the Arts, Ohio State University, 2000), pp. 25–28. The best essay on Welling's work in this regard remains Walter Benn Michaels, "The Photographic Surface," in *James Welling: Photographs 1977–90* (Bern: Kunsthalle Bern, 1990), pp. 102–13.

that is photography. Rather, they expose the passage of light itself, its temporal transformation in which all photography (the writing of its light) is its own exposure, to and from itself, the way the world reveals or exposes itself photographically.

In situating a number of Welling's photographs in *As Painting,* our aim is to bring his work into proximity to practices that share the same interests: in a materiality that is a condition of the work's visibility; in surfaces that are also the temporal re-marking of those

An *As Painting* Anthology

A Regard for Painting (*la peinture me regarde*)[1]

Christian Prigent

Untitled

"Untitled" is a title many contemporary artists give their works. Granted, many of these works do not *depict* anything (namable).

They do, however, *represent*. But what do they represent? What nature impossible to assign to the apparatus of naming under any heading? And what would authorize entitling such work? This is the question these artists of the sixties—engaged as they were in a radically analytical questioning of the codes of pictorial or sculptural representation—invite us to consider through their works.

"I do not want anything that bears a name anymore," said Jean Dubuffet. Or again: "You will free your gaze from the names given to things. You will fix it at the moment when it is not yet interpreted, not yet perverted by the names given to things. There will be no more things when there are no more names."

Painting is one of the names of this deferral of names (of assigned names, of probable titles). Thus there is no need to invent a *meaning* for paintings: their meaning lies above all in the deferral of figures, of forms, of meaning—in the display of this deferral. And if, at some level, there can be connivance, exchange, complicity, thinking (and pleasure)—it is on this ground, on the ground of an unconditional reckoning with this unstable terrain where painting places its *disorienting* signposts before our jaded eyes.

Why Make Art?

The puritanical and insolently frontal declarativity of the pieces collected in *As Painting* calls for thought. It asks basic questions: Why do this? Why make art?

A few naked truths:

First: One makes "art" because the representations that inform one about the world do not satisfy. A nagging doubt emerges as to the adequacy of language to things. One is thus forced to grapple with "style": opening up space and inventing forms.

Second: Painting represents not things but what lies between things, what articulates them (the impressionists call it "light," the action painters call it "gesture," Kosuth calls it "concept," Dezeuze would call it the "void"). For the things we re-*present* (objects of the world or moments of the body) bathe in the senseless instability of the present: time, which haunts them; the gaze, which seizes them; language, which arranges them into forms—all transform things into volumes hollowed out by enigma (*Pointless Vanishing Point,* Smithson says) and opened to that trembling confusion we call a *present* (for which Richter's blurry images provide an emblematic approximation).

Third: An artistic act is both the institution of a form and a provocation to formlessness. It denotes a paradoxical effort to fix in the finiteness of forms that which motivates one to make art: a taste for the infinite that exceeds finite forms, an attraction for the insignificant that hollows out sensible figures. This altercation of form and formlessness, of the finite and the infinite, of the full and the empty, is what generates Barré's interrupted tracings; Dezeuze's empty stretchers; Rouan's torn and rewoven figures; Viallat's nets, whose mesh catches nothing but nothingness itself: the thing, stubbornly recoiling from the symbolic.

Fourth: An artistic language does not represent what is (which is fixed in the finiteness of the figure). It represents what is done and undone in the boundlessness of dis-figuration, to which any figure is destined by the senselessness of the present. "The more one determines a figuration," says Dubuffet, "the more one diminishes its signification." One may witness this conflict between more-determination and less-signification displayed, on the one hand, in the ambiguous and indefinitely repeated form that punctuates Viallat's free-hanging sheets; and on the other, in the dispersion/coherence dialectic performed on the ground in various pieces by Bochner, showing and erasing through painting the flux of the depicted, described, informed world.

Fifth: Painting composes paradoxically iconoclastic images that free our gaze from the hold of images. Painting traverses the world's coded figures and repeats them. It makes us see something else, otherwise, behind the articulated shadows that positive knowledges, precoded representations, and the stereotyped, endlessly switching and superficial flow of mediatized images would have us take for the real.

Painting Regardless *(la peinture n'est pas à l'oeil)*

People appropriate the world through a few articulated tracings that organize it into languages. But at the same time they part with the world and dispose it in the distance of the symbolic. The painted work translates this distance into the optical gap measured by the eye, so that sensations of cut and loss invade this distance.

But a painting is also a finely worked object whose materiality suggests the attenuation of distance: this object solicits a contact with its elaborated surface, it beckons the viewer to a sensual relationship with its colored surfaces, to a tactile approach of the world's textures. It is violently invested by desire, and from the ambivalent background thus cleared emerges an energy that is variously colorful (Viallat), layered (Rouan), monochromatically condensed (Bishop, Devade), or aggressively pulverized into rhythm (Hantaï), and that violently mobilizes sight. In other words, these paintings do not show anything other than the very impulse to show. They make visible only the tension of the desire to see. They represent nothing except the dream of a symbolic appropriation that would not be fatally bound to renounce what it sought at the very moment of its finding: things, world, bodies cancelled out as soon as they are designated.

A painting requires not simply that it be seen; it assigns us to a unique point of view. Baudelaire noted the imperative nature of this assignation: "Painting has only one point of view; it is exclusive and despotic." Painting, in short, inspects us. Unless we get out of the *picture*—and this has been one of modernity's preoccupations. Witness Viallat's immense (optically unassailable) formats; Dezeuze's scatterings of tarlatane through the space of the exhibition; the optical discomfort caused by the fluid articulations managed by Bishop or Devade; the optical deception implied in minimalist strategies; or the radical frustration of the eye that so-called "conceptual" art entails.

Even if we remain at the level of the picture, though, questions arise: as soon as the words "to see," "visible," or "sight" are uttered, their meaning wavers. For what is to see? What is to show? What is to render visible? And what is there to render visible that would not have been previously "seen" (or not seen appropriately)?

Painting is the mode of being of these questions. Inasmuch as it shows something (figures, lines, colors), painting asks sight a question; it asks the question of sight; it opens up an enigma onto that screen from which shadows emerge, at once bold and shy, mutable and persistent, unstable and petrified, and which constitute for us the "world."

Of course, one may say that painters are busy making the forms of reality visible (disposing them in a space the eye can identify). But the opposite statement is just as true. The works of painting burn with the desire to disfigure (or to distort the objectal and corporeal forms we spontaneously identify and in which we recognize ourselves). They undo the numbed vision we have of things—the vision which, precisely, we call "reality": the visible vision. As a result, the very conditions of that visible vision are tinged with suspicion and thrown into doubt and confusion.

Without starting from this point, it is hard to understand these works and their stubborn rejection of the optical canons of painting—a rejection variously achieved by invalidating focalization through the expansive reach of the "all over" or the absolutely homogeneous flatness of hard-edge painting; by imposing a monochrome field which forces us, quite literally, to see *nothing but blue* (Klein), or black (Reinhardt), or white (Ryman); by spreading the canvas on the ground and thus withdrawing it from optical frontality (Bochner); by corrupting perspective (Dibbets, Rousse, Alberola); by forcing the painting out of planar space and quadrangular format through all kinds of baroque outgrowths (Stella, Gauthier); by letting saturated paint congeal, inviting the viewer's touch (Dubuffet, Poons, Barcelo); by redividing figures in the scattered cuttings of *tressage* (Rouan); by working with one's eyes shut, blindly, in the arbitrarily hidden and magically revealed folds of the deployed canvas (Hantaï); by giving up the tensed canvas in favor of soaked cloth (Louis), netlike and diaphanous (Dezeuze) or transparent (Buraglio, Degottex) or even ostensibly absent supports (Dezeuze's ladders and empty stretchers, Viallat's ropes and nets). All of these practices are ways of engulfing, erasing, or repelling any easily visualizable representation, getting a perverse charge out of evading the visible (at any rate, the merely—or wholly—visible).

In Respect of Painting (*la peinture me regarde*)

Simon Hantaï once said that the painter must "turn a blind eye." Turning a blind eye is, perhaps, to no longer want to see the visible (to no longer be able to stand, as it were, the *sight* of it). This would be to no longer want a cutting out reduced to the forms of Euclidean geometry or of the body cramped within its anatomical sack—so many objects muscularly *informed*, formalized and enclosed within petrifying codes.

And it would be instead to situate painting at the place where visibility comes undone. It would be to make sure that, if something ultimately *is* visible, it isn't so to a hypnotized eye. It would be to refuse that sight be something akin to the insatiable reflex of the optical nerve, as it instinctively sticks its tip to the focal point of the screen like a sclerotic grasshopper glued to a chameleon's tongue. It is to want sight to be anxious, to lose itself and find itself again in an unmoored and

faltering drift. For that drift is the only kind of "gaze" one can adopt when one really *regards,* that is, when one strives to grasp and to gauge painted representations from within one's *just* (equivocal and ruptured) conscience of the irresolute present of things.

What painting thus shows us and what holds us before it is the shattering of sight, the refusal of a world perpetually kept at a distance by sight, the refusal to be subordinated to an optical grasp. It is to refuse to allow vision to be that grasping which no doubt permits us to appropriate the world—but without risking ourselves in it and without losing ourselves in it, without, then, our coming to know it.

Here I am in front of (a) painting. Of course I am looking at it. But I am just as much under the threat of its gaze. Painting looks at me (*la peinture me regarde*). It sees me and keeps its eye on me. It summons me to see what I otherwise do not want to see (what I don't want to admit any regard for [*ce dont je ne veux rien savoir*]). It picks me out, anxious and undone, but also deliciously displaced, unfettered, and relieved of the weight of my own assent to the obtuse order of things. It makes me delight in a peculiar sort of fear, a fear confessed and overcome—provisionally.

1999

Translated from the French by Anthony Allen.

Christian Prigent is a poet and critic who has written extensively on contemporary French art and particularly on the work of various members of Supports/Surfaces.

1. [The French phrase "la peinture me regarde" may be translated as "painting looks at me" or "painting concerns me." Here, as in further examples, we have tried to register Prigent's play on a thematic of the gaze through words like "regard" or "respect," while preserving the French original parenthetically. Trans.]

On Painting as Model
Catherine Millet

Now that "installation" is an artistic genre, one can consider Jason Rhoades as one of its "masters." He has realized installations that are among the largest, the most open and scattered, using an array of extremely heterogeneous objects that nonetheless are held together by complex semantic relations. Reading an article on this work, I learned that the artist aimed, by means of a particular setup that placed the visitor at the center of one of his installations, to permit that spectator to experience a colored environment "like that of an abstract painting." The comparison was all the more striking because it was not the first time that an artist whose work consisted in the assembly of more or less readymade objects expressed something of this sort. This made me think of the very large number of film and theater performers and directors (including some of the most successful, who thus have occasion to be satisfied with their work) who show a real fascination for painting. Many paint as amateurs—or something more than amateurs—and many collect paintings. The appearance of installation in the domain of the plastic arts has authorized some of these actors and directors to contribute by also making installations—notably, but not exclusively, with the audio-visual material they know how to use—that have been shown in the places until then devoted to painting: museums. Peter Greenaway is one of the most brilliant representatives of this tendency. Ephemeral like theater, and even younger than cinema, and, like both, often depending in part on collective work, installation art perhaps awakens in those who practice it a nostalgic feeling or at least a desire for a perennial art, the outcome of a single will rich with a long tradition. Painting is thus, paradoxically, the more or less discernible vanishing point of a perspective in which are placed various contemporary practices once believed to be an "overcoming" of painting.

At the same time that it began to be considered dead, or at least to have been rendered obsolete by techniques that released it from various functions, painting became a sort of myth toward which many turned back, and which, in this form, played the role of a paragon. One might even reconsider the formalist theory of painting in its specificity from this point of view: painting dedicated to saying and resaying "Painting" would have served to maintain its pure presence in an epoch (that of the consumerism of the post-postwar period and the first explosion of mass media) that implicitly denied it—to maintain this until it became clear that painting could rediscover an effective role at the heart of society. In the end, don't those who use neither the tools nor the materials of painting dream of turning to their profit a small spark borrowed from its incomparable symbolic aura (and registered by the price reached by certain paintings)?

A negative consequence of this situation bears particularly on a certain type of photography, currently very much in fashion, which, in its composition, aesthetic, and iconography reinstates stereotypes long abandoned by painting. The necessarily "suspended" character of the photograph gives a modernist cachet to images that exploit a convenient narrativity or psychologism (I'm thinking of, for example, the work of Jeff Wall or Tracey Moffatt).

Photography, film, video, and synthesized images, far from discouraging painters, have on the contrary excited their competitive spirit and their desire to answer the challenge of these new modes of expression. Perhaps for this reason, in the past few years, figurative painting has shown itself the most adventurous and innovative. Figurative painting has perfectly integrated the processes by which abstract painting, on the one hand, and the nonpictorial avant-gardes on the other, have modified our way of apprehending the world. In this area, the work of Gerhard Richter is often the primary reference, but he is far from the only one. To give but one further example, a French painter of a younger generation, one might mention Vincent Corpet, whose life-size portraits, painted and modeled with altogether traditional technique, nonetheless are captured in a space as deprived of depth as an Ellsworth Kelly! Our relation to the real is definitively reversed. The world is not as representational painting reflected it throughout the tradition inherited from the Renaissance; it is as modern painting—that is to say, painting that shows itself as artifact—constructs it.

Now that we have enough distance to judge, we ought equally to realize that, against received ideas, twentieth-century abstraction has been as socially and politically engaged as figuration, and has been so from the beginning. The architectural and social extensions that Mondrian and Malevich imagined for their painting arose from an ambition much vaster than Picasso's cohabitation with the communist party. And Matisse stood aside from these struggles. Without any doubt, a deep logic linked Newman's militancy in the thirties and the conception of painting he subsequently imposed: in both cases it was a matter of "being" in the world. In France, the last strongly engaged artistic movement was that of support-surface in the seventies, all of whose members were at the time abstract painters, working precisely in continuity with postwar American abstraction. In 1973, one of the principle representatives of support-surface, Marc Devade, was enraged about a certain form of revalorization of painting:

> So, do you want me tell you that "peinture-peinture" pisses me off! . . . Enough of those small or large objects for intimate pleasure or bank accounts. . . . Swatches of canvas on the wall can transform very quickly into ribbons for the chests of colonels. . . . Paint "well," with all the "specifically" pictorial, formal, and technical acquirements—if they are not the mark of a global subjective transformation at the level of daily life and psychopathology, of a theorized social transformation, they are nothing more than adjuncts to the evolutionism proper to the bourgeois system, mere rhetoric. . . .[1]

One doesn't find much of an audience willing to affirm so radical a political conscience now. At least one can say that painters who have followed a path through the heart of abstraction are often the first to project their ideas into public space, if only across the privileged link they entertain with architecture. One can speak of a "becoming architectural" in Stella's work. Through his conception of work "in situ," Buren maintains a critical reading (in the extended sense of the term) of the institutional spaces in which he intervenes. It happens that in this confrontation, the institutional space always comes out on top, but at least the artist will have taken the risk. Even the discreet Martin Barré, in the last years of his life, didn't exhibit without carefully thinking out an altogether original arrangement of his paintings in the exhibition space. When the Jeu de Paume in Paris dedicated a major show to him in 1993, he completely redivided the space of the museum, had new walls constructed, and then hung his paintings at heights that, even if only literally, obliged the visitors to elevate their regard! I recall having visited that show on an ordinary day, at the same time as a group of young people. They passed through the show in twos and threes, retracing their steps, calling out to one another and stretching out their arms to indicate to the others a painting placed just below the ceiling, regrouping to exchange their impressions. . . . Opposing what one is used to seeing in museums—zombies filing in front of the works, often enclosed and isolated within their audioguides—Barré cut off all effects of fascination and restored to the museum its first function of being a space for a convivial intellectuality.

Recalling these exchanges, I will have a tendency to be less tolerant than I have been recently with non-pictorial practices that lay claim to a pictorial status or quality. I have no desire to return to an academic definition of painting that confines it in the use of traditional ("specific"!) materials. Instead I believe that, figurative or abstract, inscribed on the canvas or flowing onto the surrounding walls, painting finally enables less conformity than many of the "new media" and "new technologies." Because it has been called upon to respond to a multitude of attacks from outside, as well as from within, painting is an exercise in particularly severe critical thinking. And painting is, rather than a model, an excellent observation post—especially of those practices to which it occasionally serves as model.

2000

Translated from the French by Stephen Melville.

Catherine Millet is the founder and editor of *art press*. She has written, as both critic and historian, across the range of contemporary art.

1. This text appeared in *Peinture: Cahiers théoriques* 8–9 (February 1974) and is reprinted in Marc Devade, *Ecrits théoriques, II* (Paris: Archives des arts modernes, 1989).

Painting Out of Subject

Ann Hindry

> It is expressly to Manet that we have to attribute the birth of the painting with no signification other than the art of painting that is modern painting.
>
> —Georges Bataille

"Abstract practice" is an oxymoron. The term "practice" indicates first of all the setting to work of an activity in its material capacity, while abstraction in all its forms is a subtraction from the order of tangible things. As is well known, abstract painting belongs more to the vocabulary of the spirit than to that of the experience-able visual world. Nonetheless, it is only when abstract painting (or abstract sculpture) is being discussed that the accepted terminology of our modern (and later postmodern) era reaches out to the generalized term "practice." (It's enough to try out "figurative practice" to become aware of an incongruity there.) Thus: Is there, in that complex exercise in the visual realization of the idea that is abstract painting, something closer to the ground that differentiates it from the exercise of representation? Certainly, the one preceded the other, and that one had to fight before imposing itself for a long period as the flower of modernist evolution, but it's nonetheless true that the "abstract intention" seems more limited in advance, simply as an intention—as if it were a question of a project of life as opposed to the project of a life. It is of course hardly new to say that the figurative approach "renders the visible," while abstract painting "renders visible,"[1] exposes. On the other hand, perhaps one should ask about the limited character of the one as opposed to the essential interminability of the other. The emergence of the figurative artist naturally opposes the object engendered to its maker, in a well-understood system of alterity, arising from the represented external subject and thus circumscribed by it. The emergence of the abstract artist is never fully achieved because the abstract painting remains an integral part of the personal and exclusive "world" of the artist. Whatever its register, the abstract painting seems, in its very way of being, to be first of all the place of a sequential deposit of the painter's action and the motive to that action. The figurative painting is, by contrast, instantly a mirror, severed and autonomous, irradiating its subject in the face of its creator.

A slightly shifted relation of difference between the finished work and its author can thus be invoked to explain the nuanced use of the term "practice" and thus flatten out the contradiction inherent in its apposition with "abstract." In any case, by "abstract practice," one understands well enough a taking into account of the means, materials, and self-referential content of the work, and that in order to return to the moment of action or to gloss the logic of the material or to risk an interpretation, it is both tempting and dangerous to speculate much on the intention or rational origin of the approach. (Knowing that Matisse began his cutouts because rheumatism had destroyed the agility of his fingers or that Michaux was allergic to oil paint is interesting but doesn't sufficiently clarify their work.) Very schematically, for the figurative painter intention and realization can be considered two distinct givens, analyzable in view of the finished painting, its physiognomy, and its subject; for the abstract painter, the intention remains glued to the pictorial action, which is also what the finished painting presents. In other words, paraphrasing Gertrude Stein, the intention is the action is the object. It's a difficult enterprise. In fact, from the dawn of "abstract practice" to the present, it has not stopped being difficult, although the ingredients of that difficulty have evolved with the context.

Thus, in our postmodern situation of simulacra and superficially undifferentiated multiplicity, the relation to the image has become once again quasi-monolithic: the image for the image, the image as sole referent. Thus, somewhat as photography could at a certain moment have been considered as usurping the position of painting (or even sculpture) in the established relation of subject and image, so the contemporary cultural world of the always deflected image, easily overflowing the boundary of the real and the virtual in order to attain a sort of nonitemized hyperreality, has in some way usurped the position of self-referential modernist abstract painting of the image for the image's sake. The recurrent question of abstract practice thus reposes itself today in a pertinent way, on a basis that is not new but expanded.

There are two images that come to mind simultaneously, despite an immense gap in registers, when I think of abstract painting as a practice: one is of the angel rolling up a corner of the sky in Giotto's frescoes in the Scrovegni Chapel, revealing behind the emblematic blue monochrome the illusionistic representation of a place (the house of God?), substituting one representation for another, a visually intelligible figure for a symbolic nonform (the blue plane = heaven) and at the same time recalling every image to its "pellicular dimension,"[2] its destiny as a surface. The other is a contemporary cartoon, of the kind magazines love to print, by Peter Porges, where one sees a little man in a lab coat in front of a gigantic wall of electronic equipment—switches and monitors and buttons and screens, and so on—the upper corner of which is becoming unglued like painted paper, discovering the bare wall beneath. The representation of representation remains an effective strategy across the centuries, but here it is joined by the practical play of literal abstraction. Abstraction made from the image, the plane remains. The image is abstracted of all material identity; it exists only on the plane. Giotto's sky is nothing more than a pictorial sign just as the wall of computers is no more than a design. But what remains beneath when one abstracts what is above? Whether Giotto's "abstraction" opens on divine presence or the "abstraction" of the full wall opens on the absence of all human activity, the working of the opposition of above and beneath opens onto the question of pictorial specificity, of presence and absence. Bataille had already said of Manet's *Olympia* (Manet,

to whom of course one owes the premises that opened the possibility of abstraction): "The subject is nothing . . . she is the sacred horror of her presence—a presence whose simplicity is that of absence."[3]

It is between presence and absence, material reality and lived theory, image and surface, preliminary deconstruction and momentary reconstruction, that young abstract practices are going to continue to open, according to morphologically distinct paths.

In his abstract pictorial practice, Christian Bonnefoi seeks to bring about a paradoxical situation in each painting, where any dissociation of recto and verso, face and obverse, becomes obsolete. Preoccupied from an ontological point of view with the image's conditions of appearance, he seeks to escape in painting from the Saussurean shackles according to which "there must be something behind that which is in front" by betting on the specific dimension of the "plane." In interlocking plane and surface by means of a systematic and prior deconstruction of their physical identity, he looks, successfully, to restore the painting's status as object while preserving the image. The dialectical question of the above and beneath as either distinct or conflated dimensions had been taken up by a significant number of contemporary painters—François Rouan, Martin Barré, and Sigmar Polke, to name but a few and certainly not the least—but has rarely been posed in such radical terms as those of the condition of the appearance of the *tableau* as phenomenon. The irrefutable character of Christian Bonnefoi's abstract practice belongs to the way that the visual forms, which are in the end constitutive of the *tableau,* were not precisely directed by the painter in the course of the material elaboration of the work. It's not a question, however, of some kind of "automatic writing," revisited some fifty years after the fact, but of a releasing of visual control, as the artist himself puts it. What's necessary is that nothing in the pictorial act be projective, that nothing preexist, that plane, surface, and support coexist materially and temporally. For this "blind practice," Bonnefoi has put into effect a relatively simple system for binding surfaces that lets the final dawning of the painting happen only before the gaze—of the painter, as well as of the spectator. As with Giotto and as explicated in Porges's cartoon, two states of the surface coexist: the above and the beneath. But here, in the reabsorption of the chronology inherent in any process of construction, the pictorial surface is no longer abstracted from the volumetric and temporal situation of the *tableau*. Bonnefoi's pictorial practice is an abstract practice with neither allusion nor illusion, and which is not experienced as possible in the moment without taking into account the preparatory deconstruction indispensable to all its attributes. Painting as subject, and the *tableau* as a thought body.

Just where Bonnefoi takes the calculated risk of iconoclasm in making a prior material dispersal the condition of his practice, Fiona Rae practices a painting abstracted from allusions rendered deliberately incomplete by the play of purely visual dispersals of form and surface, at the risk of aesthetic abolition, of making mere "confection." In other words, Bonnefoi pushes at the ontological confines of painting through a phenomenological experimentation of the *tableau,* while Fiona Rae uses the aesthetic conventions inherited from the modernist interpretation of Kant to make the distribution of figures on the surface the identifying condition of her painting. The one deconstructs above all (abstracts his practice from conventions) while the other wagers everything on the thin edge of the ultimate equilibrium of the composition (abstracts convention from her practice). Bonnefoi's *tableau*-object and Rae's painted surfaces constitute themselves in parallel before the gaze.

This said, the allusive forms inscribed, or better deposited in a knowing swarm, with their evocations of other forms, notions, facts tributary to the history of painting, and orchestrated all across the surface of the painting with a very considered gestural violence, return to such great moments in the repertory of abstract practice as abstract expressionism or lyrical abstraction. So? A "conventional" abstract painting? Yes and

no. Conventional in its means and subversive in its effects. In a context where it is absolutely impossible to control the proliferation of cultural microreferences, Rae's colors, nonforms, and kitsch superimpositions offer a globalizing partitioning that is neither visually nor intellectually indifferent. At the same time, nothing really discernable happens except the *idea* of painting, in all its precariousness, its microscopic instant of crystallization at the edge of the abyss. A practice held by a thread.

Adrian Schiess similarly decomposes the initial ingredients of the pictorial setup. He invades the spectator's eye with a single bold color at the same time that he invests the entire space by means of a group of large *tableau*-planks, leaned vertically against the wall or placed horizontally, slightly inclined, on the ground. The precarious aspect of their "pose"—apparently a matter of trial and error—contrasts with the irredentist rigor of their installation and the perfection of their smooth and monochrome surfaces. Thus set on stage, they most fully declare their identity as objects to the extent that their material constituents—their thickness and woodenness, their weight, their symmetry—are most immediately before one's mind. At the same time, though, the haze of color that emerges from the surface of the shiny industrial paint fills the space and blurs contours. Additionally, the reflective capacity of these surfaces participates immediately in their dissolution. The *tableau* disintegrates under the gaze of the spectator only to reconstitute itself here and there along the line of the spectator's tour of these crushing panels. Color, pulverized in the space where the painting is camped, recovers, through the rectangles of mirroring surface, an autonomy no figure can arrest—since the *tableau,* as present as it may be as a real object, does not give the color its form. In contrast with Bonnefoi, Schiess performs no prior deconstruction in order to make a painting that reconstitutes itself only under the spectator's gaze; making its elaboration an ahistorical process, he dialectically engages the autonomy of color with its support, preserving, at the temporal level, the dichotomy he puts to work. The line that delimits the circuit of the *tableau,* however reified, becomes fictive in the reflective play of the mirroring monochrome surfaces and the spatial expansion of the liberated color—to such an extent that this color will not necessarily even be perceived as associated with a properly pictorial proposition.

To the question—so piercing in this period of historical fatigue, dominated by the temptation to epilogue—of the existence of a contemporary modulation of artistic practice tending to new forms, one can thus oppose some practices which, abstract as they are, are no less nourished, materially and intellectually, by the central design of making sense triumph over deconstruction.

1997

Translated from the French by Stephen Melville.

Ann Hindry is a widely published critic and curator, the French translator of Clement Greenberg's *Art and Culture,* and currently director of the Renault Collection. This essay was previously published (in French) as "Peintures hors subjet," *Rue Descartes* 16 (April 1997): 105–09.

1. I'm paraphrasing Paul Klee's celebrated proposal according to which painting ought not "render the visible" but "render visible."

2. This expression is used by Denis Hollier about François Rouan in "La peinture au défi," in *Où est passée la peinture?, art press,* hors série no. 16 (1995), a special issue of *art press* on painting.

3. Georges Bataille, *Manet* (Lausanne: Skira, 1955).

Excerpts from *The Subject of Painting*
Paul Rodgers

Simon Hantaï

On the basis of his experiment with pure automatism and a confrontation with Pollock's achievement, [Hantaï] developed an interest in systematic production by establishing the technique of folding now connected with his name. This technique is sufficiently idiosyncratic to justify a brief description. The canvas is first, so to speak, "collapsed" in a series of folds. The prepared surface is then painted while the material inside the folds is left untouched by the brush. Finally, the canvas is stretched open to reveal a picture made up of color cut out from its underlying material of white. In earlier work, the canvas was crumpled so that the automatic gesture is associated with the material's haphazard folds. In the later series, entitled Tabula, the folds take the form of regular-sized squares so that when the canvas is opened, an expanded field appears where the all-over format has been fixed in a process of repetition. Thus, interest in production as a formal device can be traced back to the process of Surrealist automatism. For Hantaï, the transition from spontaneous gesture to mechanical repetition underscores a desire for anonymity. . . .

Hantaï uses the folding method to develop a mode of almost philosophical reflection where the descent of the artist's volition to the level of mechanical repetition provokes, by repercussion, a sense of displaced identity in the mind of the viewer.

James Bishop

As for Bishop, his manipulation of rich and subtle tones of color in a discreetly charged flow of liquid energy results in an intimate and withdrawn art which seems to hint at the perception of an underlying presence. . . .

Bishop's art seems to emanate from the interior of his painting.

Daniel Dezeuze

Dezeuze began his career by exhibiting an artist's stretcher stripped of canvas and propped against a wall. Such a bald use of the painter's primary materials might well be situated in the long line of Dadaist and Duchampian provocations, or in the context of the more recent Minimalist appropriation of real space. The whole development of the artist's work since that date shows that his intention was just the opposite. Dezeuze has since used a series of ever more flexible materials, from lattice to gauze, which seem to soften and elasticate the structure of perspective and its illusion of full space, so that now his original stretcher appears as a polemical assertion of the rights of an invisible and excluded space between the planes of traditional vision. Dezeuze had clearly seen that the Minimalist occupation of three dimensions had crushed the symbolic status of art by reducing it to the level of the "real," and his whole endeavour has been to reverse this tendency in the interests of recapturing a lost sense of expansion.

1982

Paul Rodgers has written for both *Artforum* and *Artscribe* about French painting of the sixties and seventies. He has excerpted the remarks above from the catalogue text for the 1982 exhibition *The Subject of Painting: A Selection by Paul Rodgers of Nine Contemporary Painters Working in France* at the Museum of Modern Art, Oxford.

Interview with Martin Barré

Catherine Millet

CATHERINE MILLET: The most notable constant in your work is that white space on which are successively placed the geometrical forms of the first paintings, and subsequently the traces left by knife, paint tube, spray paint, the stenciled arrows, and so on. Today, our eyes are used to such a treatment of the canvas but I suppose that in 1954–55 it must have appeared scandalous because of the break away from the still naturalizing space of French abstraction at that time.

MARTIN BARRÉ: The "scandal" you refer to put itself this way: "Soon he won't be putting anything at all on the canvas." This started being said around 1957–58, and those scandalized ended by convincing themselves there was nothing there . . . That's how my work was received, in one of two ways—either enthusiastically or with total contempt. In the second case, it provoked reactions one can call aggressive: gross damage to the gallery's visitor book or sabotaging the canvases on display when defacing them with writing wasn't possible. This arose from the impression provoked by the canvases that seemed "empty," something that is no longer surprising. I've always painted thin, on the level of the canvas, while that was an era of heavily built-up paint—one might have thought painting was sold by weight, the more thickness the more beauty. But what bumped up against the taste or style of the period was not so much this lack of thickness as the impression of emptiness, of nonwork—"he doesn't press himself, that one." The fact of large empty spaces or what appeared as such meant that it was not "worked"—quantity of work, quantity of matter—the more of it, the more beautiful ("getting one's money's worth"). One couldn't think that there, where there were what one called voids, there were perhaps many things that I had decided to suppress. I think of Cocteau, who said, "It's necessary that work efface work, so that people can say, I could have done as much," or of Mies van der Rohe: less is more.

CM: How then did you come to bring this ground forward to the point of abandoning its simple role as ground?

MB: I wanted to make a two-dimensional painting. The path had been broken by Cézanne, Gauguin, Picasso, Mondrian, and others. In 1954, it's useful to recall, one was obviously not avant-garde unless one wanted to make a two-dimensional painting. This was then a painting without illusion of depth and without representation, which was not new but seemed to call forth multiple developments. If Klee and Kandinsky offered to one whole line of artists ways to exercise their various talents, it's necessary to remember that it was Malevich and Mondrian who, after Picasso, Léger, and Matisse, constructed the painting of their time. I wanted to situate myself less on the side of emotivity than on that of utility. Without always being as austere and "ascetic" as people said (praise from some, reproach from others), I remain aware that some today can reproach me for having sometimes lacked rigor. I've also been accused of making paintings that are "too intellectual"—a statement that comes from those who used to say that an artist should paint with his "guts." Happily one no longer hears that kind of stupidity. In any case, I don't understand very well what an "intellectual painter" means, or even that it means anything.

So to respond more directly to your question, I think that I did not so much bring the ground forward as I did impress into it everything-which-was-not-this-ground. I wanted everything to be together, one with another. To suppress all these "overs-and-unders."

CM: I've read, particularly in the study Michel Ragon devoted to you, about the importance of Mondrian and Malevich (especially the celebrated "black square on white ground").[1] But, to be precise, isn't the use of the white ground in your paintings different from that of the first abstract painters?

MB: Yes. First of all because it is not always white. In Mondrian's last paintings—which is to say in the true Mondrian—it's not really a ground even as it is one. Painting is really two-dimensional when it ceases to be one. With Malevich, the square is on the ground. He says it, but convinced as he was of the "absence of the object," perhaps he thought that by virtue of this the ground had disappeared . . .

CM: Were you never tempted to work on an unprepared canvas?

MB: The use of the unprepared canvas goes back to Miró and perhaps Picasso. That it was still among the possibilities of extreme reduction of means did lead me to work on the canvas itself.

CM: Certain series of paintings make use of transparency. For example, some arrows that appear transparently through a layer of white paint on which other arrows are more frankly inscribed or, for another example, the most recent paintings where such a procedure is still more systematically employed when certain hatched spaces barely rise to the surface. How do you think of this stratification in light of your will to make of the painting a single plane?

MB: I reject the illusion of depth, which means that my painting has to situate itself on a single plane. I understand your question, but the fact of wishing to show the succession of interventions, the time of production, does not create a "perspective"—perhaps a "perspective-time," but not a "perspective-space." There is no vanishing point.

It's with the canvases from 1960 that I began to see the use I could make of the traces of misfires (also in some earlier canvases, but differently), which is to say to not hide the process of paint's surfacing. Matisse, Picasso, and Rembrandt in his prints opened the way.

CM: You studied architecture before abandoning it for painting. Was that important later for your concerns as a painter?

MB: It's certain that architecture has not left my work unmarked. I often wanted to say that painting seems less a means of expression than a means of construction.

CM: Have you ever wanted to work in very large formats? To pass beyond the traditional limits of the canvas? Do you see a function for diptychs or triptychs, etc.?

MB: The dimension of my paintings is proportional to the places I inhabit . . . more or less necessarily. It's above all in the years 1960–65 that I wanted large formats, but that was a time when I had considerable material difficulties. It's curious to note that the greatest difficulties for European abstraction come just at the moment when abstract painting emerges in the United States.

Diptychs, triptychs—linked formats, let's say—have interested me, but not with a view to making large paintings in a space that does not permit them. I've used such formats in certain works in order to "link" two surfaces graphically. And with others, just to the contrary, I painted as if on a single normal canvas and then inverted each component. There are others where I left an empty space between the surfaces to create a sort of tension among them.

For a very long time now, I have used vertical formats—almost square but carried slightly higher. Since 1963 these have been constructed from a vertical Golden Section cut down by two-thirds, which gives a rectangle taller than a square, in order to affirm verticality. Presenting itself always as a height, this format—although much larger—remains what one calls and inevitably feels as a "figure" format, something that does not bother me and doesn't stop intriguing me. I think that after several centuries of representational painting, it's difficult to escape landscape-figure vision—"marine" formats being elongated landscapes and full-figure paintings being vertically oriented marine-landscapes. The square is in fact the true abstract format with the advantage of the rotation it permits. But I've made fairly few of them. I always return to the heightened (not lowered) square. The plane is detached from the wall, and the wall from which the painting comes is vertical. Every painting ought to be a statement of this fact.

CM: In general, with gestural painters there's an adequation of the trace of the gesture and color—to one pass of the brush there corresponds but one color. But it seems that in your tube paintings you sometimes felt the need to return with several colors over the same trace. What does this respond to? Is it a re-evaluation of the first gesture?

MB: The term "re-evaluation" seems to me about right. One can add "affirmation" to it. For some time I retraced the length of a color with another white trace, as if to better make it enter into the ground, fearing the ground would recede too much.

CM: Didn't you spend a considerable time paying special attention to the color brown? To the relationship of brown and white?

MB: I've always sought a large reduction in means in order to obtain the greatest concentration. So in 1954 I was using only three colors—white, Prussian blue, and Venetian red—with which I obtained grays, browns, and blacks. But the Venetian red dominated for a more extended period and that began to be a bit of a "trademark image" . . . I progressively introduced other colors.

CM: Why did you take up this technique of painting directly with the tube? Were you interested in the use of unmixed color?

MB: No. That had no interest for me. To the contrary, I finally got myself some empty tubes in order to fill them with my own mixes, and before filling them I filed the openings because I was bothered by the narrowness of the line it produced. That's why I gave up the tubes. I then had a short period using wooden sticks roughly cut from those I was using to frame the paintings (5 mm × 30 mm), but that was simply to rediscover a tool comparable to the palette knife or the brush. Then the matte black aerosol spray really pleased me because I had a larger mark that happened all at once (and no more color). When I was painting directly from the tube, it wasn't the tube that interested me but rather the suppression of the brush and palette knife I had used earlier: this in order to get a greater reduction and concentration.

CM: When you came to spray painting, having no resource beyond the contrast of black and white, did you feel as if you were abandoning the problem of color?

MB: You shouldn't see there an abandonment of the "problem" of color. It's fairer to say that I stopped making use of the element of color in order to introduce a new presence—that of the total absence of color—into my painting. But the problem posed by the "trademark image" of color came back with the black and white. Noncolors as they may have been, people wound up saying: Martin Barré = black and white. The black and white increasingly took on a useless and unforeseen importance as "elegance and distinction," if you see what I mean, while for me it was the absence of color.

CM: Are the white spaces in your paintings in fact actually white?

MB: The color that's in the process of reappearing now serves to better underline time. It plays a functional role in concentrating attention on the essential. As it bears more precisely on the color of the ground-spaces, I can say that in 1954–55, the date of the first canvases shown, the "spaces" were truly white. They created a certain useless hardness. Fairly rapidly, I let them more or less "weather," as one might say of a building. In 1959 I began leaving the canvas untouched, primed as purchased, thinking the aging would naturally assure such "weathering." As to the period of the "spray bombs," which date from 1963 to 1967, the whites have undergone various related treatments. With the current paintings, they are still more tinted and I believe that in the future they will tend to become more differentiated one from the other: the color ought not become the dominant feature that engraves itself in the memory as the "trademark image." If it is necessary to speak of color as material, it's perhaps good to say that for me the good of acrylic paints, with their rapid drying, has been to allow a more radical usage of "transparency-time," something which was practically impossible with oils.

CM: You've often been classified among the gestural painters, but your gestures have no resemblance to those of the abstract expressionists nor to those of lyrical abstraction. Instead, you've always placed the gesture into relation with nearly geometric forms. Isn't there a contradiction between the spontaneity of the gesture and the rigor of geometric forms?

MB: Around 1957–58, I progressively made my way out of a distinctly flat painting; touch was freed up . . . It's first of all the influence of Frans Hals and not of gestural painting; at the time I was giving a great deal more attention to Hals than to "action painting." From its origins to the twentieth century, art more and more appears to us as on a single plane, which is to say it seems to us contemporary. The time in which artists declared that the past smelled of decay and museums resembled nothing more than cemeteries seems happily past. But why should the gesture be necessarily opposed to rigor and control? Isn't there, in various places, a marvelous game of possibilities between a highly controlled gesture and a geometry that tries to make one forget its rigor? Any mark, any graphism, is the fact of a gesture, even a ruled line. Even an industrial design appears to me an ensemble of gestures. Without contradiction, without paradox, would there be an evolution of painting, and, without evolution would there be a painting?

CM: When you moved from painting with the tube to the aerosol sprays, was there a transformation of your gesture?

MB: One can't speak of a transformation of the gesture. On the other hand, one can say that there had not been the least need for speed. If the gesture now had to be rapid, it was for entirely practical reasons, because you had to quickly get the canvas horizontal in order to avoid drips—with the exception of the canvases (called the "Arrows") using a stencil, which were made flat on the ground.

CM: Why the arrow? Doesn't the arrow convert the gesture into a sign? Doesn't it cease to be spontaneous? Can one interpret the mechanical arrow as antigestural?

MB: All over the world, the arrow is a sign that indicates direction. There is no other symbol. I made some paintings—very few remain—in 1953 using arrows, but the series called the "Arrows" dates from the end of 1967. As a title "the Arrow" would have been more just. I don't hold with giving titles to shows, but since it's inevitable that they will get named, why not?

It's the same with the "Zebras." No one can talk about them except by calling them that.

So, that series used a stencil—a unique stencil, you understand. The idea of using a stencil came to me from photography. The series comes from a time when I wanted to make shows with photography but where the projects were beyond my financial means. I've said that for me all marks are facts of gesture—except in photography, where it's the fact (and what a marvelous one) of a trace of light or, in printing, a trace of pressure. Projecting from a spray can through a stencil (which is a negative) gives a trace and not a gesture. The gesture is situated in the displacement of the stencil on the canvas. The stencil was made from a sheet of Kraft paper larger than the largest format employed in the series.

It's important to recall that this period from 1960 to 1967 was received by many as a very antipainting period. This was true in the sense that an entire body of painting, called "lyric" or "naturalizing," was stuck in a boring academicism. Alongside their excess, what I was doing could well appear as antipainting, whereas what I wanted to show, through the traces or points of impact in a clear surface, was what a painting could be if disencumbered of object, color, and form—offering nothing more than fragments of a space existing also elsewhere than in its tangible fragments. In the recent work which continues this project, I use means more adapted to the synthesizing of earlier steps that could not but pass by these extreme limits.

CM: Doesn't this recent work appeal back to the principle of the "Zebras"?

MB: The comparison is not altogether just. With the recent canvases it's more exact to speak of space signaled by hatchings (now made with a brush), the same term one uses in speaking of drafting, whereas in 1967 the series one cannot avoid calling "Zebras" was more nearly an attempt at getting hold of a space given by a simplest gesture.

CM: How do you analyze today the period of the photographs, the "unhung objects," and the "calendar"? Is it marginal in relation to your painting? Or is it, to the contrary, a phase necessary to its development?[2]

MB: Several years ago I thought painting was finished. Let's be clear: I mean as technique. I wanted to use solely photographic material. To some extent, this can seem true if certain technical means could have been at my disposal, but that was not the case. Photography answered once again to the idea of reducing the means of painting to zero . . . But I fell back into means that were finally more complicated, at least in the current state of the technique. In any case, I did two shows using photography—very antipainting in an antipainting time, which was not notably original. But that period let me take a certain step back from my pictorial work. I always have photographic projects—it's a question of time.

CM: A new element was introduced into the paintings in your last exhibition: a formal division—in pencil and almost in filigrane—of the canvas. What is its role, particularly with respect to the gesture that this grid seems to want to limit?

MB: In an exhibition, each canvas is but a fragment just as the exhibition or the series of canvases shown in it is but a fragment of the work. We fragment by necessity much more than do architects or film directors. This fragmentary character is foregrounded in my recent work: I want one to feel how much each canvas belongs to an ensemble. The grid (a receptacle-grid) is a progressive grid that fragments the surface given. It is inscribed in that space, which is already a choice with its particular ratio of height to width and which, instead of being read by internal proportions—thirds or quarters, long diagonals, or folding back of the short side or some other customary method—is divided into squares because that is the most nonfigurative figure and because it multiplies or divides itself in the simplest ways possible. Into this grid are entered the various interventions that mark the progressive time of a crystallization and which will inscribe themselves anew in another grid or its multiple or, on the contrary, its fragmentation.

1974

Translated from the French by Stephen Melville.

Previously published (in French) in *art press,* no. 12 (June–August 1974): 6–7. An edited version appeared in *Martin Barré* (Paris: Musée d'art moderne de la ville de Paris, 1979.)

1. Michel Ragon, *Martin Barré et la poétique de l'espace* (Paris: Galerie Arnaud, 1960).

2. [Millet is referring to the work Barré showed in 1969 and 1970 at Galerie Templon. Titled *Les objets décrochés* (Unhung objects), the work for the first of these shows consisted of photographs of the gallery variously disposed within it. The second was made up of photographic enlargements of calendar pages, a new image being added to the show each successive day. During this period Barré also showed, in New York and Monschau, work that used photographs of a distant urban site to play photographic verticality off against real spatial orientations. On this work, and on Barré's career over all, see Yve-Alain Bois, *Martin Barré* (Paris: Flammarion, 1993). Trans.]

Questions for Martin Barré
Jean Clay

QUESTION: Whether it's obvious from the outline or not, doesn't recourse to the Golden Section (augmented by half of its width) to determine the format of the series dated from 1972 to 1975 risk getting carried away by an entire problematic of plastic invariables that returns us to the illusion of ideal and definite transhistorical proportions? What's more, isn't it paradoxical in invoking the Golden Section to augment its width? Isn't that simply to undo its harmonious effect?

MARTIN BARRÉ: To speak of the Golden Section, of "effects of harmony," in talking of painting seems a bit out of step in 1977 . . . Etymologically, "harmony" means "assemblage." The use of regulating outlines (of "harmonious" relationships) is thus a *means of assemblage*. There effec-

tively exist, both before and after the start of the Christian era, definite proportions that are neither "ideal" nor "illusory": a square is always a square and the Golden Section always has the ration of 1:1.618.

When I wanted to give a tangible relationship to my formats, I used the Modulor; therefore, I used the Golden Section. I *held to* this principle until the canvases of 1974–75 (as shown in the figure). In the more recent canvases from 1975–76, I used the relationship of the side of a square to its diagonal. I start from an outline—which one is not that important; it is a bit like using Talens colors or Lefranc . . . What counts is what one makes of it.

Obviously, one can do everything arbitrarily, but what does that add? I do not paint to express my soul . . . I use a rule (a "rule of the game"); I transgress it *when the painting demands it*.

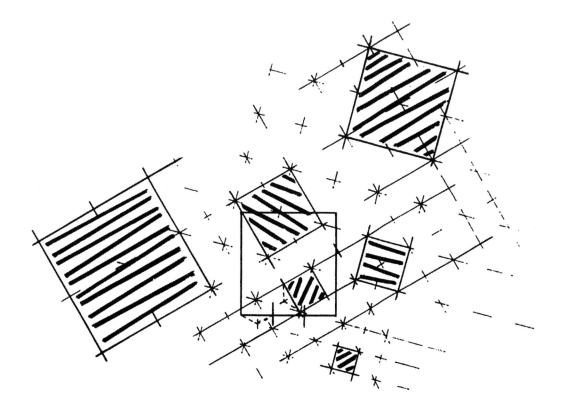

Architecture and painting have used rules of harmony (that is to say, most simply, means of assembly); the interest is not so much that they have created their rules nor that they have respected them—but rather that the subversion of these rules, of these means, leads to new ones. It doesn't matter if the way I construct a format "undoes its harmonious effects." I make use of a means of "assembly" (the Golden Section or another) to *construct* the surface best adapted to the specific work of *the* painting (I prefer to say *the*, rather than *my*). These are means that the various standard formats cannot furnish me. These formats are themselves not simply arbitrary. I don't know when they are made up, nor by whom—maybe a painter for whom they were convenient. It seems that what matters about this standardization is the service it renders to suppliers and maybe framers (these still exist). This "prior market" prefers to fabricate standard measures; it's more marketable. As for the "after-market," one knows how much the famous "point" plays a part in the business vocabulary . . . [1]

QUESTION: The traces inscribed in the quadrilateral of the canvas organize themselves according to orientations that suggest a centrifugal dynamic. In doing so, they offer themselves as things other than what they are (surfaces). Should the work generate noninscribed spaces, produce a beyond out of itself? What do you think of this 1928 reflection by the Polish painter [Władysław] Strzemiński excluding—and pushing away under the rubric of the "baroque"—all dynamism of the surface:

> The dynamic form is never bound to the surface of the *tableau*. It does not develop from the *tableau*-site (*lieu-tableau*) on which it is found. Its movement is always oriented in a certain direction that drives it beyond the limits of the *tableau*. The dynamic sliding of the form on the surface of the painting tears it away from the place where it is found, disassociating it from the

tableau, expelling it to the outside. Such sliding forms ought not exist in the *tableau*. There should be a total unity of what is painted and the surface on which the forms are painted. The forms ought to engender a total and indissoluble unity with the surface of the *tableau*.[2]

MARTIN BARRÉ: Painting always has a relationship to a planar surface and to the limits of this surface, since it necessarily has limits.

Everything that will be painted on this surface and in these limits will be flat. To this planarity is added another fundamental character, which is *immobility*.

If one has been able to speak of kinetic art, one cannot conceive of a kinetic painting, because painting cannot be mobile. When there is movement, it is a question of the illusion of movement and not real movement. What is more immobile than Balla's *Dog on a Leash*? . . . The "dynamic sliding" doesn't tear away from anything at all: there is only the illusion of such sliding. What's striking in your question is the difference between the question itself and the quote from Strzemiński. You speak of traces and spaces, whereas he speaks of *forms*. It is difficult to make a parallel with someone who always speaks of forms. Malevich speaks of the "sensibility of the absence of the object"—painting liberating itself from representation. With Mondrian, who painted until 1944, there will be a liberation from form, a *total painting*. Whereas, with the form ("sliding" or not), there are still the figurative attachments and therefore still some illusionism.

But if in Mondrian (painted) surfaces are no longer forms, the *gestures* that produce these "nonforms" are still close to those which produce forms.

If there is a "sliding," it is a real sliding of the tools on the surface. And therefore, what is given to see are the traces left by the tools (pencils, brushes impregnated with color) trailed (guided by a ruler or not) on a surface.

There is not, therefore, this illusion of sliding Strzemiński thinks of when he speaks of "baroque" (to listen to him, all painters are baroque, except him . . .).

The "noninscribed spaces" you speak of become the *placing-in-evidence* of the pictorial space itself (since the surface ceases to exist outside of its limits)—space detached from the wall, the rock face, thus bound intimately to architecture and to its origins.

Would not the first architectural act have been to create (that is to say, to *technically realize*) a flat surface? In so doing, it remakes the rock face of the first Western paintings, there where one wants to renew it, in the free air, in the light—but as flat as the water of a pond (which was no doubt the first intuition of planarity—as also of the mirror, of reflection). And so also it makes visible this surface—given to the graphic, to painting—in the pause produced by this *tearing away* that will be the *tableau* (the wall offering itself then to polychromy, or more simply to color).

This *tableau*, fragment become receptacle of pictorial inscription, would be unable to lose its *flatness,* its *tension,* its *forwardness* (its *detachment* from the rock face of its origins), without painting's losing at the same time all its specificity.

QUESTION: On the white canvas, just as it is prepared and brought from the supplier, you add to begin—at least since 1972—a fairly dense layer of red ochre. The veils of broken white that you apply successively in the effectuation of the work whiten this first layer—a progressive effacement of an underlying tint that is the chromatic base of the painting.

Should one look at your paintings as the regular degradation of a first shade by the accumulative play of white veils (modulation of value)? Doesn't this process of degradation of an "original" color imply the apposition of a rather large number of layers? And could one conceive, on this account, a *tableau* by Martin Barré in which the elaboration would be suspended after the first covering?

MARTIN BARRÉ: The first layers you talk about play a technical role. They constitute what in painting one calls the support, which becomes the surface to paint, intermediate between the canvas and that which will be

painted. As everyone knows, the pigments corrode the canvas . . . A certain thickness allows the reliner to do his job.

If painting shows us the time of its inscription interrupted at a moment that the painter chooses, decides, it is desirable that the marks of time (to come)—collisions, scratches, yellowing—alter its impact as little as possible. If the essential part of *painting* is in that *instant* of interruption (revelation; fixation), it is important that this instant seem to want to be no longer familiar with time, to be to the fullest extent possible able to subtract itself from time—and to do so without resorting to the help of glass, of the vitrine which gives to the work the look of a relic.

There is in the *surfacing* to the very air we breath something that seems to me close to this *instant*, this suspension, *time-instant,* air, light . . . The painting one moment *surfaces* . . . The painter works for this: it surfaces well or badly . . . In this surfacing to the air, to light, to something which is not fixed (warm-cool; clear-dark), the *tableau* must set forward its own *fixity* (the immobility of *Dog on a Leash*), its *instant of crystallization.* It's for this reason that its fragility, its friability, should be the least possible: it will always be necessarily too much. In every way, art and technique are the same word (because it *was* the same word). We must neglect technique only if one cannot do otherwise, if it becomes an obstacle.

There is a moment where the canvas becomes again almost white, a moment where one starts, if one can say that . . . Does the painter begin or begin again at this moment—or simply continue? Or hasn't the white canvas already begun (this white canvas that curiously some call "virgin" . . . Does a sculptor say a "virgin stone"?)? Yes, the painting could "be suspended" from the first layers.

1977

Translated from the French by Stephen Melville and Ellen Bethany Napier.

Jean Clay was one of the founding editors of the French journal *Macula* and is currently senior editor for Éditions Macula. This interview (in French) accompanied his "Le dispositif Martin Barré, L'oeil onglé," in *Macula* 2 (1977): 67–83.

1. [Barré is referring here to particular features of the French art market of the 1960s in which prices were partially based on systematic treatment of format, size, and standing of the artist. Trans.]

2. "L'unisme en peinture," *Macula* 1 (1976): 23. [For an English translation of Strzemiński's statement, see "Unism in Painting," in *Constructivism in Poland, 1923–26* (Cambridge, England: Kettle's Yard Gallery, n.d), pp. 86–95. Trans.]

How Can You Defend Making Paintings Now?
A Conversation between Mel Bochner and James Meyer

JAMES MEYER: Since the early eighties, we have been told, time and again, of the emergence of a "new painting"—this despite the numerous and quite specific critiques it has faced throughout the century: the constructivist critique, the critiques of Judd and the conceptualists, or the "Pictures" critique and attack on neo-expressionism during the early eighties. I myself have been sympathetic to this counternarrative, this discourse of painting's insufficiency. Of course, the problem is not painting as such—only that one has high expectations of it. At this point, most painters seem happy to repeat old formulas: expressionist rhetoric (painterliness), symmetrical organization, retinal play, the figuration/abstraction "tension." The space for invention in painting has become extremely narrow. Yet, precisely when the "Pictures" artists and their supporters were launching their critique, you—a leading figure of conceptualism—*returned* to painting. And you have continued to paint: your recent show at Sonnabend was primarily a painting show. How can you defend making paintings now? What is painting's relevance for you?

MEL BOCHNER: One part of that question is cultural and the other part is personal. Culturally, painting came to occupy a position that necessitated a continuous production of paintings. The so-called "relevance of painting" argument isn't so much about its relevance as art, as it is about its relevance as a sign.

JM: Do you mean its traditional identity as the ultimate art commodity, the implication that it lacks criticality, affirming the status quo?

MB: Let's just say that there's always a nail in a wall somewhere that can take a painting. But the cultural side of the question is less interesting to me. I'm more interested in how use changes necessity. Within a certain cycle, ways of using things tend to change. Personally, I had no use for the *practice* of painting in my early work.

JM: But wasn't your *Measurement* series set up as a critique of painting and its ideological implications?

MB: I would say it functioned as a question. It was important for me in early pieces like the *48″ Standards* that this question take place in the *space of painting*. The sheet of brown paper had to be hung "as if" it were a painting. I meant it to function as a proposition: what would it mean if this were a painting? Otherwise, the necessity of the use would have lost its reference.

JM: But, insofar as it was a reflection on painting and its perceptual and material conditions—like, for example, Buren's striped canvas or Weiner's wall removal—the *48″ Standards* was a critique of painting.

MB: It's only a critique of the limitations which the reading of painting at that time allowed. I can't speak for anyone but myself: it was about trying to open the boundaries of the language. What I wanted to understand was the nature of the conventions. Conventions give us the boundaries of experience. If you examine the conventions you may find where the holes are, where a leakage exists between "is" and "is not."

JM: Insofar as they were an analysis of the epistemological conventions of painting, the *Measurements* led to such subsequent projects as the *Theory of Painting* (1969), *Non-Verbal Structures: RYB* (1973), and the actual paintings on canvas you began in the early eighties and have produced ever since. All along, it's been an analysis of painting and the conditions of painting.

MB: Except, then the problem becomes, what do you have when you have an analysis of painting? What do you do with it?

Let me put it another way. Without the history of the practice of painting as the background for all my work, it becomes a series of disparate gestures. I'm not interested in pronouncements like "Painting is dead" or "Painting is alive." Either way, what difference does it make when you're in your studio trying to think about something concrete? But once you recognize that my work is an analytical attempt to rethink painting's functions and meanings, you realize that it is all one continuous investigation. In my own mind, my project has always been a kind of research based on the idea of bracketing and *unbracketing*. When you bracket you set something aside, you don't eliminate it.

JM: Or stand away from it.

MB: Yes. And so, rather than painting paintings, I was trying to work out a theoretical construct—a methodology for practice of any kind.

JM: As a reflection on painterly conventions, was your practice not, in some sense, continuous with Greenberg's modernist theory—his claim that painting's task is to explore its own conditions—the rejection of which is said to initiate the rupture into "postmodernism"?

MB: Given the way in which "formalism" is presently discussed, it's suicidal to say that there's a formal element to your art. But, of course, we know that there's always a formal element to art. Because art has to make itself visible. And to become visible, there has to be form. But there is form and there is formalist thought, which are two different things. My understanding of the formalist argument is that the form itself evolves into the content of the work. And the content of the work may not, in any way, concern itself with anything extraneous to the medium. In that sense, it's a severe example of reductivist thinking, which I'm against. For me, the medium itself has no purity. When I staple a piece of brown paper to the wall as an "instead-of painting," it is clear that the purity of the medium is not the issue. Besides, other kinds of investigation entered my work, like logic, or geometry, or linguistics, or literary theory. And that created another context which was more philosophical: in other words, what is the meaning of this activity of making art?

JM: Which Greenberg didn't want.

MB: Greenberg wanted the Kantian moment of aesthetic revelation. He said that he didn't want to "think" in front of an artwork.

JM: Yes, but there are two Kants in Greenberg: the Kant of the *Critique of Judgment,* which you are referring to, and the Kant of the *Critique of Pure Reason.* It's the latter that supports his theory of modernist painting as an analysis of the conditions of the medium, just as

Reason's task is to reflect on the conditions of itself. Now, it would seem that your reflection on painting and its physical and epistemological conditions could be discussed in these terms.

MB: The problem with that aspect of the theory, as I saw it, was this: how do you criticize a language from within? From inside you can only hope to refine and purify the known elements of the language. What my *Measurement* pieces did was step outside the language. I saw them as a kind of meta-language, a second language with which to analyze the original language. That idea of removal, of objectivizing, is distinctly anti-formalist, and against the prevailing norm of modernism at that point.

JM: But isn't that Kantian? Kant wants to step back and reflect on the conditions of philosophy's "proper" boundaries (if only, perhaps, to shore them up). There is a disassociation from the object.

MB: But what if you doubt the viability of the object of reflection itself, if you don't recognize it as having boundaries?

JM: This is what you're proposing for painting . . .

MB: What I'm proposing is to examine every possible way in which the work can be thought about. To apply pressure on a variety of fronts, both conceptual and perceptual, and to permit discontinuities to surface. I think you have to set all this in the context of the rhetoric of the sixties, which contended that all that counted existed *inside* the "framing edge." That, to me, was the repressive essence of formalism. I wondered what would change if you redrew the boundaries of the experience so that it didn't stop within the frame. How could a work reframe itself? One possibility was to focus on conceptual strategies, as in Serialism, where the work is the result of a preconceived numerical progression. Another way was to move the act of reframing to include the work's relationship to the space that contains it. All of these questions were a reaction *against* the position articulated by critics like Greenberg and Fried. What Fried criticized as "theatrical," which I would term "installational," became central to my work. A gallery is a theater; every exhibition is an installation. Why deny it? My point was this space is the prime location for an examination of the conditions of how a work of art exists.

JM: At this point, your inquiry became explicitly phenomenological.

MB: Yes. Because I wanted to uncover the premises of experience which tend to get buried in the background of theory. Phenomenology tries to surface the ways in which consciousness gives us our world. The implicit, the unfocused, the peripheral all need to be accounted for. For example, when you're looking at an artwork, are you looking up or looking down? What is happening at the edge of your field of vision? Does the work surround you? How do you account for the floor you're standing on? All of these things became crucial to me.

JM: Those of us who have an investment in what has come to be called the "Institutional Critique" tend to look back on late-sixties conceptual work as completely invested in a critical analysis of the art apparatus. For me, Benjamin Buchloh's writings have made it impossible to see this work otherwise. What you seem to be suggesting is that, at the time, your analysis was more specifically phenomenological than materialist. Or maybe you don't want to make this separation.

MB: What I don't want to do is retrofit what I was doing then to more recent theoretical models. I don't see how you can separate the phenomenological from the materialist without committing the same reductivist error as formalism. Of course, how anyone reads my work is up to them. All I can say is that bringing these issues to the foreground of the discourse was both the subject and the politics of my work in the late sixties and early seventies.

JM: How, then, do you explain the shift in your work from a contextualist analysis of painting to the production of actual paintings? Have you simply incorporated the prior reflection *within* painting, continued your investigations of the relations of perception, touch, and knowledge—what we have been calling a phenomenological inquiry—within the traditional format of paint

on canvas? As you would say, using painting as simply another "tool" for artistic investigation?

MB: Yes, I do think of painting as a tool, but, in that sense, I thought of all of my works as tools to think with. Of course, sometimes, the tool determines what you're thinking. But tools can also give you access to things to think about, which, because of the nature of the tool, you weren't able to think about before. I see my development hinging in 1973 when I completed the *Axiom of Indifference*. I had answered, to my own satisfaction, all the questions that I was addressing about how language and space intersect. The problem, in its original analytical terms, was exhausted.

JM: And you found painting to be the best site for continuing your inquiry.

MB: There were two choices: totally abandon the visual or see if I could renegotiate the terms of painting.

JM: But why is painting "the visual"? Why are they congruent? At this point in your work, you seem to privilege painting as a site—a special site for the kinds of analyses you've been doing all along. Over the past several years you've written a number of essays on painters—specifically those who, you feel, made inquiry into the conditions of painterly perception— Renoir, Bonnard, Cézanne, Matisse, Newman, artists you seem to see as precedents for your own activity. Has painting become, for you, a privileged site of investigation?

MB: I'm interested in painting as a text that is continually rewritten. One goes to painting *because* of its conventions.

JM: But you're not working in just any medium now. You're making *paintings,* and primarily paintings.

MB: Painting is the place I found where I can test certain hypotheses; where I can record and examine the developments of those speculations; where I can posit a proposition and its contradiction simultaneously.

JM: But you did that in your photography, and in your floor pieces with pebbles and coins.

MB: But you see, in my sculpture I intentionally eliminated memory. In my painting, I want to encode time.

JM: But your sculptures record the process of thought—the process of a systemic development of a proposition or mathematical concept.

MB: That's true, but painting records a physical process, a narrative of revisions which takes place *inside* the object. In my sculpture, the process precedes the object. How, or where, I have moved the pebbles around on the floor to find their exact location in the space is not evidenced in the final piece. In my sculpture the form is fixed, the process is dissolved in time.

JM: You're saying painting illustrates the time it took to do the thinking and the recording?

MB: I'm saying time becomes a subject matter. In the *Theory of Sculpture* pieces, I was testing the difference between mental and physical space, and how we know that difference.

JM: And in painting?

MB: In painting the issue is illusion. The pictorialization of space involves an illusion of time. Illusionism represents the irrational side of thought, the place where logic collapses. Only in painting have I been able to address these ideas.

JM: I have to disagree. I think your early photography—the *Perspectives* and *Isomorphs*—moves into that territory back in 1966. As an historian, it interests me how this move to confound vision by means of a "perverse" illusionism (as Lucy Lippard called it) emerges, simultaneously, in LeWitt, in Smithson (the *Enantiomorphic Chambers*), in Bell, Hesse, yourself. Somewhere around 1965–66, the "minimal" desire for an apodeictic spectatorship—Stella's claim that "What you see is what you see"—came to seem unsatisfactory. Now, it's more complex than that because implicit to this position was a radical doubt, for Judd especially, that's distinctly antipositivist: you may see what you see, but you're not going to know anything beyond this. Your circle, it seems to me, took up and radicalized the epistemological doubt implicit to minimalism.

MB: You're right, this is where the problem of doubt surfaces. Seriality was a search for a new type of certainty, because it's about one thing being necessarily af-

ter another. The following being predicated on the preceding eliminates choice, and therefore doubt.

JM: But it's a certainty that comes outside of one's decision making.

MB: Because there is no decision making after the initial choice of systems. Everything is pre-executive. But when you reach the point where you question that whole apparatus of thought, you realize that doubt is inevitable in art or, for that matter, in anything one does. The elimination of doubt by method leads to a philosophically untenable position: solipsism. Either art is the site of a philosophical investigation which is relevant to human experience or it is nothing.

JM: But art is not philosophy; you're not a philosopher.

MB: No, I'm not operating as a philosopher. Philosophy as philosophy is thought divorced from experience.

JM: Divorced because it's only operating in the space of language?

MB: Yes, and with all that that entails: grammar, syntax, vocabulary, tense, and linearity. In other words, the messiness of real thought is cleaned up to make discourse possible. For me, painting—because it is in, and of, the material world—offers an access to the *processes* of the mind, to the messiness that philosophy can't cope with.

JM: Elsewhere, you've described this as the "paradox of empiricism," a paradox you consider the "essential dilemma of twentieth-century art." Bonnard, for example, was "unable to know anything except what is given by the senses, he knew he was the prisoner of their limitations, distortions, and decline."

MB: That knowledge is precisely the knowledge that you're a human being, locked in time. It seems to me that this is a particularly twentieth-century subject in painting.

JM: What about Velázquez's *Las Meninas*? Vermeer's *Allegory of Painting*? Parmigianino's *Self-Portrait in a Convex Mirror*?

MB: The difference is between theme and subject. The problem is how to integrate this understanding into an investigation which develops these ideas as the constants of a practice. It's interesting that Parmigianino never painted another painting like the *Self-Portrait*; he never used such radical convex perspectival distortion again. I think perspective is central to this paradox. It is the most interesting ground on which to confront the mind with the senses. In my *Photo Pieces* I investigated perspective as a kind of conceptual found object. But in the recent paintings I'm trying to account for the space of the senses within the framework of perspective.

JM: By foregrounding the objectness of the work—juxtaposing four canvases, each setting up a different perspective, around a central absence or hole?

MB: By focusing on four types of space: the space of the hand—what is known by touch; the space of the eye—what is available only to sight; the space of the mind—mental oppositions like order/disorder, rational/irrational; and psychological space—claustrophobia, agoraphobia, vertigo. It's the collision of these spaces that interests me.

JM: The new paintings present a space that tumbles forward and backwards that recalls late Cézanne, Braque's *Viaducts*, the 1909 Picasso at Horta. Boccioni also breaks up space in this way to foster dynamism; Malevich and Lissitzky continued from there. Yet the rotational quality of your works and their scale displace the terms of this format. What's at stake for you in this rotational quality?

MB: The cinematic.

JM: Could you speak more to that?

MB: The cinematic is the persistence of the visual image in the mind, which is another way of saying memory. What happens between any two frames in a film? You perceive continuity where there's only discontinuity. It's Zeno's paradox, because between every two frames, there could be two more frames, and between those, two more . . . , it's endless. This is the point where cinematic time and perspective meet—at the vanishing point—or infinity. It's a mental whirlpool.

JM: Hence your rotational arrangements . . .

MB: Which can be read as a sequential rotation, but can also be read individually as a series of discrete images or, because of the symmetry of the square, as a single image. But at the moment they become a single image, they become a frame around that hole in the center. What interests me about this simultaneous continuity and discontinuity is that you can't hold the three contradictory readings in your mind at the same time.

JM: Just as in your wall painting *Non-Verbal Structures*. How much can one hold in one's perception? What can peripheral vision contain within itself? And what is the relation between focused vision and peripheral vision? In recent years, you've been exploring these tensions primarily within the painting medium. Which leads me to ask: do you consider yourself a painter at this point?

MB: In some way, I always thought of myself as a painter . . . a painter who just didn't happen to paint. Many of the forms that artistic "rebellion" has taken in the last twenty-five years have become predictable. Ironically, painting, at this point in time, has become unpredictable.

JM: Would you have said that in 1968?

MB: No. It would have been impossible. But what I can see in retrospect is that it's the absence of painting that gives definition to the *Photo Pieces*, the *Measurements*, the *Theory of Boundaries*. They all circulated around that missing signifier.

JM: Your work became well known for its investigation of systemic thought; your early criticism made a very strong case for serial organization. Even your wall paintings of the seventies and early eighties were systemically derived. Your current work is not, and I'm wondering whether it hasn't betrayed the antisubjectivist, anticompositional commitments of your early work and writings.

MB: I don't at this point find the words you're using—"subjective," "compositional"—pejorative. They were in the sixties; they were what I bracketed out. But, as my work evolved, I tried to create a structure in which these terms could be rethought and factored back in.

JM: So you're not renouncing your earlier position.

MB: No, of course not, but I'm constantly re-examining it, trying to find where it remains relevant, or where it permitted one thing, but repressed another. Systemic thinking repressed the spontaneous and the intuitive, by denying doubt.

JM: But—as we noted earlier—doubt was integral to systemic thinking.

MB: Not in terms of any internal organization that could be called "compositional," not when you knew that the system predicted the result. It was tautological—a closed as opposed to an open investigation. However, what if instead of relational I say "contextual," or instead of compositional I say "interactive?" That reopens the investigation, so that the end is no longer predetermined, but constantly mutating.

JM: At Sonnabend, there was an interesting dialogue, in the back room, between the floor sculpture—the *Rules of Inference*, organized on a rotational systemic format—and the *Painting for Four Eyes*, which had a rotational *composition*. The painting was not systemically perspicuous. For me, these works mark the transition between your systemic thinking in the past, and the opening of possibilities you seek in the present.

MB: That's a good observation, because the spiral is a form that has been a hidden substructure throughout my work. It is a means of changing the conventional reading order, of spinning things around, turning them upside down. In the sculpture the movement was centrifugal; in the painting it's centripetal, a corkscrew that pulls you into the center.

JM: The hole in the center?

MB: For me the hole in the center of the painting represents the emptiness at the center of perspective, the impossibility of any "theory of vision." Perspective, as a system, is a dysfunctional map, but one that over the last five hundred years has entered the collective unconscious. We *accept* that it represents what we see.

JM: But modernism undermined it.

MB: But did it? Multiple viewpoints, simultaneity, transparency, flatness—all the tropes of modernism seemed to be the death knell for perspective. Yet look what's happened in the past fifteen years or so, with the advent of electronic imagery—computer graphics, film animation, morphing, virtual reality—the dominant form of contemporary spatial representation is one-point perspective. Instead of repressing perspective, as it has been for the last century, I think it has to be reproblematized. This is what I mean by the cycle of use and necessity. Modernist theory led us to believe that these issues were all resolved. I want to show that there is no resolution, no firm ground; that everything that is given is immediately taken away.

JM: An undercutting . . .

MB: Or a collapse, a systematic implosion. The whole thing sucked into that hole in the center.

December 1993, New York

Excerpts from this interview have been previously published as "The Gallery Is a Theater," *Flash Art* (summer 1994): 99–101, 142; "How Can You Defend Painting Now?," in *Mel Bochner: Counting and Measurement Pieces 1966–1998* (Yokusuka, Japan: Akira Gallery, 1999), pp. 20–25; and "How Can You Defend Painting Now?," in *Mel Bochner* (Rio de Janeiro: Centro de Arte Hélio Oiticica, 1999), pp. 58–59.

The Objection That the Obscure Makes to Painting
Christian Bonnefoi

In general, different analyses of collage focus on its "extensions," on the manner in which an innovative technique (touching not only on the elaboration of the image but on its very presentation) leaves the terrain of its initial proposition (painting and, more precisely, cubism) in order to extend into extension—space—itself. Collage becomes montage (Eisenstein), construction (Tatlin, Lissitzky, Moholy-Nagy), then readymade (Duchamp).

If this development through extension turns out to be correct logically, it ought to allow us to state that conceptual art and installation, via Duchamp, proceed from collage, and thus from painting; and that which has been announced at different times as the overcoming of the art of painting is only in fact a way of its continuing.

For my part, I would like to insist on another nonthematic possibility of interpreting cubist collage, which I will define as its *intention:* the development of *intensity* or, more exactly, the extension specific to the intense, *extensive intensity.*

I would like to show how the intensity that produces its extension is an appeal to the *tableau,* an underlying, nonappearing structure that is masked by the stylistic successions of painting, which are then gathered together in a totalizing history of art.

And I would like to show how, in the extended space that cubist collage sets up, intensity installs itself from one side of a gap to the other, between the surface and the added element (from where?), not only without ever abandoning the terrain where intensity has been given body (how?) but still consolidating it.

From there, another displacement occurred with Mondrian, giving us something else to consider: no longer a matter of form or "innovative technique" but of the consolidation and deployment of the principle of extensive intensity—the *tableau.*

1. Picasso's pin "collages" dissociate the preconceived unity of the surface. To the syntagmatic division of the surface (according to the extensive and lateral mode specific to the occupation of space), the pin "collages" oppose a paradigmatic division, of one plane (*plan*) on another (a mode of the intense spreading into thickness: Mondrian). Surface and division change nature: their outcome is entangled (*elles sont mises en destination*).[1]

2. Paradigmatic organization of the *tableau* supposes a fundamental modification of the rapport with the visible that Georges Didi-Huberman terms the "caesura of the visible," dividing the visible under our eyes and the visual in withdrawal, underlying, nonappearing, thus assuring the first its mobility.

This is what I called "division of division" in an interview, "On the Appearance of the Visible," published in *Macula.*[2] A limit reached by extensivity forms a break (*franchissement*); touched by intensity, it forms a sharing out (*partage*), a division within itself, a delimitation.

A limit thus divided opens the intention and site of its motif or motive (*motif*). My essay on "the destruction of the surface entity" demonstrated that what I call the plane is the division and nongeometrical destining of the surface—that is, the possibility of the recto and verso of the same surface coexisting in the same place and at the same time.

If there is thus caesura, dislocation, withdrawal, mobility, and destination, it is because a modality specific to time intervenes.

3. A conception of the *tableau* as modality of the plane, time, and the invisible substitutes for the conception of painting as an art of surface, space, and the visible.

4. This means that the sense of cubist collage lies in the interstice, the nondisjunctive spacing between glued elements, between what comes from elsewhere, from the future, that which cannot be figured, and what comes upwards from underneath, from the ground.

The interval is the site of expectation—of the event, and of enigma.

5. Historically, cubist collage introduces a poetics or productivity of place for receiving the unknown and unforeseeable future that I call, in a positive sense, the Obscure. The latter is not what disappears into light's absence but what, as an autonomous world, holds itself before the light.

6. This infinitely small (almost nothing) that defines the interstice of collage resonates with Mallarmé's "nothing will have taken place but the place" (*rien n'aura eu lieu que le lieu*) in *Un Coup de Dés*. This "place" that is the "nothing" that "will have taken place" will find form in *The Tomb of Edgar Poe* in the sentence: "Calm block fallen here below from an obscure disaster" (*Calme bloc ici-bas chu d'un désastre obscur*).

7. At first, collage's aspiration toward exteriority separates and frees up the elements of painting, whose surface organization has exposed a lack and thus the need of an object. What we call an "installation" is the extreme realization in which this need of an object is satisfied, through its passage outside of itself, breaking out of the surface, and thus securing the adequation of the visible and the object in a totalizing space.

But in a second moment, collage prepares a return *toward* the surface, toward proximity, through the constitution of a new unity according to the modalities of the plane (i.e., the paradigm of thickness, the division of the division). What is near is not undone, and what returns, responding to the objection that gives it its limits, does not occur at the same place from which it starts. The response is the division of the division.

The need of the object thus opens itself to the desire of that which orients the response to objection. In considering objection, which follows Malevich's "world without object," what is announced is the overcoming of abstraction (a problematic of painting) by the question of the *tableau* (a problematic that considers objection to be something to which a response is a necessity).

The movement that "aspires to" exteriority has freed up the elements of the *tableau,* and the movement initiated from objection in the form of what returns leaves it open to the event of the future.

On the occasion of an exhibition that conceived the *tableau* from the point of view of a ternary structure, 1-2-3 or, more precisely, 1-3-2 (the 3 assuring the function of an interval), I said that the 4 is the internal movement of this ternary structure, the combination (*chiffre*) that conveys the possibility of a temporal movement in the folds of the work's thickness, a thickness that is given over to the modalities of what comes into appearance.

If one confers on "disaster" the Mallarméan sense produced by the addition of "obscure" ("obscure disaster"), one could say: the 3—the nothing—in between the 1 and 2 that limit it, is illuminated in the disaster (*dés-astre*) of the 4.[3]

The "novelty" of collage is the invention of a specific place of "what rises up from beneath" and what comes from elsewhere.

With Mondrian, the aspiration to exteriority is no longer necessary. Attention is focused on the second term: the paradigmatic division specific to the plane in its unbroken thickness as "block." In terms of their structure and not what is visible, the plane assures the cohesion of the elements in their destination.

The plane reactualizes the surface otherwise: the surface is that which is given by and in the opening of the plane at the very moment it is taken into consideration (division of the division).

In stressing what is beyond sight, collage aims at something different from what is traditionally considered a motif or motive (*motif*) in the "visual arts"; it aims at the *other* as that which has not taken figure in the visible.

It brings to light the limit of the work as reason of the work. This extreme limit is an objection. To paint is "to address oneself to" in considering objection. To hold oneself in this position is to speak, to conceive relation as discourse.

The unveiling specific to cubist collage brings to light a question without delivering the secret.

To the withdrawal of being corresponds an absolute reserve, the alterity of the other. The Obscure, the mode of the future, positions itself in the face of a clearing (*l'éclaircie*), the mode of presentation.

Through the unveiling specific to cubist collage, the objection borne by its essential exteriority is now exposed as the reason that modifies form in the history of styles and the history of art, at least from the moment that art is destined to a task other than giving things form. This other task sets the formal elements off into their destination, a liberation through objection of an initial motivation, a modality that the form contains at the cost of a totalized aesthetic experience. Paraphrasing Emmanuel Lévinas, one could say that liberty as spontaneity is arraigned by objection, which is justice.

The spontaneity of modern iconoclasm (Van Gogh, Seurat, Picasso, and abstraction) attends to the voice of the Obscure in the disaster of the elements and their entry into destination.

The Obscure is the modern mode of what Georges Didi-Huberman terms "dissemblance," the "setting into mystery" (*mise au mystère*),[4] allowing the thought that the work, whatever its period, thinks itself as originating in the call of objection, and so interrupting any exclusive concern with stylistic production.

This is not a way in which the work turns back in on itself, nor a willful obstinacy. Through objection, opening the present (the three forms of the present) to the test of the future, the temporal conversion of spatial extension is assured. Extension (whose pictorial model is the series) enters into destination through the determination (intention) of intensity. Intensity is the modality, *contained* in a single point, of the possibilities of appearance.

Extensive intensity is, without leaving its place, a bringing to light (extensity) that does not release itself (intensity). The mode of showing specific to extensive intensity—as a temporal conversion of space, responding to objection and inscribing it intensively within its preoccupation without containing it there—this showing releases its extension (its consent to appearance) in a paradigmatic dimension, at right angles, as it were, to the surface.

The point of intensity, at the very moment it releases its extension as a site of inscription, *simultaneously* stops any form of paradigmatic escape. This point is the beginning of a rapport with—and relation to—objection. This beginning is the opening specific to the division of the division.

To begin without leaving this site (tradition) is to position oneself differently (modernity) on the paradigmatic axis enclosed in the point. For example: cubist collage, through what it sets into destination, does not break free of the surface and installs the interval (1-2) whose relation counts as three (*le trait du trois*). In relation to collage, Mondrian poses thickness as arrested on the paradigmatic axis, its point of intensity, determining outside of appearance the new conditions of appearance internal to the new surface: this "outside" that is "in the interior of" the surface is the future of the 4 deploying its temporality in the presentation of the 1-3-2.

The preceding sentence can thus be modified: if 1 and 2 are the edges of the caesura, 3 is their setting to work in response to the objection of 4, the Obscure.

In the spontaneity of his drip paintings, Pollock encounters this objection, as witnessed in the small cardboard formats, divided by cutting and collage.[5] The objection leaves traces of a division of the surface that is envisaged by Pollock but never realized.

However, this suffices to understand the meaning of the original intention: gesturality (which corresponds to what is set into destination) is answered by composition as a division of gesture (the way a gesture can turn back onto itself, which submits spontaneity to further consideration). It is now a question of beginning to think through the coincidence and coexistence of a spatial covering and its temporal exposition.

Or rather: how does the economy of the 4 demand to be understood within the economy of the 3?

The *tableau* (in its conception as a renovated icon, not exclusively answerable to the laws of painting) assumes responsibility for the intention announced by collage at the moment when, in its incessant effort to break free of itself, it strikes against (*bute*) the objecting obstacle. Striking against the objecting obstacle is the maximal sign of its effect: its end. The counterthrust (*contre-coup*) divides the end as limit, frees the cause, and initiates a beginning. The beginning is the initiation of a relation to objection. Initiative is said of a positional act of discourse . . . "rapport of truth which at once severs and dis-severs distance" (*rapport de vérité qui à la fois franchit et ne franchit pas la distance*)—Emmanuel Lévinas.

Changy, November 1990

Translated from the French by Philip Armstrong.

This essay was first published (in French) in *Christian Bonnefoi: Oeuvres graphiques, 1973–1996* (Alès, France: Musée-Bibliothèque Pierre-André Benoît, 1996).

1. See Christian Bonnefoi, "A propos de la destruction de l'entité de surface," first published in *Macula* 3–4 (1978), reprinted in *Ecrits sur l'art (1974–1981)* (Brussels: La Part de l'Oeil, 1997), pp. 109–14. [For a further reading of Bonnefoi's reference to Picasso's pin collages, see Yve-Alain Bois, "The Pin," in Christian Bonnefoi, *La stratégie du tableau* (Madrid: Alfredo Melgar Editions, 1992), pp. 14–17. Trans.]

2. See the interview with Yve-Alain Bois and Jean Clay, "Sur l'apparition du visible," first published in *Macula* 5–6 (1979), reprinted in *Ecrits sur l'art (1974–1981)*, pp. 159–217.

3. [In light of commentaries on Mallarmé by both Blanchot and Lévinas, Bonnefoi is playing on the "*dés-astre de 4*" by suggesting "disaster" (*désastre*), "chance" (the roll of the dice—*dés* in French, as in Mallarmé's *Un Coup de Dés* cited above), and the "stars" (*astres*). For further exploration of this reading of Mallarmé, see in particular Maurice Blanchot, *The Writing of Disaster*, trans. Ann Smock (Lincoln: University of Nebraska Press, 1986), p. 2. The reference to numbering here recalls Derrida's various readings of Lacan, as well as his text on Sollers's *Nombres* in *Dissemination*, trans. Barbara Johnson (Chicago: University of Chicago Press, 1981). The same reference to numbering might also recall Damisch's essay on Rouan's *tressages*, at least as this essay also sets itself in relation to Lacan. See the introduction to Lacan's text on Rouan in this catalogue. Trans.]

4. See Georges Didi-Huberman, *Fra Angelico: Dissemblance and Figuration*, trans. Jane Marie Todd (Chicago: University of Chicago Press, 1995).

5. [Bonnefoi is referring to such works as Pollock's *Cut Out* (c. 1948–50) or *Cut-Out Figure* (1948). Trans.]

Ebbs and Flows, Fragments (for Simon Hantaï)
Alfred Pacquement

Emplie de plis.

—Henri Michaux, *La vie dans les plis*

As is well known, though maybe not so well known here in the United States, Simon Hantaï withdrew from public life in 1982. Sensing a time when art would become the object of excessive commercial speculation and when cultural events would become nothing more than political stakes—while modern art, long marginalized, would henceforth play a strategic role opposed to the artists' initial objectives—Hantaï approached this new phase in a radically critical mode: that of absence. Deliberately going against the grain of the media-driven and mercantile exasperation of the "roaring eighties," and because art had become an object of common consumption, Hantaï withdrew, stopped producing, and refused to exhibit and diffuse his work. He worked otherwise, intellectually.

Some, of course, incredulous at first, will consider this withdrawal to represent a passing doubt (it is not the first time that Hantaï temporarily stops working) or a sense of failure, perhaps of closure, which might lead to a new phase. In a way, this is a fitting impression in the case of an artist who shares with certain writers and philosophers the necessity of doubt, the choice of a "writing of the disaster" (Blanchot), but it is an impression that overlooks Hantaï's stubborn determination. Although he reached a point in the beginning of the eighties where his explorations had become fairly widely acknowledged, Hantaï ignored all kinds of solicitations, obstinately assuming this absence, this "painting strike," that nevertheless left ample room for the action of thought.

For absence is not silence or, more accurately, muteness. In this sixteen-year period, Simon Hantaï read philosophical texts and revisited his former works in different forms: cutouts, as in the *Laissées* series; photographic distortions (more *Laissées*, this time as silkscreens); *domestic foldings* with kitchen rags; readings, writings, classifications, reorderings, destructions, burials. The relation to painting, to his own painting, remained a continual activity throughout this extended period in which Hantaï disappeared and stopped exhibiting. The very person who had already spoken of working "with his arms severed and his eyes shut" carried on, in spite of the self-inflicted mutilations that were the deep conditions of his work to that point.

During one of our recent meetings, Hantaï mentioned a short miscellany by Samuel Beckett, recently published and entitled "Three Dialogues."[1] These, in the event, are writings about art, loosely inspired by conversations with the critic Georges Duthuit about three painters: Pierre Tal Coat, André Masson, and Bram van Velde. Whereas Duthuit strives to positively reconstruct the artist's intent and puts his trust in it, whatever the cost, Beckett repeatedly insists on that impossibility, on the necessary failure implied in the pictorial act. He denies painting the expressive power one ordinarily imputes to it, situating the artistic act outside that field. Two formulas, among many others, illuminate this argument: "impoverished painting, 'authentically fruitless, incapable of any image whatsoever'"; and "[he] who, helpless, unable to act, acts, in the event paints, since he is obliged to paint."

This is to say that Hantaï is not alone, or less alone than one might have been led to believe (of course, it would be much simpler to turn him into a marginal figure poised in lofty and haughty solitude). Indeed, others have, at certain times, come to similar positions: from Pollock to Giacometti—and closer to Hantaï, Michel Parmentier—from Beckett to Blanchot, to Deleuze as well (who quotes Hantaï in his *Abécédaire*), intellectual correspondences abound.[2] They sustain the mental activity that allows Hantaï to pursue his thinking. Nevertheless, Beckett's words, addressed to Bram van Velde, do not suit Hantaï who, as far as he himself is concerned, is able to act, which may include a claim for moments of nonproduction, without necessarily being obliged to paint.

Nonetheless, through this uncompromising position advanced in 1982, Hantaï willingly isolated himself from the artistic circles that had learned to attend to his progress. For example, the artists who had a continuing relationship with him were rare, whereas in the preceding decades (the "folding" period), those who kept regularly in touch with him or with his work were numerous. Almost twenty years later, Hantaï's withdrawal has left a gap, even though the 1998 exhibitions proved how much his painting remained present as soon as it was made public again.[3]

Given that the American public is for the most part discovering his work for the first time, it seems important to provide some background and to emphasize the considerable impact Hantaï has had on his contemporaries in France. From his conflictual relationship with André Breton, and his contact (or lack of contact) with the abstract painters of the fifties, to the role he played for the artistic generations of the sixties and after, Hantaï is one of the artists most often mentioned on the French scene in the last thirty years. As often happens, these parallels simplify complex relationships; they tend to insist on a few aspects, often too formal in nature, to the point of producing an inaccurate reading. The best example of this simplification is the use made by the Supports/Surfaces painters of unstretched canvas, which appeared as the manifesto of a painting freed from its former constraints and often went hand in hand with the practice of folding clearly borrowed from Hantaï. To infer a direct parallelism between them, as has often been done, is profoundly erroneous. Hantaï's method does violence to the surface, folds it and crumples it, but in his case the painting (*Tabula*) calls for a smoothing, refuses the unevenness of the surface, needs therefore, *in fine*, for the canvas to be stretched on a stretcher (though some of the big canvases were sometimes shown, against the painter's wishes, without that support).[4] In a comment from 1985, Hantaï himself cautions against an excessively conjunctive reading of his work: "I have always lived and worked in the margin, and the spotlight in which my work was thrown at the time of Supports/Surfaces' success reflects only certain aspects of it, actualizable and generalizable in that moment."

The role Hantaï played for this generation of painters is nonetheless considerable, and it needs fuller understanding. Logical in his approach, Simon Hantaï does not accept this role—unlike so many other artists, he does not attempt to claim a place but on the contrary strives to remain an outsider. My remarks, therefore, will not unfold according to an established order, nor in the strict chronology one might expect, but rather as fragmentary notes, so as to avoid presenting Hantaï as a master surrounded by disciples—that would be ludicrous—or even as an artist who imposed a representative style at a given period. We must respect the painter's will, all the more so because he may be leading us on a trail more conducive to certain insights, however disordered they may be. Hantaï's place is, in effect, much more complex than, and in its own way as essential as, that of any "founding" artist.[5] In the end, this critical stance Hantaï assumes toward the place he occupies in the art world appears all the more legitimate because his position was always inscribed in the margins; one recalls the first preface André Breton dedicated to him in 1953: "It was almost necessary to force him to exhibit his work, so loath is he to get caught in the commercial circuit, which, nowadays, is the Conqueror Worm of artistic expression."

Hantaï's painting does not present itself simply, and it cannot be shown with indifference to circumstances. It is not structured in a finalized history, or at any rate, that history remains to be written. There are entire layers (*pans*) of his work that remain to be discovered, as if the foldings had literally veiled certain parts; or as if the observation of the work, inscribed in a much too linear structure, had sidestepped moments of consequence that remained invisible merely for lack of someone's eye chancing upon them. Examples abound, and Hantaï has been accumulating them for a while, to the point of seeming like the one orchestrating the various phases of his own rereading: the tall

1958–59 painting, which was recently entitled *A Galla Placidia* and bequeathed to the Musée d'art moderne de la ville de Paris, after hanging in the studio for a long time without anyone noticing it,[6] even though it is part of a major moment; other paintings of the same period, a period critical for the rest of the work, which have been exposed little by little when the occasion allowed;[7] the cuttings of the early nineties (*Laissées*), which were revealed for the first time in March 1998 during the Renn espace show in Paris; and long-hidden traces which similarly anticipate a later approach, such as the foldings or rubbings of 1950 (thus prior to his surrealist phase). All of these examples say a lot about Hantaï's way of upsetting the historical labels attached to him.

An even better example: though the key date of 1960 is well identified, since it marks the beginning of the folding method that guided Hantaï's pictorial work from then on, it was in Münster that he reconstituted for the first time an ensemble close to the exhaustiveness of the *Mariales* of 1960–62, and this for the first time since their original presentation at the Kléber gallery in 1962. Much remains to be done to situate a work whose author precisely disallows any—necessarily reductive—situating.

Rather than accumulating facts and inert comparisons, it would be better to turn back to the paintings and attempt to approach these ebbs and flows. Let's reject, from the outset, the schematic reading of Hantaï's work, with its supposed three periods: surrealist, expressionist, and finally, "folding." First of all, there is a period before the so-called surrealist years, one in which Hantaï encounters Matisse's work and experiments with folding, among other ways of mistreating the traditional status of the painting. This still ill-defined period must be taken into account (as should the early work realized before his departure from Hungary). Second, the years of transition (1958–59) that precede the folding phase are an essential moment about which almost everything remains to be written. Third, since 1982, Hantaï has entered a period that critics tend to exclude from any commentary, because it

is aproductive. Whether this extensive last phase, now almost as long as the folding phase that preceded it, does not illuminate the painter's research as much remains to be decided. What is certain, in any case, is that this aproductive period speaks volumes about the artist's position, and thus can no longer be ignored.

One formula can summarize Hantaï's work from 1960 on, since the adoption of folding as a method: "the unpainted made active." There are other, even more radical variants, such as "the unpainted painted." Through folding, Hantaï strives to put on the same plane and fully join the destructured and restructured surface of the painting to the space in reserve—the *unpainted*. It took some time for the painter to embrace the zones in reserve as an integral part of the work, and more time still for the viewer to accept them as such (as evidenced by misunderstandings with certain artists, who saw them as spaces to transform anew). If one had to trace the trajectory of Hantaï's work as a series of musical movements (we may recall that he realized a group of *Etudes*), one could describe the gradual acceptance of the unpainted as a succession of "tempi," all the way to the *Tabulas-lilas* that complete the "active" phase of the folding period.

Painting thus becomes an ensemble of relations from which prettiness, the mastery of the gesture, and talent have been banished. The material is treated crudely: a rag, a crumpled piece of cloth, will do. Behind this indigence, however, lies the strength of a thought, a philosophy in which painting holds its place in the world, in which the memory of art and the founding concepts of aesthetic thought remain present. Hantaï paints, as he has often repeated, "blindly" (recall too the apt expression of "retinal silences," a response to the nonretinal art proclaimed by Duchamp), but the reflection he has been engaged in for almost twenty years leads one to think that this impoverishment of the pictorial method (to the point of interrupting it) goes hand in hand with a call for lucidity and an effort of memory. All sorts of facts signal this interpretation: from the carefully ironed apron his mother used to wear in Hungary before the war, preserved with its impeccably square folds; to the paintings buried in the garden and exhumed much later, so as to discover their traces deteriorated by the weather;[8] to the dedications of the paintings recently bequeathed to the Musée d'art moderne de la ville de Paris, in which he makes references to Ravenna and the Venetian Tintorettos, as well as to the two remarkable paintings of the Virgin Mary by Enguerrand and Piero.

Let us return to before 1960, to that essential although still little studied period of 1958–59, as determined, among other things, by the tall *Ecriture rose* in the Musée nationale d'art moderne, Centre Georges Pompidou—a kind of negative painting on the surface of which Hantaï recopies the liturgical and philosophical texts he associates with a few symbolic signs (the cross, the star of David, . . .) over the course of an entire year and to the point of illegibility. During this period of interrogation into the foundations of pictorial practice, a whole ensemble of processes emerge tending toward the disappearance of mastery, the refusal of the authority of gesture, and resulting in a slowing down of the hand, in effacement. Hence the quasi-integral covering of the painting's surface by a uniform writing; the repetition of small identical signs overwhelming the surface; and elsewhere, finally, the covering of the surface with gold leaf to envisage a monochromatic space. A little later, Hantaï develops what he entitles the *Torchon* (rag): the surface of a painting, mistreated as it is elaborated, only resuming its shape through unfolding.

This approach, which goes against the grain of lyrical abstractions of all sorts, where it was rather a matter of "overpainting"—except maybe with Pollock and his rudimentary method (Hantaï talks about Pollock's "stick")—will deeply mark younger artists in the mid sixties, such as Buren, Parmentier, Buraglio, Meurice, a little later Viallat, and with him, most of the members of Supports/Surfaces.

On January 3, 1967, four artists exhibited their work at the Salon de la Jeune Peinture. Or rather, they did not exhibit, because—after having painted in public

according to their respective, extremely reductive "codes"—they took the canvases off the walls and left nothing but an empty space, adorned only with a banner reading: "Buren, Mosset, Parmentier, and Toroni are not exhibiting." A number of flyers accompanied the action. In a letter addressed to the art world, to which this series of demonstrations were announced, one may note the following phrase: "to present the trace of our activity, but above all to make manifest the mechanics from which it proceeds."[9] Hantaï's method is evidently germane to such claims.

Buren and Parmentier had known Hantaï for a while when they started producing their radical work of 1966–67. Each had met with him often, had talked with, or rather listened to, Hantaï. In Buren's words: "At the time we saw him, he worked completely against the grain, in Paris at least. On the questions that mattered to us, he was as critical as we were. He shared the same ferocious perception of the Parisian art situation: cinetism, new realism, Ecole de Paris abstraction. Simon had the same reticence, and he knew that situation better than we did. He was the only person to concur with us; his example, his orientation reassured us. Moreover, he was a part of History. We knew of his past, his relationships with Breton. We knew he was isolated. Everything he said or did was respectable; his image was not deceptive . . ."[10]

At that time, Parmentier was operating through horizontal foldings, covering the folded canvas with a single sprayed color (blue in 1966, gray in 1967, red in 1968). The hand gesture was neutralized by the pictorial process, the "facture" impersonal, the formal system of horizontal foldings always the same. Unlike Hantaï, he left the folds visible and did not stretch the canvas on a stretcher, but his pictorial process was directly borrowed from the painter of the *Mariales*. Parmentier speaks of his work as "an insistent mute monologue," an expression that obviously compares to Hantaï's formula of "painting blindly."

Buren started using the striped canvas in the fall of 1965. He firmly refused that period's expressive and embellished abstraction and found Hantaï's painting on his path. The elaboration of Buren's approach—neutralizing the gesture, depersonalizing the act of painting, and soon contextualizing the work in situ—happened in proximity to Hantaï—an intellectual and aesthetic proximity, as well as a geographic one, with both artists living for a while in neighboring homes at the Cité des Fleurs in Paris. At first the stripes were undone by rounded paint overlays, which were soon transferred onto the edges of the canvas. Later, the striped fabric, with only the outermost white bands painted, stood in for painting, with no other artifice. In the interview quoted above, Buren talked about Hantaï and, precisely at that founding moment of his approach, about the "proximity of a conscience," acknowledging his interest for Hantaï's method.

In Paris, Jean Fournier's gallery has been entirely identified with Hantaï's trajectory, ever since the violent rupture with André Breton.[11] This is where the *Alice in Wonderland* exhibition was held in 1955, organized by the critic Charles Estienne. This is also where Hantaï, after several personal exhibitions following one another in rapid succession, showed a group of *Mariales* (May–June 1962), which were seen by many of the younger artists I've mentioned. The first foldings had without doubt a considerable impact on these artists, who were less than twenty-five years old and were trying to escape both the surge of fashionable narrative images and an expressive, overly personalized abstraction. A little later, Jean Fournier's gallery also fostered an interesting and unique attempt to link two generations, for the first time taking a new lineage of abstract painters into account. *Tryptique,* an exhibition from 1966, brought Riopelle, Tapiès, and Hantaï together with Buren, Parmentier, Buraglio, and Meurice.

At the same time—between 1964 and 1968—Pierre Buraglio was in effect experimenting with recoverings, or with the cutting of old canvases whose fragments were stapled together, or with camouflages. Each of the pictorial operations engaged by the artist takes its distance from the *tableau*. They were negatives, or refusals that lead to destruction: covering, cutting, camouflaging. At this time Buraglio encountered Hantaï's painting and spoke about it: "Between his emotion and the form or tableau, Hantaï places a mechanical operation on the canvas to be painted which then distances him from that form, from that *tableau*."[12]

Much later, Buraglio, following his own approach of recuperating found materials, reused the scraps of canvas or stained grounds Hantaï provided him and reintroduced them in his own work, loyal to the "economy of recycling" that characterizes it.

At that same time, Jean-Michel Meurice was working in a more American vein (under the influence, for example, of Morris Louis), letting color spread on the surface and ultimately saturate it. A little later, he opted for painted aluminum crumpled surfaces, or folded and cut vinyl, surely marked by Hantaï's painting. He also wrote several articles about Hantaï from 1965 on, and a little later directed two films in which Hantaï is seen painting.

In one of these films, Dominique Fourcade reads a long excerpt from Cézanne's famous conversation with Gasquet, at the request of Hantaï, who seems to know it by heart. This is precisely a passage where the space of the *unpainted* enters painting: "For a long time I remained unable to paint, not knowing how to paint Sainte-Victoire, because I imagined the concave shade like the others who do not see, whereas, see, look, it is convex, it flees from its center. Instead of contracting, it evaporates, becomes fluid. It participates, blue, in the ambient breathing of the air . . ."[13]

In 1968, Parmentier stopped painting. He would only resume his work sixteen years later, at the point where, in a way, he had left it, and would work only intermittently from then on. Parmentier's extreme position cannot be assimilated to Hantaï's, who stopped exhibiting in 1982 after having consecutively put on a personal exhibition in the big nave of the capcMusée d'art contemporain in Bordeaux and a presentation of his recent paintings in the French pavilion during the twentieth

Venice Biennale. Neither the contexts nor the trajectories of the two artists are the same, but the common fact of withdrawal is sufficiently exceptional, as a matter of "proximity of conscience," to bear remarking.[14]

At the beginning of the seventies, art in France was strongly marked by the Supports/Surfaces movement, whether one considers the members of the group itself (Viallat, Dezeuze, Pincemin, Bioulès, Cane, Devade, etc.) or those in its orbit and subsequently distanced from it by circumstance (Rouan, Jaccard, as well as Buraglio and Meurice). We would need to add to this group the names of Buren, Parmentier, Mosset, and Toroni, who had become visible in this context a little earlier but who were radicalizing a similar pictorial proposition in order to reverse it and ultimately negate it. For all these painters, Hantaï is not a master but, in Buren's words, a "conscience," more or less close to each of them: the person who, perhaps, offers, for those especially close, a way to go on. The other pictorial references of this generation were mainly drawn from postwar American art. The "folding" process then became a widespread act favored by this new generation of artists, who saw in it a clearly stated method of deconstructing the *tableau*. Besides Parmentier, who first took it up, one can mention Cane, Arnal, Saytour (who, like Parmentier, leaves the traces of the folds), Dolla, or Jaccard.

Such examples—which could be multiplied— give an account of the strong impact of Hantaï's work in the seventies, but also perhaps of a somewhat narrow approach which will not be without consequence—as is my claim—on the painter's later stance. The fortune of a formula like "folding as method," echoed from critical texts to catalogues, has likely induced a much too materialist reading of Hantaï's work, at least during those years of deconstructing painting in which neutrality, the free canvas, and all sorts of purely formal attitudes were adopted. This excess of visibility, focused on the "mechanical" process rather than on its meaning, may have, as it were, led Hantaï to silence,

thus better exposing it as a lack. One ought to have looked elsewhere.

Antonio Semeraro, for example, nourished by numerous encounters with Hantaï, would later succeed in giving the unpainted its unqualified place in the work, following a "paradox of proximity." Semeraro's huge empty surfaces, traversed by precisely adjusted colored cuttings, display a precarious balance, close in spirit to Hantaï's *Blancs*.

Michel Parmentier, in turn, would find just words for Hantaï's absence in speaking of his attempt at "escaping the trap of a sovereign speech—sovereign and insidiously utilitarian—served to us by a certain notion of modern art."[15]

A long silence thus follows, punctuated by nonevents, such as the little-known pages Deleuze devoted to Hantaï's *unfolding*.[16] From one rupture to the next (with surrealism, gesturality, the sign, production), Hantaï has for the most part either preceded or countered his contemporaries' stances. Through this impoverishment, however, he reached a philosophical position that may be activated anew for other artistic approaches. An example? A model? These words won't do. An aesthetic, even political program. A conscience, perhaps.

"No! Under no circumstance!" writes Hantaï after reading this text, "absolutely no 'eloquent conscience,' but rather a concern for the consequences of an ateleological choice."

1999

Translated from the French by Anthony Allen.

Alfred Pacquement is widely noted as both critic and curator. Formerly director of the Galerie nationale du Jeu de Paume and of the Ecole des beaux-arts in Paris, he is currently director of the Centre Georges Pompidou. This essay was previously published (in German translation) in *Simon Hantaï: Werke von 1960 bis 1995* (Münster: Westfälisches Landesmuseum für Kunst und Kulturgeschichte, 1999).

1. [Samuel Beckett, *Disjecta: Miscellaneous Writings and a Dramatic Fragment* (New York: Grove Press, 1984), pp. 138–45. Trans.]

2. [*L'Abécédaire de Gilles Deleuze, avec Claire Parnet,* a series of televised interviews from 1996, shown in France on the TV channel Arte. Trans.]

3. *Laissées et autres peintures,* Renn espace, Paris, March–June 1998; and *Donation Simon Hantaï,* Musée d'art moderne de la ville de Paris, 1998.

4. See Hantaï's note in the catalogue *Donation Simon Hantaï* (Paris: Musée d'art moderne de la ville de Paris, 1998), p. 32.

5. Or "initiators" (*embrayeurs*), as Anne Cauquelin calls them in her book on contemporary art in the *Que sais-je* series, combining in that term artists (such as Duchamp and Warhol) and art dealers (such as Castelli). One sees where such simplifications of history lead, once the margins are excluded. [See Anne Cauquelin, *L'art contemporain* (Paris: Presses Universitaires de France, 1994). Trans.]

6. See Hantaï in *Donation Simon Hantaï,* p. 24.

7. For instance, in a group exhibit at the Musée d'art moderne de la ville de Paris, at the same time as the exhibition at Münster. [For the catalogue of the Münster exhibition, see *Simon Hantaï: Werke von 1960 bis 1995.* Trans.]

8. See Georges Didi-Huberman, *L'étoilement: Conversation avec Hantaï* (Paris: Minuit, 1998), pp. 107–11.

9. In a letter dated 24 December 1966.

10. Daniel Buren, in Daniel Buren and Michel Parmentier, *Propos délibérés* (Lyons: Art Edition; Brussels: Palais des Beaux-Arts, 1991), p. 46.

11. This gallery was initially called Galerie Kléber and took Jean Fournier's name after moving from the Avenue Kléber to the Rue du Bac.

12. In *Beaux-arts* 1115 (January 1966), reprinted in Pierre Buraglio, *Ecrits entre 1962 et 1990* (Paris: Ecole nationale supérieure des beaux-arts, 1991).

13. In *Conversations avec Cézanne* (Paris: Macula, 1978), p. 112.

14. Let us note that Pierre Buraglio also stopped painting in 1968, but as a militant act in the service of political activism. He resumed his work as an artist in 1974.

15. See the catalogue *Michel Parmentier* (Paris: Centre national des arts plastiques, 1988).

16. [Gilles Deleuze, *The Fold: Leibniz and the Baroque,* trans. Tom Conley (Minneapolis: University of Minnesota Press, 1993), pp. 33–36. Trans.]

Letters to Georges Didi-Huberman
February 1997–January 1998
Simon Hantaï

Paris, 2/19/97

Dear Georges,
Here's what happened to us, unforeseen, unpro-
grammed, noncalculated.
A gift, then?
Your call to invite me to visit the *Empreinte* exhibit
greatly touched me. After 15 years of retreat and 3
years of incapacity, I don't know if that visit would
have been possible otherwise.
During that short period of time, I tried to see (what
does that mean: to see?) less the localized objects than,
if possible, in a fluctuating, peripheral way (when I
paint, I don't see the part hidden behind the flattened
folds—a way of seeing I modified by choice: I put my
eyes out)—and even the spreading of colored matter is
done with little direct attention, but rather with my
gaze wandering outside through the window,—where it
snows and rains. For the problem is neither the artistic
treatment, nor the desire that indulges in it, but its absence and the working through and realization of that
absence: letting something happen which the pleasure
of painting prevents from happening.
This is what I was also trying to do during the visit to
the exhibition, and if I didn't pay enough attention to
your words—please forgive me. To see the thought that
underpins the show as clearly as possible, its knowledge, its taste, and even more the element of active un-
knowing, the wager and the risk.
I am glad about this unforeseen development. Your
generosity, your wager are precious to me, I like it, it
was as it ought to have been, as I would have wished it
to be, appearing in public of my own accord after my
long absence.
Let's call it a throw of the dice, then. Agreed?
With affection,
Yours, in friendship,
Simon H.

Dear Georges,

here are some small clues, confused and fragmentary, but which may perhaps also, hopefully, provoke something, even if only on the rebound.

Alright. Here on the wall are my handprints, dipped in a pile of powdered color, remains from a stack of accumulated paintings exposed to the winter weather, decomposed, rotten powdered color turned into = caput mortuum.

As you can see—a lot of accumulations—in the corner of the garden, where compost is prepared—a layer of paintings, leaves and earth on top, and so on—a lot of paintings have disappeared in this way—most of all in '94 and '95, photographed here.

The background of what remains.

Critique of painting, of artists—Bataille, Duchamp. What these critiques address or do not address.

The importance of knowing this.   Where and how did painting encounter the important points in itself: always and again, the scissors and the stick dipped in color [Matisse, Pollock]. Not as variations in the *former context:*

Many things from the '20s and '30s. Variations within a well-known aesthetic. But the letting-happen of a new "context." What needed to be *let fall* for it to happen.

If folding and unfolding: (no) more connection   the connections are torn   the near is distanced   the closed opened   interrupted   one paints blindly   groping   on the off chance   throwing the dice   one plays and puts at stake.

The articulated is disarticulated.

The hidden   the fault   the shattered   the scattered. Inattention   distraction   attention   scattered fluctuating   peripheral   decentered   delocalized crack   breach   break   to interrupt

to inter rupt
"through the breach of the retina . . ." (Freud).

The blind spot (thought)   painting without seeing
while looking elsewhere   vacant   absence of
value   of content   unoccupied   incapacity   vague
wave   slit   to be dispossessed   detached   cutting
aimless   untied   thresholds   unfavorable   unpredictable . . .   the gut   process of stepping back
regressive   mutilated.
Oh! music again and forever.

But I can't do it any differently. I talk about what painting has taught me. In a certain way, I even correct other
people's verbal expression in the name of that experience. Perhaps you remember it, in the palm of my hand,
my *Hohlwege*,[1] but Freud's *screen* of the dream as well.
And Bataille and Duchamp, that is what we should be
able to do, that is our necessary impossibility, provided
we do not want to wallow indefinitely in the idle talk
of our context. What would an unprecedented "yes"
to Duchamp look like, and what fundamental point
would it address, which is no longer only of the moment? And Bataille too. And the indices of that. This is
why one should read the others with passion.
One does not see, one sees words.

Calm down, hold your horses, especially as this is more
about a *withdrawal than an "active autism,"* whose exhibition is essentially bound to the other who speaks in
my place, if it is to be the exhibition of a "we." I know
the *shifting,* back and forth, interminable—and spent
my painter's life on all fours
And even lower—
Now for a little chinoiserie:
A lepedöt leteríti, behajtjá és *négykézlab* lelapitva, par-
lagosan bemeszeli széltölszélig, szépséggond nélkül,
*gond*talanúl félrenézve, oda ki, látva amint hull a hó.[2]

"He had been so sick, they had already prepared his shroud."

Freud (The Wolfman)

Here is one of the big paintings hanging at Bordeaux (Entrepôt Lainé in '81).
Torn apart in '95, in the summer, photographed by Antonio Semeraro, my friend, my great
friend of those years of retreat (15 years).
Visible the cut in the big hanging violet one. The upper right-hand corner.

The second and third pictures were taken at Maisons-Alfort, in '81, by Kamil Major, who helped me with the handling and preparation of the canvases. The *black* element was used to realize the largest silkscreen presented [in *L'Empreinte*] at Beaubourg.
Folded and painted   half-unfolded   unfolded
hung   cut   put back on canvas.

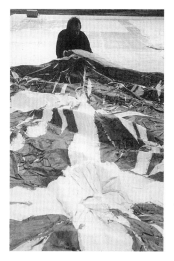

Once the violet one was cut and even the white border removed, I realized after the fact that the white strip was missing. I had to put it back. The rest is now at Berri's. You have seen it.

The eye. Through folding, I put my eyes out   one-eyed
blind reckoning   bet on its blindness.
To finish with the screen.   Will be part of . . .
modifying myself

Speaking of autism, one day I will show you a text by H. Michaux about a drug experience. Surprising.

Neocortex unfolds like a mantle of cloth folded and folded over   the frog does not have a cortex   blind person's vision   blind touch   out of sight   tact   ears
the feet   the knees   the hand lost (in the pocket)
put the eye in parenthesis   the severed hand

the possibility of an inversion of sense   "dregs" (*la lie*)

the canvas, bed sheet, on the ground, on the earth, folded, flattened, in a pile, down, not in a dictionary sense, but outside of contraries, not opposed but desired, awaited, a joy, something that finally arrives, a "no more than that," a happy "yes" to this "no more than that"   A "that's it" . . .   it's there . . .   just above the level (*au ras*) of things   *Rohmaterial*[3]   innards.   Shows what hides   folded into the reserve   Wandering Swabian   white shroud   *the slit in Cézanne's studio*[4]

rather studied than praised

"We other, we deal with the negative." K[afka]

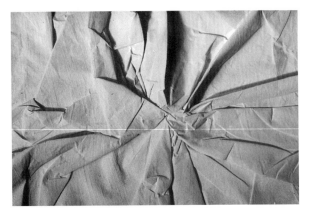

You told me about "starring," like the cracking of glass (*étoilement*): a big, folded canvas (*toile*), on the reverse a knot at the meeting point of a vertical and a horizontal line.

On the other photo: the beginning of the opening, of the unfolding. A knot appears. Afterwards: totally opened and hanging at Bordeaux. It is one of the *two* paintings, kept, separated and bound by the starring? Not a sun. What else, then?

Don't forget this is about folding. Setting in motion of a process that takes charge at a certain moment: 1960, a limit reached in painting, and nothing else than that; scissors and a dripping stick.

The canvas ceases to be a *projection screen,* becomes a material, cutting within itself, etc.

the invaginated   the involuted   the flattened mountain   the painted and the hidden   folding and unfolding.

between tracks   between lines   between knots   between blows   entry   door chain   interlacing   to search in between   half-closed   interlaced   between knots

—I'm going off the rails. Let's return to starring.
dialectical   bursting open   spatializing
                          diffusor   dilaceration

knot: *more or less large* (It changes everything. It's actually the only element through
which modifications have been produced in
my work since 1973.) Essential enlarge-
ment. Material support for the unpainted. One square
meter of blue is bluer than fifteen square centimeters of
blue. (M[atisse]) Hence my metrical enlargements,
which paradoxically lead to nonmetrical structural
modifications. This is only possible through folding.
Reworked   around   the   remains   of   something
irreducible.

Let's return to starring once again
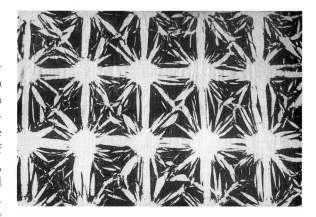

        knot   gives this   unfolded
        void that severs and binds
        to spangle with stars   starring   starry sky
        crossing   *intersect*
intersecting   crosswise

mountain flattened under/by the feet   interval
just above the earth   iron (D[uchamp])   the in-
between   the between   the crack notch   slash [*en-
taille*]   linking   undoing
—let's stop. You've heard the song before.   Power,
masters, privileges, triumph etc.
to place in parenthesis.   And phantasm too?   Ah that
fan.
In the Hungarian language, there are nice things about
that.
The black photo of that painting, preserved   There is
nothing more important . . .

Sunday, 7/6/97

Here you see the cutting of the Bordeaux canvases, in '95 (photos by Semeraro), in the summer, in blinding sunlight. The white light, so impossible for the camera, yields these disorienting results. Lower, on the wall, the journal of those years, with the background references, which have been there forever, the white mountain and its dislocating action, the scissors and the dripping stick.

The inventory of things accumulated in the attic for many years, their discovery or destruction.

The sticks ‖‖ are traces (30 years) of these refusals. Hundreds destroyed. And about those cuts, that you know, what remains to be said?

Extractions, maybe.   Thoughts depending on my strengths

I paint so as to look at   what a prodigiously simplified material   limited   the in-between has assumed all consistency, its own autonomy and its own direction

"you sang blankly" (K[afka: Josefine])   "an end to flowers" [Beckett]   to pluck the parrot   active autism aphasia   anexact

inexact, to designate thus something exactly

I tried for a long time to control disorder, instead of taking it as my subject

Ulysses' dogs, Cézanne's and Lévinas's, guide dog for the blind watched the grass grow for a long time.

linen (angyalrúgta fü—angel—kicked grass)

Cézanne born in '39, in '61 (21 years old) admires Meissonier, Cabanel (letter) the withered hand involuntary sifting, involuntary appearances   animals' soul   blind, archaic vision   the frog (doesn't have a cortex)

Visibility since a blinding experience

invagination   infolding retreat   to leave "my day in the sun"   dislocations through pleating   szemfo-gyasztó (belittling eye)   taking the crown off

suspense of the "against"   the baker's transformation

map of the brain   fault   never wanted to "hold" a
rank in the institution   intaglio (*intaille*)   low without an opposition to height   expels itself from (the)
painting   there is nothing behind it.

Sight close to the ground   touch   the baring of the
relation   more than the neutral vessel   the very material of the work

Drawing = hierarchy   no more separate
drawing   theory in praxis, plastic thought
working   develops itself in it
rabatment of the axis   painting with one's feet
innards   the body remembers   hands behind the
back . . .   I'm not up to the problem (folding)   cutting and opening coincide   I lost the vowels   clum-
sily and as well as I could   people blind from birth
animals   were playing dice   *The holes between the
apples* (C[ézanne])
sandless desert   did I cheat?

"table" reverse

painted

open

At Berri's you asked me: what do you prefer: pictures [*tableaux*], paintings or . . . I forgot the third one and I replied: paintings. That was too hasty. Since '73, I call them tables.

 square first ('73) small (15 cm)
the frame joins the dance (M[atisse])

Noting the embarrassed silence—raising the tone: *tabula*. But all of them together then, with their change in time and in the plural? Simply tabulas. The guard dogs start howling. You can't do that! Of course you can! Of course you can! You can, since it's done, and being in common use for more than twenty years ratifies [the word]. Tabula, therefore, is my answer to your question.

Simply the name of things, as it results from the confrontation of the random and the metrical, which are usually separated genres. Not for or in the folding. That is precisely the question.
It isn't even new. Already in Novalis, for instance.
I don't have enough space here to enumerate the oppositions he envisaged. I'm hurrying.
What about the consequences of this bet?—
The logic of proximity is no longer defined, and can be achieved in an infinite number of ways
the elements divide and change each time in nature.
With the increase of dimensions, separations interweaving . . .
Your starring?
Beyond the results in time, the idea persists, tied to the conditions which yielded these results.
The idea, and the means of these ideas, blind realization.
To reveal a knot invisible thus far.

(1) the parrot before the unfolding
(2) unfolded
(3) hanging at Bordeaux ('81)
(4) Both elements, above (blue) and in the middle (violet), are now at Berri's after cuts and changes in the white parts.

Deleuze: negativity of the positive and positivity of the negative
Lacoue-Labarthe: active neutrality of the in-between
Nancy: the in of the in-between
Derrida: (among many others) linking of the unlinked at the heart of unlinking
or: the rupture of the connection is the connection
Nietzsche:—look into it. What are we talking about? What painting gave me.

Dear Georges—I have no other picture of this painting. Therefore, I am sending you this postcard, sent to me with obvious intentions by Antonio Semeraro (as I said, and I repeat: my very good friend, companion of solitude and sharing).

Mantle with large folds, painted
what is going on under the mantle is blindingly clear
Opens sight to its limit

The Louvre Pietà as well

[postcard: The crowning of the Virgin, Enguerrand Quarton, Villeneuve-lès-Avignon
Dear Simon and Zsuzsa   Very deep emotions while visiting Cézanne's studio. Thinking of you, affectionately
Antonio + M(ara)]

 Cut out a window into writing paper

The painted mountain flattened out. Almost . . .
The Mont Sainte-Victoire is painted at the bottom
"I am as dead" Cézanne
The exact quotation by Cézanne is:
There isn't enough room here. I am copying it on another sheet.*

     *Cézanne's letter to Camille Pissarro:
L'Estaque, 2 July 1876,

". . . It's like a playing card [. . .] The sun here is so vivid that it seems to me that objects are always outlined, not only white or black, but blue, red, brown, violet. I may be wrong, but it seems to me that it is the limit of modeling . . . "[5]

Monday, 7/7/97

Dear Georges,
here is something for the chocolates. I hope I didn't
bother you too much.
Yours, in friendship,
Simon

One day I will tell you about the Charcot file at
Salpêtrière hospital. Not the file you discussed a little
while ago, but the other one, the one still buried, despite my entreaties to Binet, about the work done on
patients concerning the alteration of color perception,
which goes back to Empedocles, through Goethe and
Buffon, down to Cézanne, Flaubert, Matisse, to other
colors, solicited, not materially expressed, but also,
through Hegel's glass raised to Goethe's health, to the
beginning of industrialization in England under a pink
light. Ouff! Not to mention some aspects of my studies,
up to the white-on-white works called *Tabulas-lilas*
(from the back). Or delocalized colors, the opposite of
localized ones (Bragg effect)—triggered by the mos-
quito virus and going all the way to the Ecclesiast,
This time—Pouff!!!   Irony knows—maybe—

Paris, December 17, 1997

Dear Georges,
Your great gift profoundly moved me—an unexpected
jolt, especially since, at the time you wrote it, I had myself been trying to elaborate for several years, from elements and phenomena scattered in painting and in
other realms, knots, compared with Charcot's experiments with alterations in color perception on hysterics
at Salpêtrière hospital and on a number of people suf-
fering from nervous illnesses. In contrast, the text on
hysteria and art published in *Macula* at the beginning
of the '80s irritated me. Probably wrongly.
But your *Invention of Hysteria* is fully, and even more,
for me.[6]

We will talk about it again one day, and decide whether
we can get my larva out of its chrysalis and see if it is a
stillborn.
Thanks. Your friend
Simon

Paris, December 19, 1997

Dearest Georges,
I found the paper with the inscription on Tintoretto's
tomb at Madonna dell'Orto, copied in June 1982. The
paper is quite faded, barely legible. Jérôme got started
on it yesterday afternoon, when he dropped by. An important day for me, indelibly inscribed.
Two paintings, narrow and high, hitting up against the
 vaults, only visible from underneath, dirty,
carelessly painted with a broom, outside
norms, already Greco. It's on the right.
Look closely at the blue at the bottom, etc.
. . . My first encounter with Tintoretto.
Very strong. Afterwards, at the Accademia
and at San Rocco, a new look at his other paintings.
Rose, Rose, Rose . . . T.'s tomb—
soaked—upon returning, towards the end of the day,
sudden shock—saw the absolute black, of pure light,
on the façade of S. Maria dei Miracoli. The next day,
while wanting to see that black again, I got lost: I didn't
recognize anything. Outside Venice? And suddenly,
that black. Transfixed. Decided to move forward, sliding my feet on the ground, *inch by inch,* my eyes fixed
on nothing, waiting. Then it comes *from everywhere.*
Blindly follow these piercings. Street after street. In the
corners, left or right at the pace of a snail depending on
these apparitions, memorizing their forms, locations,
street names. Saw and remembered only that. I will not
paint with color anymore. What duration? More than
the whole morning. Came late for the opening of my
show at the French pavilion. The next day, came back
with Jacqueline Hyde to photograph the place. Find
those photographs again. I know, I knew, that it is
about questions of sculpture. To invent. Dell'Orto

too is, in this way, a black unpainted garden of lights, but . . . —Another chrysalis and
on that note I'll sign off with affection

Simon

During this journey inch by inch, the passers-by (I saw them as ghosts) surely saw me as a lunatic to avoid. Salpêtrière story, the alteration version, one more time. I shall stop here. I must.

VENETI APELLIS
IACOBI ROBUSTII
COGNOMENO
TINCTORETTI
CINERIS
HOC MARMORE CLAUDUNTUR
IS MAGNUS NATURAE AEMULATOR
   MUTAM POESIM
INGENIO VEHEMENTI REDDIDIT
   ELOQUENTEM
DIVINO SI QUIDEM PENICILLO SOLI
   COELIQUE INCOLAS
SUIS IN TABULIS SPIRARE COEGIT

Friday, 2 January 98

Dear Georges,
After our telephone conversation today, these fragments, which captured my attention yesterday and last night.

Bataille: inversion of action into nonaction
   the work's absence
   one must denounce the belief in this reality
   as responsible itself for this reality
   prepare its *atrophy* [*étiolement*] in the long
   run
debilitate, drain, exhaust
emaciated (*étique*) "any free manifestation of the mind is obscene"
least inclination
greater resistance nonpure

atrophy is also an inversion of doing into nondoing
just like "I would prefer
not to" is a "leaving-work" without conclusion, swallowed violence, identifiable incandescence, by default, empty power, empty place, aberration, underwork

"I strove to put everything nicely in place, while keeping quiet about it."

And for the Koran: "key for understanding, one for which tradition has the beautiful
and modern name of *starring* (tanjîm)." When a hadith (a word of the Prophet) says that "the Koran was revealed according to (a flow [*un débit*]) *a star*" . . . then articulated by the Prophet *on the occasion* (sabab) of a specific event, of a question asked . . .

On the off chance, without any justification but friendship

Simon

A Magyar nép müvészete. [From: *The Art of the Hungarian People*]
volume IV.
Malonyay Deszö   = author
Franklin Tarsulat Kiadása   = publisher
Budapest.
page 155:
. . . s így szabálytalan *csillagok* maradtak a vászon . . .
. . . they fastened stones onto the white canvas with strings, and placed the canvas in dye (indigo). Once it was blue, they took off the strings and *irregular white stars thus remained on the canvas, untouched by the indigo dye*

below
underneath
atop
already reversed
ironed   flattened
"there is a" *Meun*   underneath
                       spread out on top of that
blindingly clear   Poe, Freud, etc.
one does not see, not yet
one does not see E. Quarton's painting
my painting   reveals it
               Meuns reveal it/will be able to re
               veal it, etc.
the purloined letter and other similar ones
M.   the virgin has a mantle of/from
               Meun
               Meun like mantle

1997–98

Translated from the French by Anthony Allen.

Simon Hantaï's letters to Georges Didi-Huberman were first published in Simon Hantaï, *Werke von 1960 bis 1995* (Münster: Westfälisches Landesmuseum für Kunst und Kulturgeschichte, 1999). They are reproduced here courtesy of Hantaï. Two exhibitions are worth recalling, since they figure in several of the letters: *L'Empreinte,* an exhibition Didi-Huberman curated at the Centre Georges Pompidou in 1997, which included several works by Hantaï; and Hantaï's exhibition *Laissées et autres peintures,* curated by Alfred Pacquement and shown at Renn espace in 1998 (the space was formerly owned by Claude Berri, who is also mentioned here). Didi-Huberman's public "response" to Hantaï's letters is published as *L'Etoilement: Conversation avec Hantaï* (Paris: Minuit, 1998). For their help in preparing the translation and publication, we would like to thank Simon Hantaï, Georges Didi-Huberman, and Erich Franz.

1. [In German in the original. Trans.]

2. I spread the bed sheet on the ground, fold it and, on all fours, flatten it out, coat it, buried talent, edge to edge, looking aside, there, outside, watching the snow fall.

3. [In German in the original. Trans.]

4. [See Simon Hantaï and Antonio Semeraro, "L'oeil de l'aiguille," in *Où est passée la peinture?*, art press, hors série no. 16 (1995): 128–29. Trans.]

5. [Paul Cézanne, *Letters,* ed. John Rewald, trans. Seymour Hacker (New York: Hacker Art Books, 1984), p. 154. Trans.]

6. Georges Didi-Huberman, *Invention de l'hystérie: Charcot et l'iconographie photographique de la Salpêtrière* (Paris: Macula, 1982).

Six Comments

Sherrie Levine

Since the door was only half closed, I got a jumbled view of my mother and father on the bed, one on top of the other. Mortified, hurt, horror-struck, I had the hateful sensation of having placed myself blindly and completely in unworthy hands. Instinctively and without effort, I divided myself, so to speak, into two persons, of whom one, the real, the genuine one, continued on her own account, while the other, a successful imitation of the first, was delegated to have relations with the world. My first self remains at a distance, impassive, ironical, and watching. (1980)

The world is filled to suffocating. Man has placed his token on every stone. Every word, every image, is leased and mortgaged. We know that a picture is but a space in which a variety of images, none of them original, blend and clash. A picture is a tissue of quotations drawn from the innumerable centers of culture. Similar to those eternal copyists Bouvard and Pécuchet, we indicate the profound ridiculousness that is precisely the truth of painting. We can only imitate a gesture that is always interior, never original. Succeeding the painter, the plagiarist no longer bears within him passions, humors, feelings, impressions, but rather this immense encyclopedia from which he draws. The viewer is the tablet on which all the quotations that make up a painting are inscribed without any of them being lost. A painting's meaning lies not in its origin, but in its destination. The birth of the viewer must be at the cost of the painter. (1981)

In the seventeenth century, Miguel de Cervantes published *Don Quixote*. In 1962, Jorge Luis Borges published "Pierre Menard, Author of the Quixote," the story of a man who rewrites the ninth and thirty-eighth chapters of *Don Quixote*. His aim was never to produce a mechanical transcription of the original, he did not want to copy it. His ambition was to propose pages which would coincide with those of Cervantes, to continue being Pierre Menard and to arrive at *Don Quixote* through the experience of Pierre Menard. Like Menard, I have allowed myself variants of a formal and psychological nature. (1983)

We like to imagine the future as a place where people loved abstraction before they encountered sentimentality. (1984)

I like to think of my paintings as membranes permeable from both sides so there is an easy flow between the past and the future, between my history and yours. (1985)

In "The Death of the Cathedrals," Marcel Proust imagines a near future when the Catholic mass will be reconstituted as a theatrical display, actors performing the roles of the clergy as well as the faithful. He wrote and rewrote this essay between 1904 and 1919, a period contemporaneous with the development of abstraction and the readymade, which were disparate attempts to reclaim art from the realm of representation and imitation. Reading his ruminations on the loss of the real, I was reminded that this anxiety, which we now call postmodern, is precisely what motivates my work. (1996)

The comments dated 1980–85 are from Brian Wallis, ed., *Blasted Allegories: An Anthology of Writings by Contemporary Artists* (New York: New Museum of Contemporary Art; Cambridge: MIT Press, 1987).

The comment dated 1996 is from *Cathedrals* (Cologne: Galerie Jablonka; Los Angeles: Margo Leavin Gallery, 1996).

Did You Say "Ethics"?
Michel Parmentier

> I speak of an art turning from it in disgust, weary of its puny exploits, weary of pretending to be able, weary of being able . . ., of going a little further along a dreary road.
>
> —Samuel Beckett[1]

> In girum imus nocte et consumimur igni.
>
> —Guy Debord[2]

One may be dispossessed of words, ideas, or approaches (including the most unconditionally important, the most serious) by people who least understand them, who are least familiar with them. These words and attitudes are tossed at sea like so many messages in a bottle and come back in a hundred different guises, lavishly labeled, trivialized, only to keep critics and journalists afloat for several years, so long as they take care to make these things fit every possible occasion. So it is with "ethics," a word that, in the realm of painting, can be used only rarely with any pertinence, and not without rhyme or reason; likewise, a reference to a writer or a philosopher is emptied of any meaning when it is taken over and worn out by media exposure. Blanchot's *The Writing of the Disaster* cannot pop up just anywhere without losing some of its substance, and "ethics" cannot emerge from the pen of a journalist[3] addressing the use of new materials and new technologies without provoking outbursts of laughter. Is Nam June Paik supported by an ethical position? Then so is a hamburger.[4]

This is offered by way of precaution. Another caution: if there is a moral dimension—or even merely a moral approach—in this or that work in the plastic arts, it can only be revealed in praxis, can only be brought to light by praxis. One may think that I am stating the obvious here (and it is a commonplace, but not one I share with many people—except for Daniel Buren and Simon Hantaï in France, in different ways of

course). This seems to me to be a dialectical, or perhaps Marxist, thought—simple good sense.[5] This inseparability of ethics and praxis (reflected/made) is opposed equally to idealism, determinism, and art for art's sake; with a little luck, it should even preserve us from the spectacular and, with more luck still, from the *beautiful*. The notion of beautiful being evidently subjective, it is better not to dream.

Despair is never better expressed than as humor (Why did I like Kierkegaard's *The Concept of Anxiety* so much? Why am I so moved—to tears—by a Jewish joke?): laughter is shock therapy.

The word "despair" is no doubt excessive here. In this context, it should be left to others, elsewhere, yesterday, today, and likely enough tomorrow, to the victims of genocide, of massacres, of earthquakes, or of AIDS. I withdraw it immediately: more humbly, let's say "doubt" or "continual dread"—this should suffice.

Doubt, which is partially—but fortunately never entirely—resolved in praxis, has the particularity of always being reborn. It is a fatal disease. Only the supposedly politically committed artists escape it—let us leave them to their torpor, their illusions, their parasitical opportunism.

It is time to do away with that overlong history of servile breakthroughs (*déhiscence*), as well as with the now entirely obsolete concepts of modernity and the avant-garde; some have already claimed that there is no progress in art, but rather, in a recurring fashion, always pauses of stagnation, even of regression. Today, one can see that, symptomatically, the avant-gardes are for the most part as reactionary as the academicisms: the dozens of artists who work on "installations" today feed on a new (for how long?) logic of regressive "déhiscence,"[6] sidestepping the real problem of the void, just as the supporters of the return to the image, representation, or *craft* have done and continue to do; the "installationists" either prudently borrow from the new technologies (which are essentially exogenous to ethics), or they repeat a Duchampian posture. Picasso himself, for all his talent, did nothing else in the end when he reappropriated and updated *Las Meninas;* the move is brilliant, but a little daft too, because it relies exclusively on talent and ignores all doubt.

The new problematic was already opening up in Pollock's drip painting, even before the previous vista was gloriously closed with Matisse. Pollock's disorder and excess (which one might call Sadian) returns us to Bataille, and to Blanchot in the realm of writing. Matisse gives us his sumptuous *Blue Nudes* . . . but sumptuous in the way Racine's writing is, and that's where the shoe pinches.

Still, everything remains to be lost, again.

It is not iconoclastic to claim that we must absolutely forget everything in the act of painting; we must amputate ourselves. This claim does not imply that self-taught artists are better disposed than those who have learned and who have worn out their shoes in the museums; quite to the contrary—a single lightning bolt, a single epiphany can lead them to lazily engineer a whole career, and examples abound. Nonculture is never equal to the rejection of culture.[7]

The "I would prefer not to" of Melville's Bartleby, and its more radical variant "I prefer not," should give us much food for thought.

Perhaps doubt, brought forth as it is by and through certain gestures (and above all, never dissolved in them) provides a basis for questioning, whereas other painted gestures (sometimes sublime ones) offer *answers*. It is within this opposition—or, at the very least, this alterity—that the fracture between ethics and aesthetics, between fear and pleasure, is revealed; in the best of cases, aesthetics and pleasure are not a rupture in, but a continuation of, historical legitimacy and the logic of the breakthrough (*déhiscence*).

> I relapse . . . into my dream of an art unresentful of its insuperable indigence and too proud for the farce of giving and receiving.[8]

Beckett wrote this as early as 1949, echoing, while lamenting it, da Vinci's *disfazione* from the *Notebooks*.

What is there to add? Perhaps something still *less*, again. But *still*.

October 1999

Translated from the French by Anthony Allen.

1. ["Three Dialogues," in *Disjecta: Miscellaneous Writings and a Dramatic Fragment* (New York: Grove Press, 1984), p. 139. Trans.]

2. ["We go round and round in the night and are consumed by fire." This palindrome is the title of Debord's 1978 film. The script has been published in translation in Guy Debord, *In girum imus nocte et consumimur igni* (London: Pelagian Press, 1991). Trans.]

3. In the French weekly *Figaro Magazine,* a stupid right-wing publication (pardon the pleonasm).

4. I only speak for the present moment and do not prejudge the future of technologies. In a few years, who knows? These technologies will perhaps be our keys out of the old territory, as long as their users are able to transform the gadgets that currently fascinate them into tools of reflection, as long as they stop playing around and get tired of bluffing.

5. Those who still confuse Marxism and the Gulag are generally the same people who consider Warhol's work as the manifestation of a moral sense.

6. I use this word in the very particular meaning that Beckett gives it: open to receive in order to give back (the "giving and receiving").

7. The former is a (miserable) *predicament,* the latter is an *action* (imprudent maybe, impudent no doubt, but which may allow us to catch a glimpse of a hypothetical new point of departure).

8. ["Three Dialogues," p. 141. Trans.]

Notes on the Work of François Rouan

Jacques Lacan

with an introductory note by François Rouan and
commentary by Stephen Melville

The following pages reproduce in facsimile Jacques
Lacan's contribution to the catalogue of a 1978
exhibition of François Rouan's work. They are
accompanied by an English translation. François
Rouan has provided this introductory note.

Introductory Note

On the occasion of this letter's republication, I'd like to
make two remarks:

Jacques Lacan never, it seems to me, went to look
at the back of the *Portes*, the paintings on which I was
working at the time, so I am astonished at his noticing
that I had taken the trouble of filling in the "holes" created by the tension of the vertical and horizontal bands.

If Jacques Lacan speaks well of the two bands
constitutive of weaving, he says nothing of what constitutes the reprise in painting of a third, fourth, or even
a fifth band—each of these painted.

—François Rouan

François Rouan peint sur bandes

Si j'osais, je lui conseillerais de modifier ça et de peindre sur tresses

La tresse à trois vaut d'être relevée

Aucun rapport entre trois et tresse. C'est à mon étonnement ce que m'affirme le Bloch et von Wartburg, dictionnaire étymologique auquel je me réfère. On y trouve au contraire une évocation de θρίξ, τριχός, évocateur de la natte qui est la matière habituelle de la tresse à trois.

Je ferai retour à la peinture sur bandes ; cette nouveauté — frappante — qu'introduit François Rouan.

Voici comment je la schématise

Fig. I

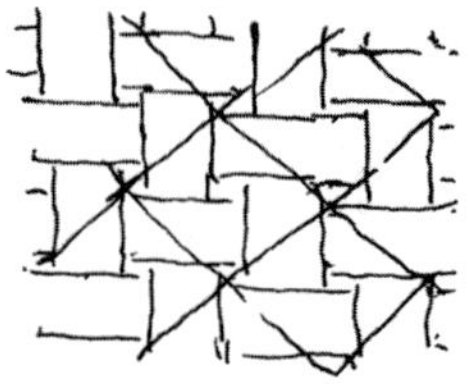

François Rouan paints on bands.

If I dared, I'd advise him to modify this and to paint on braids. The three-stranded braid is worth raising.

There's no relation between three [*trois*] and braid [*tresse*]. This is, to my astonishment, what Bloch and Von Warburg, the etymological dictionary I consulted, affirms. One finds instead a reference to thrix, trixos, evocations of the tress that is the customary material of the braid.

Let me return to painting on bands—the striking novelty introduced by François Rouan. Here's how I schematize it.

Les petits trous n'existent pas Ils sont confondus
Néanmoins je crois devoir les mettre en évidence
et même souligner qu'il y a des ~~dextrogyres~~ lévogyres
que je ~~mets au centre des~~ reprends de ~~des~~ lignes obliques. ~~et~~
~~des lévogyres et des lévogyres que je désigne~~
~~par ces lignes~~. Le dextrogyre central serait aussi
porté par des lignes analogues (= obliques).

Venons.en à la tresse

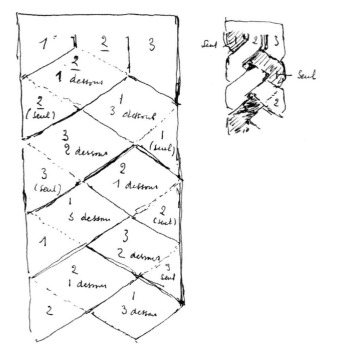

The little holes don't exist. The bands are married. Nevertheless, I thought it better to make them evident so as to emphasize the levorotation by connecting them with oblique lines. The central dexorotation is likewise carried by analogous obliques.

Now we come to the braid.

[*dessous* = strand beneath; (*seul*) = strand folded against or over itself]

Le bâti du tableau le prend en haut et en bas
Nul besoin de fixer ce qui est latéral :

Il y a d'autres propriétés de cette trame
nommément la propriété dite borroméenne
qui tient à ce que' après six mouvements
(de nattage), ces bandes peuvent être mises
en cercle et qu'une étant coupée, libère
les 2 autres : je veux dire qu'elle les rend
indépendantes l'un de l'autre

Ceci se renouvelle après 12, 18, 24.
36 mouvements .... Comme le montre la
figure suivante :

Fig. III

Ce qui n achève circulairement
de la façon suivante

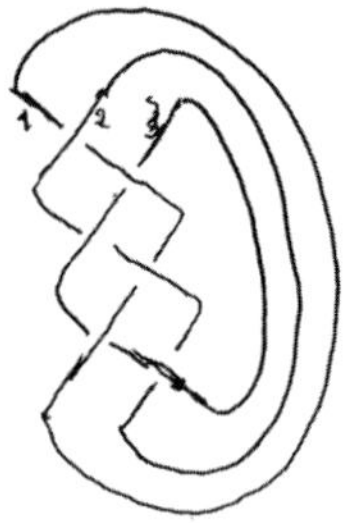

laquelle tresse se transforme de la manière
suivante par rabattement du 2

Fig. IV

The framework of the *tableau* anchors it at top and bottom. There's no need to anchor it laterally.

Such a braid has some further properties—namely those called Borromean, which arise from the way in which, after six passes, these bands can be joined in a circle such that if one band is cut, the two are freed—by which I mean made independent of one another.

This repeats after 12, 18, 24, 30 movements, as the following figure shows:

which becomes circular as shown below

which braid is transformed by folding back 2:

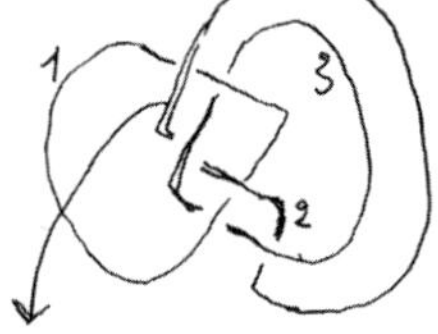

Après que le rabattement de 2 complète la question et il saute aux yeux que la section d'un quelconque Fig. V de ces cercles laisse les deux autres superposés, c'est-à-dire non noués en chaîne.

À remarquer que, plongés dans l'espace, les trois cercles se croisent également. Ils ont pourtant moins de croisements. Alors que, mis à plat, ils ont 6 croisements Fig. VI la figure VI (en perspective) montre que dans l'espace ils n'en ont que quatre

De même il y a une tresse à quatre et à cinq, à six, voire à ce qu'on appelle infini, c'est-à-dire impossible à nombrer. Telle est la figure VII dont on voit le principe : un Fig. VII cercle étant coupé, n'importe lequel des autres est indépendant, c'est-à-dire n'est pas en chaîne : c'est une chaîne mais réduite à ses éléments

---

After the folding back of 2 the proof is complete and it's readily apparent that cutting any one of these circles leaves the other two superimposed—that is to say, not knotted in a chain.

It's worth noting that, placed into space, the three circles cross one another equally. Nonetheless, there are fewer intersections. While in flat projection they have 6 intersections, figure VI (in perspective) shows that in space there are only four.

In the same way, there are braids of four, five, six strands—up to what one calls infinity (i.e., impossible to number). Thus figure VII, where one sees the principle: one circle being cut, all the others are independent, not forming a chain. It is a chain but reduced to its elements.

To conceive this, I'm going to represent it (the Borromean chain) in perspective. Here's a chain of four. It's easy from this to imagine it with five, six, in fact without limit. It stays true that a break (or cut) in but one of these circles frees *all* the others. This representation is in three-dimensional space (thus our reference to perspective).

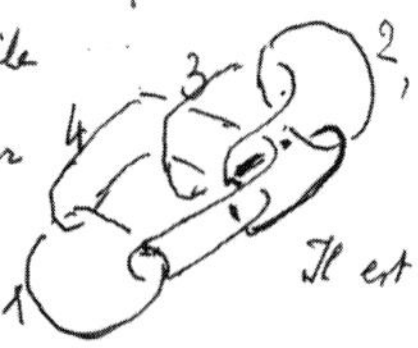

How does the presentation from figure II work out for the chain of four? It looks like this:

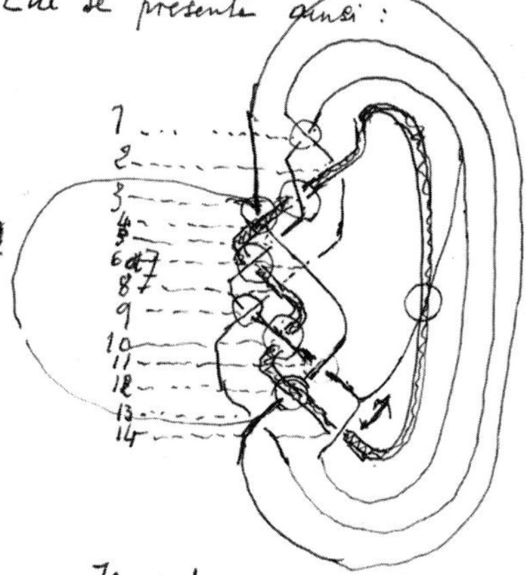

It's striking that this flattening suffices to maintain the same number of crossings—14—while in space there are only eight (as circled in figure IX).

Starting from these three circles there are 4 positions that permit its knotting

4 passes over 1
    under 3
    over 2

The result in space is Fig. XI

This happens in space as

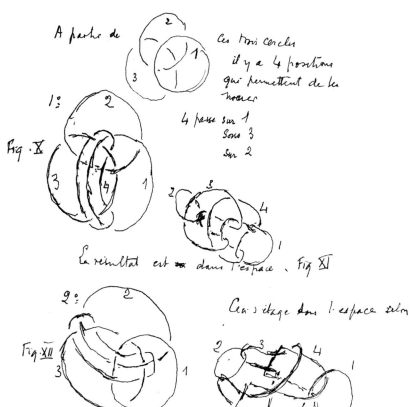

The two following are:

Les deux suivants sont :

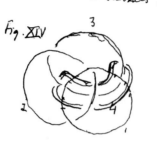

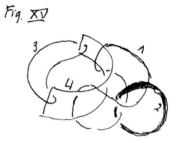

and then

et après

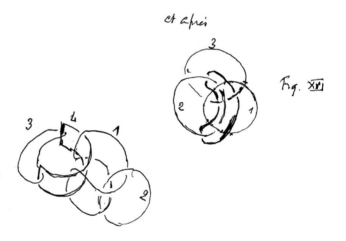

I offer this for the consideration of the public that will go to see the paintings of François Rouan.

Je livre ceci à la méditation du public qui ira voir les tableaux de François Rouan

Originally published in *François Rouan* (Marseilles: Musée Cantini, 1978). Translated from the French by Stephen Melville.

Some Commentary

These seven handwritten pages are the last text published by Lacan during his lifetime, written at François Rouan's request for the catalogue of his 1978 exhibition at the Cantini Museum in Marseilles. By 1978 Lacan was showing the effects of what appears to have been a series of strokes, and the text is clearly unfinished: it is unfocused, repetitious, grammatically perilous, physically shaky, and seems finally to lose itself in Lacan's obsessive drawing and redrawing of the passage between the flat projection of his Borromean chain and its three-dimensional realization.[1]

For all these obvious problems, the text does nonetheless have some points of considerable interest, both for those interested in Lacan's psychoanalysis and for those interested in Rouan's work and the imagination of painting at work in it. To take up, then, several points very briefly:

Diagrams

Diagrams and related forms (borrowed logical or mathematical notations and the like) play a large role in Lacan's teaching and writing throughout his career. His use of them suggests that he particularly values such things for both their clarity and their opacity (he regularly works the difference between reading them as transparent notations and as pictures), as well as for their complex relation to the text in which they appear (where he treats them as working both the difference between text and image and the difference between word and letter). A further frequent feature of Lacan's employment of such things is a marked interest in the difference between what can be shown flat and the actual three-dimensional form of which that would be a projection. Thus his well-known "Schema R" is redescribed in a footnote in Lacan's *Ecrits* as the flattening out of a Möbius strip; in the retrospect provided by these pages and Lacan's other late meditations on Borromean knots, it is probably worth noting that a simple line drawing of a Möbius

strip can also be taken more or less as two circles superimposed on but independent of one another. Lacan's various later diagrams, including those in this essay, are probably well taken as revision or further thinking through of the terms of those earlier diagrams.[2]

Psychoanalysis

One of Lacan's earliest quasi-diagammatic excursions involved demonstrating how a random sequence once notated, and thus remarked, was immediately generative of complex higher orders that describe a law or set of laws at work within that sequence without giving any predictive access to it. This thought of three orders, one brute and contingent, one lawful, and one arising as the impossible image of their possible harmony or synthesis, is a version of Lacan's central distinction of the three registers of the Real, the Symbolic, and the Imaginary. "Registers" here can be taken to mean something close to ways the world happens (rather than divisions of it), and the Unconscious is, in this light, an inevitable consequence of the fact that the world happens all at once in three registers that are at once independent and deeply intertwined. A failure of any one register to establish itself results in all these floating free of one another, a psychotic condition that amounts to a failure to establish an inhabitable world. The contrast Lacan offers in these pages between the braid that is capable of determining its own limits and the weaving that expands obliquely without limit thus appears to be a version of the contrast Lacan offers elsewhere between his Schema R and the unanchored variant of it he offers in diagnosis of Freud's patient Schreber.

Painting

Lacan's remarks evidently assume some interesting equivalence between the structure of painting and the structure of persons and implicitly critique Rouan's painting for falling short of this equivalence—that is, presumably, falling short both of the appropriate kind of autonomy and the appropriate kind of finitude (the finitude marked in us by the existence of the Unconscious). In "La peinture est un vrai trois" (Painting is a true three), written for an exhibition of Rouan's work at the Centre Georges Pompidou, Hubert Damisch argues that in painting on his woven bands Rouan does in fact make something structured as a braid (Lacan is, in effect, so fascinated by the surface that he fails to come to grips with the painting, both the thing and process of its making), and thus Rouan's paintings have a dimension answerable to that marked by the Unconscious in us (an argument picked up by Rouan in his remarks introducing Lacan's text here). Republished as the culminating essay of Damisch's 1984 book *Fenêtre jaune cadmium, ou les dessous de la peinture,* this essay was an important exploration of the structure of the painted surface and the nature of its depth, the implications of which for *As Painting* go well beyond the particular issues raised by Rouan's *tressage,* of which Damisch was an early and articulate champion. This general view is worth comparing with that laid out by Christian Bonnefoi in "The Objection That the Obscure Makes to Painting," elsewhere in this catalogue; Bonnefoi's remarks about the "'ternary structure' of the *tableau*" appear directly responsive to the issues posed here as between Damisch and Lacan.[3]

1. Further details on the relation between Lacan and Rouan and the circumstances of this publication can be found in Elisabeth Roudinesco's *Jacques Lacan (European Perspectives),* trans. Barbara Bray (New York: Columbia University Press, 1997), pp. 379 ff.

2. Lacan's "Schema R" can be found in "On the Possible Treatment of Psychosis," in *Ecrits: A Selection,* trans. Alan Sheridan (New York: W. W. Norton, 1997). The diagram mentioned below and produced in considering the case of Schreber is also to be found in this essay. The treatment of randomness and order, also mentioned below, is to be found in the appendices to Lacan's "Seminar on 'The Purloined Letter,'" in the French edition of the *Ecrits* (Paris: Editions du Seuil, 1966) and has not been rendered into English. This volume also includes a translation of Jacques-Alain Miller's useful "Commentary on the Graphs."

3. For a short, appreciative overview of *Fenêtre jaune cadmium, ou les dessous de la peinture* in English, see Yve-Alain Bois, "Painting as Model," in *Painting as Model* (Cambridge: MIT Press, 1990).

The Ineffable—About Ryman's Work
Daniel Buren

It is always perilous to write about the work of an artist, particularly about the work of a painter. It becomes even more so when the artist in question has been one of your friends for nearly thirty years! But the most difficult of all is to write about another artist's work, being yourself an artist; in this case, the author's outlook is critical, self-interested, knowledgeable, reciprocal and envious. And in my case, also admiring!

A direct exchange of ideas, asking questions whose answers enhance or interfere with the comprehension of the work, expending the energy to understand the other's work, sometimes without even exchanging a single word—all this does not encourage me to write about this work.

What perils does a text of this kind present?

The first question and a fundamental one for me, is to ask: Why write about an object—painting—whose very virtue is to abolish language, or at least to do without it, but also, in Robert Ryman's work, to impose silence? This leads me to a another question: Are there elements in this work that can break this silence without diminishing its own "statement"?

Is it possible to discuss things that are not directly in the work, but which contribute to it and can therefore help to understand it?

Are there one or several ways to talk about a work which would be both useful to its comprehension and remain separate from it? In other words, a way to discuss all sorts of aspects, none of which actually exist in the painting?

Assuming that writing about a specific work is neither absurd nor redundant, the process appears to me to be paradoxical. The danger is that a work which can be completely captured in writing no longer has any visual or plastic interest. In this case, the writing would literally exhaust the work.

Robert Ryman and I first met through the work that we were exhibiting. Indeed, when we look at another artist's work—when it raises important questions—it is no longer the work that is exhibited, but also the person looking at it who finds himself exposed to the work of the other.

The first time I was therefore "exposed" to Bob's work—in the same way one is exposed to cold, to the sun or to X-rays—was at Konrad Fischer's in Düsseldorf in November 1968, where I was preparing a one-man show scheduled to be held in the same exhibition space at a later date. I had never before seen any of Ryman's work, with the exception of a few totally meaningless reproductions.

This "exposition" was thus reciprocal, and since that day, this work continues to expose itself, as I am exposed to the multiple questions that it raises, year after year, in one exhibition to another.

I refuse to discuss what is intrinsically visible and painterly in this work; I will limit myself to the so-called, although essential, "technical" aspects—an approach that does not take away from the painting itself.

Robert Ryman himself does not diverge from this approach, and when he writes about or discusses his work, he always—with a few rare exceptions—talks about techniques, his brushwork, how he hangs the paintings, the materials he selects. It is always extremely precise and in direct relationship to a specific object or painting.

He always limits himself to this type of question and never deviates from his subject by, for example, discussing the effect created by a certain brush, support or technique. He always indicates in a very practical way what it is that motivates him to work in a certain way. He never talks about the intrinsic visual aspect of the work or its possible meaning or meanings. Nor does he delve into the emotions created by this alchemy either within himself or the viewer.

He is among those artists who fully respect the viewer and who—although they provide all the necessary keys to understanding their work in a certain way—never draw any conclusions concerning the value or the meaning of the produced work, or explain the feeling that the viewer is supposed to experience.

If he is looking for a fine or very fine brushstroke, he explains how he tries to achieve it and what materials he may use.

He generally discusses how an unsatisfactory experiment motivates him to return to the same problem or even how the same experiment, undertaken with an entirely different purpose, takes him along a previously unknown path. Or he may discuss the choice of a material—a rough surface may require a certain type of treatment—or explain why a specific surface of a piece of Plexiglas was sandblasted to hold pastel colors better and why he thought this would help the work. That is all, but it is already a great deal. He says what can be said. I challenge exegetes or other art historians to do more than this!

The reader will understand that I have no desire to further discuss either the emotion or the lessons I have learned from Robert Ryman's paintings. He already provides many of the elements underlying his painting and his approach to it.

I will now discuss several facts that say much about the way we perceive, assimilate and understand things.

Who today could credibly claim that Ryman's work is not that of a painter? Even those who—although they are generally uneducated, blind and sometimes stupid, like a certain Domecq and some of his pitiful companions—saw nothing other than a repetition of totally empty, white surfaces, now consider these works to be paintings. Yet this has not always been the case, even though the most obtuse among the denigrators of this kind of art in the early 1960s—which they confused slightly with Conceptual Art—now seem ready to proclaim loud and clear that they never questioned the intrinsic value of these works as paintings!

At the start of his career and through the end of the 1960s, Ryman was not even classified as a painter. Indeed, one of the first international exhibitions in which his work was allowed to be shown was called *When Attitudes Become Form*. This was in Bern in the spring of 1969; what is interesting is the subtitle of the exhibition: *Works, Concepts, Processes, Situations, Information*. Nowhere was the word "painting" visible! It had been banned from the vocabulary and the painters along with it. In other words, Robert Ryman, who participated in this exhibition, was not considered by the curators of the exhibition to be a painter. Furthermore, his own catalogue, published jointly by the Tate Gallery and the MOMA in 1993, contained the following text about the same exhibition: "The exhibition helped to disseminate American Conceptual Art, Minimalism and Post-Minimalism in Europe." This is an astonishing comment in more than one way: Does this mean that the theme of the exhibition was primarily to introduce the latest forms of a certain American art into Europe? And exactly which movement would Ryman's work belong to, in the view of the authors of his own catalogue? It was nice of them to inform us of this some twenty-five years after the fact, especially in that there were as many Europeans as Americans participating in the exhibition! They could just as well have written that the Europeans were only selected and included in the exhibition to provide an attractive backdrop for their American colleagues!

Although most agree that as a movement Minimalism was created in the United States—even if its roots are certainly in Europe—it is absurd to maintain that Post-Minimalism was also born there, and even more idiotic to insinuate that Conceptual Art was an American-inspired movement, which it absolutely was not.

Furthermore, the very first exhibition of artists who showed under the title *Koncept Art* was held just a few months later, in September 1969, in Leverkusen, West Germany; it included an equal number of European and American artists.

The purpose of this digression is to emphasize that the hegemony of American propaganda will use even the most amazing and insidious untruths—in this case, just a few lines in the middle of Ryman's catalogue—to monopolize everything interesting that comes within its grasp. It is also a fairly illuminating look at how art history, even the most recent, is reinterpreted in the United States. For the majority of U.S. art schools, the history of international contemporary art is an exclusively American history!

The fact that this history is made elsewhere than on American territory, primarily in Europe, can only be interpreted as if American artists were the only ones exhibited around the world, and that we are thereby granting them the homage that is their due! Yet most American artists over the last thirty years owe their international reputations, and for many—especially those artists still unknown in their own country—even their livelihood, to galleries, major group shows, museums and collectors in Europe.

This brings us to the heart of the subject: in 1969, the various curators of international exhibitions in no way considered Ryman to be a painter, but rather as a Post-Minimalist, or even a Conceptual Artist.

These were the early days of this movement, an ideal catch-all that encompassed a few unclassifiable emerging artists, before it became a formal, academic category, with its hierarchy, masters, theoreticians, followers and imitators of all stripes—indeed, an exclusively American specialty. This said, it is surprising that work like Ryman's could have been considered anything other than painting, especially as he has never attempted to hide that fact that he is a painter, and even dates the start of his professional life in terms of a painting made in 1955, entitled *Orange Paint no. 1*. Yet this visual and mental confusion is extremely enlightening. On the one hand, it denotes the originality of this painting, which so "blinded" the curators at the time that they did not recognize it as such. On the other, the relevance of this unidentified object must have been extremely intriguing to have captured the interest of these curators!

It is also surprising to see such a work appear at that particular time, insofar as painting was not particularly in fashion; it was not spectacular, affected, beautiful, ugly, expressionist or even innovative—although painters did exist and exhibited, albeit rarely, in the major group exhibitions organized between 1968 and 1972. Meanwhile, all around the world, everything else was or tried to be—with a few exceptions—new, never-before-seen, exaggerated or even purely and simply provocative to the petit-bourgeois!

There is none of this with Robert Ryman, and yet his work was already present, not for what it is, but more certainly for what it is not, for the incomprehension it provokes. It was included through a total misunderstanding. Nobody really knew what it was, so it could safely be categorized with Conceptual Art, a wonderful grab bag of art movements!

This also teaches us that a profound, analytical and sensitive examination of a painting as an object can be so innovative, rich, complex and unexpected that, initially, no one will see it as painting in the true meaning of the term. One could even risk saying that true painting, in other words, a true work of art from any movement whatsoever, in the most noble sense of the word—innovative, intriguing and beautiful to boot—cannot initially be seen as such. This was such a powerful argument that the fiercest critics would claim that Ryman's work could in no way be considered painting; and indeed, that it is even a pure negation of it, an anti-painting!

What they all forget, of course, is that this type of painting cannot be appreciated at first sight as a painting, even if its creator swears that it is nothing but that! This work overturns commonly held beliefs about painting to such an extent that it cannot be immediately assimilated as such. At worst, it is considered to be an insignificant object; at best, as an intriguing, therefore undefined and unclassifiable object. Accepting it as painting would mean a re-examination of the painting that preceded it, but would also expand the inner vision that we have had about art up to this time.

For this same reason, one could logically affirm today that, although Ryman's work is certainly linked to a historical movement in Western painting, it is also disassociated from it to such an extent that we can speak of the history of painting before Ryman, and its history after Ryman.

A threshold had been crossed, as was the case with the work of Picasso, Malevich, El Lissitzky, Matisse, Mondrian, Brancusi, Pollock, Duchamp, Barnett Newman, Yves Klein, Carl Andre, Léger, Manzoni, Tony Smith, Weiner, Michael Asher, d'Anselmo, Palermo, Stanley Brown or several others.

I would add that there are fundamental artists who, although few and far between, have altered the course of art. And alongside these essential artists are legions of others who are highly talented, sensitive, imaginative, skillful and intelligent, but who basically carry on the legacy of those in the first category to the best of their abilities. Artists in this second category are often far more famous and their work more expensive than those in the first.

In my view, of course, Ryman is one of the few rare artists in this category. This classification does not mean that his work appeared out of the blue, that he did not have other influences, far from it. In terms of art history, it is clear that Ryman owes—and recognizes— a debt to Mark Rothko. This powerful influence is not, of course, a formal one.

I will let the attentive viewer discover this as well as other influences that can be detected in his work. I would like to discuss an essential element of Ryman's work, that of the intrinsic painted object and how it hangs on the wall.

In January 1974, I made a special trip to Amsterdam for the opening of a Robert Ryman retrospective at the Stedelijk Museum. We visited the exhibition together and talked about the works one by one. I had a thousand questions and was insatiable. Suddenly, as we walked through a room, I saw an absolutely splendid series of diaphanous works, like *Adelphi-1967* and the series of *Surface Veils-1969/1970*. Some of these works originally used the wall as a support and were taped over it or glued directly to the wall by the paint that had

spilled over the edges. Many already belonged to collectors, who had had them elegantly framed before lending them to this exhibition! I hesitated before raising my question, afraid that he would take it as an implicit criticism, but finally I dared ask him if he didn't think that these works, exhibited in this way, had lost something of their fundamental interest?

His reply was direct. He was very angry and acknowledged my criticism. A long discussion followed concerning the ways of hanging paintings and how to remedy this alteration, in this case due to what can only be called a conservative outlook on the part of the collector who, fearful of losing an acquired work, solidified it by covering it with Plexiglas or some other protective frame. It thereby "resembled" the mediocre idea of what he or she held of painting in general, forcing Ryman's work to be compared with this mediocrity.

How many works of art end up in museums around the world and then no longer express what they were intended to express, but rather what the manipulators want it to express, once they have appropriated it for themselves? I feel that painting, more than any of the other arts, is sensitive and delicate in terms of the use made of it, especially in that most artists in general, and painters in particular, admit that once a piece has left their studio, they no longer look at it.

Robert Ryman seems to me to be an entirely different sort of painter, and I believe that he was dismayed by this retrospective at the Stedelijk in Amsterdam; as a result he decided to tackle the problem head on.

First of all, when he can and when he is asked to do so, Ryman has found techniques to exhibit some of his extremely fragile and delicate works from this period in a new way by attaching them directly to other materials, such as "featherboard," a flat, inert and lightweight material, making it easier to hang them on the wall.

This visual transformation made by Ryman has nothing to do with the manipulations I discussed earlier, and although it modifies the original work somewhat, it betrays neither the spirit nor the integrity of the work. Furthermore, although he did not interrupt his research and remained interested in different ways of hanging his paintings, from this point on, he integrated the method of hanging the work as one of the visual elements forming the painting itself, so that the collector or museum curator would have no choice but to respect the integrity of the work, thereby drastically reducing the risk that it would be formally transformed.

From this moment on, nails, hooks, screws, frames, guide strips, metal rods, nuts—centered, off—centered, offset, symmetrical and asymmetrical—made of iron, aluminum, wood, stainless steel, became as much a part of the painting as the support and material—the paint—placed on it.

These objects had already been used on Ryman's painted surfaces, but for other purposes: anecdotal, gratuitous, imaginary, or directly incorporated into the material. The novelty here was that these tools and objects were systematically used as the visual means by which the painting would be hung on the wall, and became part of the interplay produced by the painting.

With this, Ryman developed an entire alphabet with which he could skillfully play, while remaining discreet as in *Expander-1985;* or he could invent other systems of hanging the work, so that the painting would hang a few inches away from the wall, like *Journal-1988;* or he would use two blocks of wood, so that the painting no longer appeared attached to the wall, but disconnected from it, like *Initial-1989.*

These methods were added to the hundreds of different surface treatments, incorporated into the hundreds of different materials forming the surfaces themselves, a process that gradually created one of the richest pictorial works ever made.

On the subject of hanging the paintings, it must be added that, up to that point, Robert Ryman had been interested in the object itself and in its external appearance, wall and attachments included, but not in the position of the work on a particular wall. He trusted others—collectors and curators and museum directors—letting them place the paintings on the walls. In his shoes, I'd be more careful!

Another aspect that is completely foreign to Ryman's work, but is nonetheless extremely important: the problem of photographic reproduction. Just as the artistic world was not at first able to classify his work where it belongs—as painting—photography is extremely revealing about the work in question, its characteristics and its limitations.

I believe in the following axiom: that no work of art, and especially no painting, can be photographed. Once said, of course, this statement must be clarified and somewhat analyzed. First of all, anything can be photographed, of course, including a work of art. What cannot be transmitted by a photograph, however, is the essence of the work itself, its intrinsic qualities and its very existence. At best, a work of art and its reproduction have the same relationship to each other as does a family photograph or portrait to its model. The flesh, scent, movement and life are absent.

The undeniable dilution from a work of art to its photographic reproduction is even more dangerous in that, as they are two inert objects, the loss of one when reproduced by the other may seem to be minimal to an untrained eye. Yet this loss is great, as the result is a kind of substitute, and some people, once they have viewed the photograph, believe they don't need to see the artwork at all! If they believe that, then they will never be able to understand. It reminds me of André Malraux; when he was General de Gaulle's Minister of Culture, he dreamed of making full-scale, color photo reproductions of European painting masterpieces.

According to Malraux, these reproductions would bring art to everyone, as they would be exhibited from village to village, city to city, as a sort of infinitely reproducible museum. This is even worse, in fact, than an imaginary museum, worse than the reproduction of the Lascaux cave paintings. Had this incredibly stupid project ever been realized, it would have been a sort of discount museum, which, created through the laudable pretext of educating the largest amount of people, would in fact have permanently perverted those who fell for the idea.

From this point of view, painting is different from sculpture. Although the inherent process of the latter allows for a certain dose of reproducibility through a sort of cloning, painting cannot be copied, with the exception of certain works, such as Warhol's, for example. Some painting, of course, can be reproduced more easily than others. In short, one could say that any figurative painting, when reproduced, transmits a certain resemblance to the original and leaves the impression of remaining fairly close to it. This similarity decreases, however, with reproductions of non-figurative painting. As it cannot connect with anything solid, the reproduction becomes some kind of joke. In both cases, of course, the essence of the work is lost forever, in various degrees, simply because it does not exist in the reproduction.

Robert Ryman's work is among the most difficult of all artwork to photograph as the film cannot capture what it is supposed to memorize. It eludes any means of reproduction. It is, of course, photographed, but the result is so meager that I wouldn't be surprised if these reproductions were a serious handicap to the dissemination of the work itself. On the other hand, whether they lose all or some of their essential interest as soon as they are photographed, it is undeniable that an artwork that has been reproduced is remembered more easily that those that have not been.

Skimming through a catalogue of Picasso's works gives the agreeable impression—even though the very essence of the reproduced objects is lost—of looking at a pretty album of images that are frozen, diverse and yet homogeneous. Looking through a catalogue containing reproductions of Robert Ryman's work, on the other hand, leaves the reader with the impression of looking at a series of senseless images, ones that are frozen, but flat, repetitive and dead. In the first case, the reproduction invites the reader to go and see the original work—even to be disappointed, if, for example, it is not as large as one thought, the colors are not exactly

the same, and so on. In the second case, the reproduction obviously says absolutely nothing about the work and does little to make it comprehensible. It does not incite the reader to go see it. It is far too remote from the original subject, which remains stubbornly opposed to any photogenic treatment. In reproductions of the first type, photography remains a friendly ally of its subject; it is extremely dangerous, as the seduction it produces takes away from the work. In the second type of reproduction, photography is paradoxically less dangerous in that it does not flatter the work. It always reflects less than the reality and, although it interferes with the visual dissemination of the work, it can never be a substitute for it. This is why Robert Ryman's work cannot be reproduced photographically. This comment says much about his type of work, which absolutely requires direct physical contact.

Robert Ryman creates a resistant type of painting. It resists any spectacular, exaggerated or manipulative techniques, concerning how it is hung on the wall, poorly adapted frames and photographic reproduction.

Photographs of Ryman's work do exist, of course, in art books and catalogues. They tend to show the works alone, emerging from the page, without wall, floor or ceiling, as if totally immaterial, floating in the middle of a white page. Yet, starting in 1967, Robert Ryman became increasingly interested in the way his works were hung on the wall, and he started pursuing research in this direction, with direct collages, scotch tape projecting beyond the painted work, hooks, and so on. From this moment on, photographs—as incapable as ever of capturing the painting in question—also had to include these artifices invented by Robert Ryman to hang his works, since they were an integral part of it. Eliminating them would be like arbitrarily cutting off part of the work.

Some reproductions have a sort of frame which was invented by the photographer and added around the reproduced work so that the nuts, clips and other elements can be seen. This new type of masking device, which floats as aimlessly on the page as the reproductions, is nonetheless interesting in that it illustrates the color and texture of a small piece of the wall on which the painting has been hung.

Robert Ryman is extremely careful to integrate the importance of the wall to his painting, using the hanging devices as necessary visual elements. The photographer, then, is forced to include—although timidly, to be sure—the wall supporting the work in the reproduction of the work itself. And whenever this is not required by the work itself, the photographer quickly eliminates it. The complexity of Robert Ryman's work seems to be accentuated even more by the emptiness of the transmitted image. As it cannot be captured, it teaches us once again of the absolute necessity of seeing a work of art in person.

The paradoxical beauty of this work resides in part in the fact that, by remaining constantly linked to the material nature of his work, he has thus gradually and pragmatically produced a body of work which in this century can be counted among those that have achieved the highest level of spirituality.

Mexico, 1999

© Daniel Buren

Reprinted with the author's permission from Daniel Buren, *The Ineffable—About Ryman's Work,* trans. Lisa Davidson (Paris: Editions Jannink, 1999).

Checklist of the Exhibition

In dimensions, height precedes width precedes depth.

Polly Apfelbaum

Spill, 1992–93
Synthetic crushed velvet, torn sheeting, dye, safety pins
9 sections, dimensions variable
Courtesy the artist and D'Amelio Terras, New York

Enigma Machine, 1993–95
Synthetic velvet and dye
Dimensions variable
Courtesy the artist and D'Amelio Terras, New York

Still Life: Green/Orange/Blue, 1997
Synthetic velvet and dye
Green: 43 $^1/_4$ × 21 $^3/_4$ in. (110 × 55 cm); Orange: 44 $^1/_4$ × 20 $^1/_2$
in. (112 × 52 cm); Blue: 44 $^1/_4$ × 23 in. (112 × 58 cm)
Courtesy the artist and D'Amelio Terras, New York

Bones: Large, 1999
Synthetic velvet, dye, cardboard roll
4 pieces, 48 to 60 in. (122 to 152 cm) each in length; overall
dimensions variable
Courtesy the artist and D'Amelio Terras, New York

Commissioned installation, 2001
Dimensions variable
Courtesy the artist and D'Amelio Terras, New York

Martin Barré

61-T-15, 1961
Oil on canvas
46 $^7/_8$ × 31 $^7/_8$ in. (119 × 81 cm)
Private collection, Paris

63-Z, 1963
Glycerophtalic and acrylic paint on canvas
31 $^7/_8$ × 21 $^1/_4$ in. (81 × 54 cm)
Private collection, Paris

72–73-F-108 × 100, 1972–73
Acrylic on canvas
42 $^1/_2$ × 39 $^3/_8$ in. (108 × 100 cm)
Private collection, Paris

74–75-B-113 × 105, 1974–75
Acrylic on canvas
44 $^1/_2$ × 41 $^3/_8$ in. (113 × 105 cm)
Private collection
Courtesy Galerie Laage-Salomon, Paris

74–75-D-113 × 105, 1974–75
Acrylic on canvas
44 $^1/_2$ × 41 $^3/_8$ in. (113 × 105 cm)
Private collection, Paris

75–76-B-174 × 164, 1975–76
Acrylic on canvas
68 $^1/_2$ × 64 $^5/_8$ in. (174 × 164 cm)
Courtesy Galerie Laage-Salomon, Paris

James Bishop

Untitled, 1974
Oil on canvas
76 $^3/_4$ × 76 $^3/_4$ in. (195 × 195 cm)
Courtesy Galerie Jean Fournier, Paris

Roman Painting IV, 1975
Oil on canvas
76 $^3/_4$ × 76 $^3/_4$ in. (195 x 195 cm)
Collection of the artist

Mel Bochner

F-4, 1966–67
Gelatin silver photograph mounted on Masonite
53 × 80 in. (135 × 203 cm)
Courtesy Sonnabend Gallery, New York

Perspective Insert (Collapsed Center), 1967
Gelatin silver photograph mounted on Masonite
48 × 48 $^1/_2$ in. (122 × 123 cm)
Courtesy Sonnabend Gallery, New York

48" Standards, 1969/2001
Brown wrapping paper stapled to wall, tape, and Letraset
Dimensions variable
Courtesy Sonnabend Gallery, New York

Studies for Theory of Painting (One–Four), 1969
Graphite, colored pencils, and pen and ink on 4 sheets of graph
paper
4 sheets, 8 $^1/_2$ × 10 $^1/_2$ in. (22 × 27 cm) each
Collection Sarah-Ann and Werner H. Kramarsky, New York

Rome Quartet II, 1992
Oil on canvas
4 panels, 55 $^1/_4$ × 55 $^1/_4$ in. (140 × 140 cm) each
Courtesy Sonnabend Gallery, New York

Christian Bonnefoi

Occasion, 1974
Collage on paper
10 $^1/_2$ × 8 $^1/_4$ in. (27 × 21 cm)
Collection Jan and Ben Maiden, Columbus, Ohio

Hyperion 2, 1977
Painting and collage on canvas
78 $^3/_4$ × 102 $^3/_8$ in. (200 × 260 cm)
Courtesy the artist

Machine 78, 1978
Metal frame and polymer
11 $^3/_4$ × 11 $^3/_4$ in. (30 × 30 cm)
Courtesy Galerie de France, Paris

Babel II, 1979
Oil and graphite on canvas
76 $^3/_4$ × 51 $^1/_8$ in. (195 × 130 cm)
Courtesy Galerie Jacques Elbaz, Paris

Eureka IV, 1997
Acrylic on canvas
89 $^1/_2$ × 64 $^1/_2$ in. (227 × 164 cm)
Collection of Nancy and Dave Gill, Columbus, Ohio

Commissioned installation, 2001
Dimensions variable
Courtesy the artist

Daniel Buren

Peinture aux formes indéfinies, 1966
Paint on canvas
57 $^1/_2$ × 44 $^7/_8$ in. (146 × 114 cm)
Courtesy Galerie Jean Fournier, Paris

Peinture aux formes variables, 1966
Paint on canvas
88 $^3/_4$ × 78 $^1/_2$ in. (227.5 × 199 cm)
Courtesy of Daniel Buren

Planches de contre-collé colorées, 1991
Formica and wood, 23 boards, white and colored
78 × 78 in. (200.1 × 200.1 cm)
Courtesy of Daniel Buren

Commissioned installation, 2001
Dimensions variable
Courtesy the artist

André Cadere

Barres de bois carré, 1970
Painted wood
12 bars, 73 $^1/_2$–79 $^3/_{16}$ × 1 $^1/_2$–1 $^3/_4$ × 1 $^3/_8$–2 in. (188.5–203 × 4–4.5 × 3–5 cm)
Courtesy Galerie L. & M. Durand-Dessert, Paris

Six barres de bois rond, 1975
6 bars of 12 cylinders in painted wood
6 bars, 47 $^1/_4$ × 3 $^1/_8$ in. (120 × 8 cm) each
Collection Centre Georges Pompidou, Paris
Musée national d'art moderne/Centre de création industrielle

Jean Degottex

Papier-Plein no. 7, December 14, 1975
Paper glued on canvas
31 $^1/_2$ × 47 $^1/_4$ in. (80 × 120 cm)
Collection Marcelle and Maurice Benhamou, Paris

Lignes-Report, 1977
Acrylic and glue on linen
17 $^7/_8$ × 23 $^7/_8$ in. (45.5 × 60.5 cm)
Collection Marcelle and Maurice Benhamou, Paris

Pli × Pli III, August 1980
Acrylic and brick powder on cotton
58 $^7/_8$ × 55 $^7/_8$ in. (149.5 × 142 cm)
Collection Marcelle and Maurice Benhamou, Paris

Oblicollor, 1983
Acrylic and glue on canvas
85 $^7/_8$ × 84 $^5/_8$ in. (218 × 215 cm)
Collection Marcelle and Maurice Benhamou, Paris

Daniel Dezeuze

Echelle de bois rouge et brune, 1975
Wooden lath with red and brown stain
208 $^5/_8$ × 54 in. (530 × 137 cm)
Collection of the artist, Sète, France

Gaze découpée et peinte, 1980
Gauze, pulverized paint, tape, felt marker
68 $^7/_8$ × 50 $^3/_8$ in. (175 × 128 cm)
Collection of the artist, Sète, France

Cube, 1997
Wood, metal
61 × 61 × 61 in. (155 × 155 × 155 cm)
Fonds national d'art contemporain, Puteaux
Carré d'art—Musée d'art contemporain, Nîmes

Moira Dryer

Headline, 1989
Casein on wood
46 × 48 in. (117 × 122 cm)
Collection Barbara Schwartz, New York

The Wall of Fear, 1990
Acrylic on wood, grommets
84 × 96 in. (213 × 244 cm)
The Estate of Moira Dryer
Courtesy Gorney, Bravin + Lee, New York

Untitled, 1991
Acrylic on wood
48 × 46 in. (122 × 117 cm)
Collection of The Newark Museum, Gift of Leonard Lieberman
in honor of Arlene Lieberman, 1996

François Dufrêne

Dessous d'affiche, 1962
Underneath of poster glued on canvas
5 ¹/₈ × 3 ¹/₂ in. (13 × 9 cm)
Courtesy Galerie Véronique Smagghe, Paris

Où je perçois personnellement en perspective persane, 1973
Underneath of poster glued on canvas
39 ³/₈ × 31 ⁷/₈ in. (100 × 81 cm)
Courtesy Galerie Véronique Smagghe, Paris

Simon Hantaï

M.c.8, 1962
Oil on canvas
145 ⁵/₈ × 86 ⁵/₈ in. (370 × 220 cm)
Collection of the artist, Paris

Blancs, 1973
Acrylic on folded canvas
16 ¹/₈ × 10 ⁵/₈ in. (41 × 27 cm)
Collection Musée d'art moderne de la ville de Paris

Tabula, 1980
Acrylic on canvas
91 ³/₄ × 136 ¹/₄ in. (233 × 346 cm)
Collection of the artist, Paris

Laissée, 1981–89
Acrylic on canvas
109 ¹/₈ × 95 ¹/₄ in. (277 × 242 cm)
Collection of the artist, Paris

Laissée, 1981–95
Acrylic on canvas
121 ¹/₄ × 90 ¹/₂ in. (308 × 230 cm)
Collection of the artist, Paris

Stèle (en mémoire de Denis), 1984
Canvas and wood
54 ³/₈ × 19 ⁵/₈ × 19 ⁵/₈ in. (138 × 50 × 50 cm)
Private collection, France

Donald Judd

Untitled (Progression), 1965
Purple lacquer on aluminum with light cadmium red boxes
8 ¹/₄ × 161 × 8 ¹/₄ in. (21 × 409 × 21 cm)
Collection Wexner Center for the Arts, The Ohio State
University; purchased in part with funds from the National
Endowment for the Arts

Untitled, 1978
Cadmium red oil on American Douglas Fir plywood
19 ³/₄ × 39 × 19 ³/₄ in. (50 × 99 × 50 cm)
Courtesy Paula Cooper Gallery, New York

Untitled, 1987
Plywood and red Plexiglas
118 × 98 × 19 ³/₄ in. (300 × 249 × 50 cm)
Courtesy Paula Cooper Gallery, New York

Imi Knoebel

Schattenraum 4, 1988
Masonite panels, acrylic on wood
Wall panels: 118 ¹/₈ × 141 ³/₄ in. (300 × 360 cm) overall;
cube: 114 ¹/₈ × 141 ³/₄ × 118 ¹/₈ in. (290 × 360 × 300 cm)
Collection Centre Georges Pompidou, Paris
Musée national d'art moderne/Centre de création industrielle

Sandwich 2, 1992
Wood and acrylic
98 $^{1}/_{4}$ × 66 $^{3}/_{4}$ × $^{3}/_{4}$ in. (249.5 × 169.5 × 1.8 cm)
Collection of the artist, Düsseldorf

Odyshape I, 1994
Acrylic and aluminum
42 $^{1}/_{2}$ × 41 $^{7}/_{8}$ × 5 $^{3}/_{8}$ in. (108 × 106.5 × 13.8 cm)
Collection Six Friedrich, Munich

Sherrie Levine

Presidential Profile, 1979
Slide, projector
Dimensions variable
Collection of the artist, New York

Untitled (President: 5), 1979
Collage on paper
24 × 18 in. (61 × 46 cm)
Collection The Museum of Contemporary Art, Los Angeles;
Purchased with funds provided by Councilman Joel Wachs

After Ilya Chasnik, 1984
Casein and wax on mahogany
24 × 20 in. (61 × 51 cm)
Collection of the artist, New York

Cathedrals (1–9), 1995
Black-and-white photographs
10 × 8 in. (25 × 20 cm) each
Courtesy the artist and Margo Leavin Gallery, Los Angeles

After Blinky Palermo, 1996
Paint on wall
Dimensions variable
Courtesy the artist

Untitled, 1999
Graphite on walnut
18 $^{1}/_{2}$ × 3 × $^{3}/_{4}$ in. (47 × 8 × 2 cm)
Collection Paula Cooper, New York

Untitled, 1999
Graphite on walnut
18 $^{1}/_{8}$ × 3 × $^{3}/_{4}$ in. (47 × 8 × 2 cm)
Collection Steven P. Henry, New York

Agnes Martin

Untitled, 1962
Acrylic priming, graphite, and brass nails on canvas
12 × 12 in. (30.5 × 30.5 cm)
Collection Museum of Contemporary Art, San Diego; Museum purchase, 1976.18

Untitled, 1975
Oil on canvas
72 × 72 in. (183 × 183 cm)
Collection Herb and DeeDee Glimcher, Columbus, Ohio

Michel Parmentier

5 octobre 1966, 1966
Lacquer on canvas
109 $^{1}/_{4}$ × 95 $^{3}/_{16}$ in. (280 × 244 cm)
Collection Bénédicte Victor-Pujebet, Paris

30 octobre 1966, 1966
Lacquer on canvas
109 $^{1}/_{4}$ × 95 $^{3}/_{16}$ in. (280 × 244 cm)
Collection Bénédicte Victor-Pujebet, Paris

17 juillet 1988, 1988
Pencil on paper
121 $^{11}/_{16}$ × 85 $^{13}/_{16}$ in. (312 × 220 cm)
Collection Bénédicte Victor-Pujebet, Paris

20 novembre 1999, 1999
Paint on paper (4 sheets)
119 $^{5}/_{8}$ × 118 $^{1}/_{8}$ in. (304 × 300 cm)
Courtesy Galerie Jean Fournier, Paris

Gerhard Richter

Doppelglasscheibe (416), 1977
Glass and gray paint
78 $^{3}/_{4}$ × 59 $^{1}/_{4}$ × 19 $^{5}/_{8}$ in. (200 × 150 × 50 cm)
Collection Musée départemental d'art contemporain de Rochechouart, France

I. G. (790-4), 1993
Oil on canvas
28 $^{3}/_{8}$ × 40 $^{1}/_{8}$ in. (72 × 102 cm)
Private collection

I. G. (790-5), 1993
Oil on canvas
28 $\frac{1}{2}$ × 32 $\frac{1}{4}$ in. (72 × 82 cm)
Private collection

Abstraktes Bild (825-10), 1995
Oil on canvas
20 × 24 in. (51 × 61 cm)
Collection Mark H. Williams, Los Angeles

François Rouan

Papiers gouachés et découpés, 1965
Glue, paper, gouache, paint
63 × 47 $\frac{1}{4}$ in. (160 × 120 cm)
Courtesy the artist

Tressage quatre toiles, gris, rose, bleu, et blanc, 1967–69
Mixed tressage techniques on canvas
78 $\frac{3}{4}$ × 65 $\frac{1}{8}$ in. (225 × 165.5 cm)
Private collection, France

Tressements de 4 surfaces, 1967–69
Graph paper, ink, wash
9 $\frac{1}{2}$ × 9 $\frac{1}{2}$ in. (24 × 24 cm)
Collection of the artist

Porta Latina, 1971–74
Oil on canvas
78 $\frac{3}{4}$ × 67 in. (200 × 170 cm)
Collection Mrs. Maria Gaetana Matisse, New York

Queequeg III, 1999
Oil on canvas
100 $\frac{3}{4}$ × 66 $\frac{1}{8}$ in. (256 × 168 cm)
Courtesy the artist

Robert Ryman

Stretched Drawing, 1963
Charcoal on stretched raw canvas
14 $\frac{1}{2}$ × 14 $\frac{3}{8}$ in. (37 × 37 cm)
Collection of the artist, New York

State, 1978
Oil on cotton with metal brackets
88 × 84 in. (224 × 213 cm)
Collection Albright-Knox Art Gallery, Buffalo, New York;
George B. and Jenny R. Mathews Fund, 1979

Robert Smithson

Untitled, 1966
Mirror
8 $\frac{1}{4}$ × 4 $\frac{1}{2}$ × 1 $\frac{1}{2}$ in. (21 × 11 × 4 cm)
Collection Whitney Museum of American Art, New York; Gift of
the Estate of Robert Smithson, 92.2.3

Pointless Vanishing Point, 1967
White paint on folded steel
40 × 40 × 8 in. (102 × 102 × 20 cm)
Collection Herbert F. Johnson Museum of Art, Cornell
University; Gift of Virginia Dwan, 86.122

Mono Lake Non-Site (Cinders Near Black Point), 1968
Painted steel container, cinders, and map photostat
Site map: 40 $\frac{1}{4}$ × 40 $\frac{1}{4}$ in. (102 × 102 cm); container: 7 × 39 $\frac{3}{4}$
× 39 $\frac{3}{4}$ in. (18 × 101 × 101 cm)
Collection Museum of Contemporary Art, San Diego; Museum
purchase, 1981.10.1–2

Slantpiece, 1969 (original)/1976 (reconstruction)
Mirror and rock salt
48 $\frac{1}{8}$ × 59 $\frac{3}{4}$ × 48 $\frac{1}{8}$ in. (122 × 152 × 122 cm)
Collection Allen Memorial Art Museum, Oberlin College; Gift of
the Buckeye Trust in memory of Ruth C. Roush, 1980

Anne Truitt

Grant, 1974
Acrylic on wood
7 $\frac{1}{2}$ × 144 × 9 $\frac{1}{2}$ in. (19 × 366 × 24 cm)
Courtesy Danese, New York

Elixir, 1997
Acrylic on wood
81 × 8 × 8 in. (206 × 20 × 20 cm)
Courtesy Danese, New York

View, 1999
Acrylic on wood
81 × 8 × 8 in. (206 × 20 × 20 cm)
Courtesy Danese, New York

André Valensi

Objet d'analyse, 1970
10 cotton cords
78 $\frac{3}{4}$ in. (200 cm) each
Collection Musée d'art moderne, Saint-Etienne; Gift of
Vicky Rémy

Claude Viallat

Filet, 1970
Rope
98 ³/₄ × 78 ³/₄ in. (251 × 200 cm)
Courtesy Galerie Daniel Templon, Paris

Untitled, 1971
Acrylic on canvas
85 ³/₈ × 59 in. (217 x 150 cm)
Courtesy Galerie Jean Fournier, Paris

Sans titre no. 130, 1997
Acrylic paint on assorted fabrics
98 ³/₄ × 73 ³/₄ in. (251 × 185 cm)
Courtesy Galerie Daniel Templon, Paris

Jacques Villeglé

Plateau Beaubourg, 1960
Torn posters on canvas
31 ³/₄ × 39 ¹/₄ in. (80.5 × 100 cm)
Collection of Howard and Pamela Holtzman, Chicago

Métro St.-Germain-des-Prés, 22 September 1964, 1964
Torn posters on canvas
19 ⁵/₈ × 12 ³/₄ in. (50 × 32.5 cm)
Courtesy Zabriskie Gallery, New York

James Welling

Gelatin Photographs, 1977–80
4 black and white photographs
19 ⁵/₈ × 15 ¹/₂ in. (50 × 39 cm) each
Collection Frac Bourgogne, France

Diary/Landscape #199 from *Diary of Elizabeth and James Dixon (1840–41)/Connecticut Landscapes,* 1977–86
Gelatin silver print
3 ³/₄ × 4 ⁵/₈ in. (10 × 12 cm) (framed dimensions 15 × 18 in. [38 × 46 cm])
Courtesy the artist

Diary/Landscape #178 from *Diary of Elizabeth and James Dixon (1840–41)/Connecticut Landscapes,* 1977–86
Gelatin silver print
4 ⁵/₈ × 3 ³/₄ in. (12 × 10 cm) (framed dimensions 18 × 15 in. [46 × 38 cm])
Courtesy the artist

LIV, 1988
Polacolor ER print (unique)
24 × 20 in. (61 × 51.8 cm)
Collection The Museum of Contemporary Art, Los Angeles; Gift of Peter and Eileen Norton, Santa Monica

IJWC, 1989
Chromogenic print mounted to Plexiglas
23 × 19 in. (58 × 48 cm)
Courtesy the artist

Lousianne, 1998
Vegetable dye on rag paper
34 ⁵/₈ × 26 ⁵/₈ in. (88 × 68 cm) (framed dimensions 62 × 39 in. [158 × 100 cm])
Courtesy Donald Young Gallery, Chicago